The Politics of Life

In the series
Asian American History and Culture
edited by Sucheng Chan

The Politics

 Four Plays by

of Life

Asian American Women

Edited and with an
introduction and commentaries by
VELINA HASU HOUSTON

Temple University Press
PHILADELPHIA

Temple University Press, Philadelphia 19122

∞ The paper used in this publication meets the minimum requirements of Ameri-can National Standard for Information Sciences—Permanence of Paper for Printed Library Materials, ANSI Z39.48-1984

Printed in the United States of America

Photo of Velina Hasu Houston by Peter Martin.
Photo of Genny Lim by Bob Hsiang.

Library of Congress Cataloging-in-Publication Data
The Politics of life : four plays / by Asian American women ; edited and with an introduction and commentaries by Velina Hasu Houston.
p. cm. —(Asian American history and culture)
Contents: 12-1-A ; The chairman's wife / Wakako Yamauchi — Bitter cane / Genny Lim — Asa ga kimashita / Velina Hasu Houston.
ISBN 1-56639-000-1 (cloth : alk. paper). — ISBN 1-56639-001-X (pb : alk. paper)
1. American drama—Asian American authors.   2. American drama—Women authors.   3. American drama—20th century.   4. Asian Americans—Drama.   I. Houston, Velina Hasu.   II. Yamauchi, Wakako. III. Lim, Genny. Bitter Cane. 1993.   IV. Series: Asian American
PS628.A85P65   1993
812′.540809287—dc20   92-13090

To Setsuko and Kiyoshi

Contents

Acknowledgments *xi*

Introduction *1*

Wakako Yamauchi *33*

12-1-A *45*

The Chairman's Wife *101*

Genny Lim *151*

Bitter Cane *163*

Velina Hasu Houston *205*

Asa Ga Kimashita (Morning Has Broken) *219*

Acknowledgments

FIRST AND FOREMOST, I express my gratitude to Sucheng Chan and Roberta Uno, whose support for and belief in my creative and academic vision enriched and encouraged the development of this book. I give special thanks to Sucheng Chan for her editing expertise. I also express my appreciation to the playwrights for writing these plays, allowing them to be included in this volume, and providing supportive information about their backgrounds and careers. In addition, I express my thanks to Janet Francendese, senior acquisitions editor at Temple University Press, for her enthusiastic support of my efforts to create this book, and to Shirley Geok-lin Lim for her insightful critiques of my plays and her permission to quote her in this book. I also thank Marc Thomas King, my research associate, who helped in processing some of the written text to computer and whose general support of two of my creative projects this year has been invaluable.

For the artistic support and development that has led me to my peculiar position in international, American, and Asian/Pacific American theater, I express my heartfelt obligation to the following: my mother, Setsuko Takechi Perry, who encouraged me to write poetry at the age of six; my artistic family at the Old Globe Theatre—Craig Noel, Jack O'Brien, Thomas Hall, Mark Hofflund, Bill Eaton, and others—who give me the rarities of love and nurturance in the American theater; my artistic family at Manhattan Theatre Club—Lynne Meadow, Barry Grove, and others—who nurture my vision and art; Norman Fedder, Joel Climenhaga, Harold

Nichols, Theodore Apstein, Richard Walter, Michael Gordon, Robert Brustein, David Hillbrand, Mako, Keone Young, Alberto Isaac, Momo Yashima, Tisa Chang, Leon Denmark, Douglas Turner Ward, the late Samuel Barton, Count Stovall, Judith Nihei, Emilya Cachapero, Ernest Abuba, Tom Szentgyorgyi, the late Jonathan Alper, Julianne Boyd, Olympia Dukakis, Louis Zorich, Patricia Yasutake, Jessica Teich, Gordon Davidson, Akira Wakabayashi, Naomichi Fujinobu, Gwenn Victor, Peggy Shannon, Susan Albert Loewenberg, Emilie S. Kilgore, Julia Miles, Juli Thompson Burk, Dennis Carroll, Gene Shofner, Michael C. Donaldson, Gary D. Kaufman, Phylis Geller, the late Steve Tatsukawa, Mary Jane Eisenberg, Dana Ardi, Bobbi Thompson, Robert Kelley, Randy Adams, Yuriko Doi, Robert Alpaugh, Howard Allen, Gary Gisselman, Tomas Hernandez, Ron Sossi, Jan Lewis, Lucy Pollak, Jody Roman, Richard Toscan, James Day Wilson, Herbert Shore, Melissa Meyer, Bonita Matthews, Margie Smilow, Donna Marie Carolan, Lois Berman, Lee Grant, Cedric Scott, Sidney Poitier, James Clark, Arthur Storch, Barbara Trembley, Yvonne Styles, Deidre Berthrong, Bob Myman, John Ritter; and my wonderful literary agents, Mary Harden of Bret Adams, Ltd., and Merrily Kane of The Artists Agency.

I also must thank the people in my personal life who provide spiritual, cultural, and artistic encouragement, without which this book never would have been realized: my mother, Setsuko, and my stepfather, Homer L. Perry; my son, Kiyoshi Sean Shannen Houston; H. Rika Houston, Brian Ten and family, Victor Wortman, Frances Young and family, Tohta Tomizawa and family, Haruko Takechi and family, Donald Nahaku, Kazue and Daniel Logan, Joji Kawada Houston, Teresa Kay and Tracy Jay Williams, Steven Kent Brauer, Sandy Alpert, Philip Tajitsu Nash, Arlene Derenski, Donna Marie Carolan, Barbara Broman, Patsi Graham, Natalie and Harlow Ginright, Honey B. Friedman, Yuri and Bill Kochiyama, Bonnie Oda Homsey, Takayo and Sy Fischer, Olga Varga, Lori Rika Inano, Camille Hamilton, David Silverman, Irving and Nancy Pearlberg, Mark Utzinger, Chi-en Telemaque, Patricia Ayame Thomson, Melanie Hughes, Ruth De Sosa, Dura Temple, Sheri Bailey, Ann Ng, Joyce Nako, Wakako Yamauchi, Momoko Iko, Sharon Maeda, Jude Narita, Sue Kunitomi Embrey, Emma Gee, George Toshio Johnston, Phyllis and Galen Murakawa, Marilyn Tokuda, the Reverend Gary London, Allison Erkelens Shutler, Alison and Jordan Frank, Kathrin and Alexander Seitz, Richard R. Isaacs, Walter Allan Bennett, Mari Sunaida, Paul F. Moore II, Corinne Asaeda-Ramirez, Freda Foh Shen, Tara Marchant, St. Augustine's By-the-Sea Genesis House Church, all of my Amerasian brothers and sisters who struggle as people of color in America, and others who are too numerous to mention. I also owe thanks to my maternal grandmother, Fusae Takechi, whose spirit living through my mother and through me has renewed me again and again, both personally and artistically. Last, but certainly not least, I wish to thank all the theater artists and technicians who continue to bless the theater with their enriching talents and help to bring dramatic literature to life, and the readers and audiences who give their attention to the page and the stage.

I feel grateful to be a part of a vital and flourishing theatrical expression that is only beginning to show its colors in these increasingly diverse United States and in the ever-shrinking global village.

To quote the late poet Delmore Schwartz: "God is in love, in love with possibility."

Introduction

I fire at the face
Of the country where I was born . . .
As the waves splash, moment by moment,
I stand ready to fire
With the pistol of confession.
                                        —Kazuko Shiraishi

JAPANESE POET KAZUKO SHIRAISHI'S poem "I Fire at the Face of the Country Where I Was Born"[1] reveals the feminine experience as a political experience—as an existence belabored by the dogs of history, the senility of history, contemporary societal perspectives about women, and the need to manage the rage often catalyzed by these burdens. The pistol of confession aimed at our beloved country—that is the reality at which the Asian American woman playwright sooner or later must arrive, because the history of oppression of people of color and women in the United States leaves her no other truly honest route. She is compelled to mine her soul and come to grips with who she is in relation to society. The confession of Shiraishi's poem is a pistol because without such assertive behavior—without breaking the limiting boundaries of stereotype and prejudgment—she remains unheard. It is confession because we, as multicultural beings, are frequently at odds with America. We must challenge America's understanding of our history and her

---

[1]Kazuko Shiraishi, "I Fire at the Face of the Country Where I Was Born," in *Women Poets of Japan*, ed. Kenneth Rexroth and Ikuko Atsumi (New Directions Books, 1977), 110–11. Reprinted with permission of New Directions Publishing Corporation.

1

perceptions about our present and future. We must confess the angst and fear and rage that oppression has wrought while sustaining our relationship with America as proud citizens. *Confession* means we have developed a rich voice and we must be heard. It means we challenge all manifestations of oppression. The playwrights in this volume wield their own unique pistols, firing in different directions, but never missing their marks. The politics of life challenge us to maneuver within and around the bastion of European American patriarchy and to manage our lives and the accompanying rage with clarity, imagination, honesty, integrity, and resolve amid the erosive elements of racism, sexism, and antifeminism.

WAKE-UP CALL

In 1980, when I was a master of fine arts student of playwriting at the University of California at Los Angeles, I wrote a play entitled *Asa Ga Kimashita* (*Morning Has Broken*). One of my playwriting teachers, a European American, told me that the play had no place in the American theater because American theater audiences had no desire to see a play set in postwar Japan that focused on the fall of a Japanese patriarch. He said that I would never become a "real play-wright" unless I began writing for a "wider" audience. I was not certain if the professor said "wider" or "whiter," because the fan in his office diminished the sound quality, but there was no need to ask. In this case, the words were synonymous. The play went on to win several prestigious national awards and other honors. Apparently, American theater audiences do have an appetite for more than just meat loaf and apple pie.

The waves continue to splash on the faces of Asian American women playwrights as we carve new places for ourselves. One would like to believe that the civil rights movement rid America of racism, but that is a naive, if not ignorant, view. One would like to believe that racism is put aside as repugnant, something for the right-wingers to practice inconspicuously, like a sand flea crawling onto the fragmented continents of our lives. But I certainly feel the itch. I feel the prickle. In my life as a playwright, there are a great many wake-up calls that alert me to the fact that my being Amerasian and female *does* make a difference, no matter what the idealists profess. And, often, I am one of those idealists.

My life defies placement in any singular or traditional category. I am Amerasian, which means that I am neither Asian nor American (and yet both) and that I am neither native Japanese, Blackfoot Pikuni, nor African American (and yet all three)—truly multiracial and multicultural. My rendering categories useless also is true of my artistic and academic worlds. I have been writing plays for twenty-one years and enjoy a career as a playwright and screenwriter. At the same time, in my academic career I lecture in the United States and Japan on theater, playwriting, Japanese culture, Amerasian identity, and Japanese American culture and teach at the University of Southern California's School of Theatre. I am an amalgam of three cultures, two countries, and three races; I also am an amalgam of the artist and the academic. The spirit that fuels my art feeds my love for teaching; this blend of artistic voice and academic vigor shapes this volume. The plays in this volume reflect, for the most part, an artistic consciousness of the significance of the essential elements of drama. I am familiar with many plays by Asian American women. The works in this volume were chosen because the playwrights are pioneers; their work in the American theater has opened avenues of opportunities for other Asian American women playwrights to have their work presented. Wakako Yamauchi's *And the Soul Shall Dance*, Genny Lim's *Paper Angels*, and my play *Tea* have been ground breakers, being widely produced and often at theaters that had never produced a play with an Asian American theme, for example, the world premiere of *Tea* at Manhattan Theatre Club.[2] Other Asian American women playwrights whose work includes this artistic consciousness are Akemi Kikumura, Linda Kalayaan Faigao, Victoria Nalani Kneubuhl, Karen Yamashita, Rosanna Yamagiwa Alfaro, Jeannie Barroga, Elizabeth Wong, Cherylene Lee, and Karen Huie. Their plays are dramatic literature that go beyond the temporal nature of theatrical entertainment. Other interesting and provocative theatrical material exists, but it eludes classification as a play, as dramatic literature. As this book goes to press, new

---

[2]Momoko Iko also fits this category, but the rights to her plays were not available to include them in this anthology.

voices are emerging that will enrich the offerings of Asian American women in this category.

The women in this anthology have managed to be unconventional and still maintain essential elements of drama, an approach that has created genuine dramatic literature that will stand the test of time and not be simply adventurous explorations later relegated to the status of experiments or fads. These are writers who have paved the way for Asian American women who write prose or poetry or who act—such as Amy Hill, Jude Narita, Brenda Aoki, Jessica Hagedorn, Chungmi Kim, Mari Sunaida, Marilyn Tokuda, Patty Toy, and Szu Wang—to test the waters of the playwriting world successfully.

THE AMBIGUITIES OF LANGUAGE AND DEFINITIONS

Many terms in this introduction, at first glance, might seem familiar to the reader but, with deeper examination, might become confusing. The ambiguities and limitations of language can be startling when people resist the categories imposed on them. At its best, language—just like race, politics, or geography—is nothing but labels that are defied by the subjectivity of the human mind. For example, the U.S. Bureau of the Census labels Tongan Americans as Pacific Islander Americans, yet they are not found gracing Asian American cultural festivals; they are found, rather, showing their wares at the African Marketplace in Los Angeles's Crenshaw District. When I questioned a Tongan American at the 1991 marketplace, he answered that the Tongan cultural artifacts he had to sell were more African than Asian and that he felt "more comfortable" with African Americans. His presence at the African Marketplace leads people to guess about his race. What is he? Asian or African or Pacific Islander? Does he decide or does the observer or the government or biology decide? Similarly, *race* can be a rather useless and nonspecific term. My race often is identified incorrectly—from Polynesian to South American to Malaysian—as strangers feel compelled to guess my origins. At a seminar sponsored by the Dramatists' Guild, I was amused to hear several artistic directors of Los Angeles–area theaters state that they preferred New York playwrights to California playwrights, prompting a Los Angeles–based, award-winning playwright to ask how her status would change when she moved to Brooklyn. I wondered about myself. Having been transplanted in California from Kansas, am I a midwestern playwright or a California playwright?

What is a play? My definition begins with Aristotle's *Metaphysics*: "The world must be understood as a unity, not portrayed as 'episodic.' " The remainder of the definition, formulated over years of literary, philosophical, and cultural journeying, hinges on this idea of connectedness.

A play must have a plot, a premise, characters, meaningful language, conflict that rises to a climax, and a conclusion/resolution. Plot is the composition of events.[3] The characters must include a protagonist with a clear and compelling dramatic objective; often, this protagonist may be a double protagonist or a multiprotagonist. By the play's end, the protagonist must experience a transformation. If the play has supporting characters, their compelling needs must be catalysts for conflict with the protagonist. Every principal character must have something at stake. All speech must be useful; it must move the plot along and/or reveal character. "Character discloses choice: it shows the kind of choice in cases in which it is not obvious what a man [person] is choosing or avoiding. That is why there is no character in speeches in which the speaker has nothing to choose or to avoid. Mind is exhibited where people argue that something is or is not the case, or make some general affirmation."[4]

A play is not performance art, a poetry recital, or disconnected episodes. These latter alternatives do not provide the catharsis that makes theater *theater*. Says Renford Bambrough, "The aim of the dramatist can therefore best be achieved by constructing a plot in which there is an intelligible sequence of events, one in which the spectators can see why the later events naturally would or inevitably must follow from the earlier."[5] To quote Aristotle, "Even the beauty

---

[3] Renford Bambrough, ed., *The Philosophy of Aristotle* (Mentor Books, New American Library, 1963), 412–20.
[4] Ibid.
[5] Ibid.

and exhilaration of brilliant speeches and episodes fade quickly and ultimately mean little without plot and a considered arrangement of events."[6]

Playwrights must clutch these necessities in the fists of their gifted craft and then begin to explore/stretch/manipulate/knead the boundaries. A "considered arrangement of events" does not necessarily mean that a playwright must write the "well-made play" with two or three acts that unfold like old English drama. A good play does not have to be linear or naturalistic or Elizabethan to be well made; but every good play is blessed with the essential dramatic elements that make it a play and that take both the characters and the audience on a journey that moves the soul. A play without the essential dramatic elements is like a human body without a brain, heart, lung, or spine. The blood of the play does not travel and it has nothing to say.

In my playwriting classes, I tell my students that, in certain respects and on a simplistic level, writing a good play is like trying to get from one destination to another. For instance, to get to New York from Los Angeles, a path must be set. It may be a different path from the one someone else takes, but it *is* a path, a plan with basic rules of the road that keep one on track. Once that path is set, one is free to wander off of it, do somersaults, run in circles, explore, fly, crawl; but, ultimately, the markers one sets must be followed or one will never get to New York—and neither will one's readers or audience. To follow other markers is to set a new path (not to go without a path). In writing for the theater, the "markers" or "path" are the aforementioned fundamental dramatic elements, whether organized in traditional or peculiar ways or tucked away in soaring lyricism that makes the observer believe they are not there. That is the secret—having markers but letting the flesh and blood of the play keep the audience from seeing the skeleton.

What is mainstream theater?   The mainstream American theaters are major theaters that largely produce plays written by European American male playwrights, or by deceased European playwrights. By *major*, I mean theaters above the Equity-waiver, Off-off Broadway, and ninety-nine-seat theater level. This includes Equity houses from Off Broadway to regional League of Resident Theatre

[6]Ibid.

(L.O.R.T.) theaters to Broadway to other large commercial houses around the country. It also includes smaller theaters, especially in Los Angeles, New York, Chicago, and San Francisco, whose artistic successes have created high profiles for them, such as the Odyssey Theatre Ensemble, The Magic Theatre, The Second Stage, and Steppenwolf Theatre Company.

Plays by persons of color are usually dubbed *ethnic theater,* although the reality is that *all* American theater is ethnic theater. Discussing the marginalization of the works of playwrights of color by mainstream theaters that produce plays portraying "a relatively homogenous society, with white males as the centers and prime movers," playwright David Henry Hwang said, "This is ethnic theater [too]—but the theater of only one ethnic group."[7] Indeed, even European Americans—be they of German, Italian, Irish, etc., descent—possess ethnicity, based on their ancestral origins. What is important about plays by Americans of color is that they are truly a sign of the growth of a modern theater genuinely native to America, in terms of our history and future as a country in which colors and cultures collide.

What is a major playwright? *Major* means superior in importance, rank, or stature. The heart of the matter is that the norm for comparison in America is what I call the Great Eurocentric Yardstick. Generally speaking, society perceives playwrights of color as minor relative to American playwrights overall (except for a few African American mega-playwrights such as Lorraine Hansberry and August Wilson or Chinese American playwright David Henry Hwang). This minority position is based on the fact that a majority of the plays being produced in mainstream American theater today are written either by male Europeans or European Americans. When playwrights of color, such as Wakako Yamauchi in the world of Asian American playwrights, are considered in their ethnic subset, they become mega-major, if you will.

About eight years ago, *People* magazine was considering doing an "up-and-coming" style article about me, but the editors were indecisive as to whether or not I was a sufficiently important playwright. The editor, who was interested in my literary prolificacy

---

[7]David Henry Hwang, *Broken Promises: Four Plays by David Henry Hwang* (Avon Books, 1983), xi.

juxtaposed against my youth, subject matter, and craft, asked me in an apologetic tone, "How can you tell when a playwright is important?" He noted that a great many playwrights existed who, like me, had been produced in New York and had several other productions around the country. "Who, exactly, should be considered major?" the editor asked. The answer to that question is almost always subjective, except in the cases of a few high-profile, affluent playwrights. In terms of living American playwrights, after Arthur Miller who is to determine who is major? Despite the editor's uncertainty over my standing as a playwright, the magazine published the article. His question could not be answered objectively because no objective definition exists.

The kinds of plays that are important to me are plays that give something to the world in which we live, that recycle our emotions, spirit, and intellect to refuel and improve the world—not destroy it. Important plays are rich with cultural and political substance. They reflect a social consciousness without losing a sense of the personal. Their vision remains inextricably tied to the never-ending exploration and excavation of the human condition. For theater should not only entertain but also enlighten. Cuban American playwright Maria Irene Fornes also believes art has educational value. In her plays, she said, people always are learning and "trying to find a way out, rather than feeling a romantic attraction to their prison." She explains, "The play is there as a lesson because I feel that art ultimately is a teacher. You go to a museum to look at a painting and that painting teaches you something. You may not look at a Cezanne and say 'I know now what I have to do.' But it gives you something, a charge of some understanding, some knowledge that you have in your heart."[8]

I use the term *political* in a way that is not limited to the actions of government. It relates to the negotiations of power, economics, ethics, emotion, culture, race, gender, class, relationships, intellect, art—that is, the politics of life. In this sense, Momoko Iko, Wakako Yamauchi, Genny Lim, Frank Chin, Philip Kan Gotanda, Walter Allan Bennett, Maria Irene Fornes, Marlane Meyers, Samm-Art Williams, George C. Wolfe, Jeff Stetson, Luis Valdez, and others are

[8] Maria Irene Fornes in *In Their Own Words: Contemporary American Playwrights*, ed. David Savran (Theatre Communications Group, Inc., 1988), 55–56.

important playwrights or "major" American playwrights. In general, a playwright is an unknown entity to the average American. We have movie theaters in most of our cities and towns, but the attendees rarely know the names of the screenwriters. We do not have major theaters in most of our towns, and even in the cities in which they do exist, the playwrights' names do not trip off the tongue. So when I use the term *major playwright*, I am referring to individuals who may not be household names.

What is an "Asian," an "Asian American," or an "Amerasian"? An *Asian* is someone who is native Asian. An *Asian American*, on the other hand, is *not* Asian. An Asian American is an American of Asian descent, born and reared in the United States. An *Amerasian*, a term coined by Pearl S. Buck, is someone who is half Asian (usually native Asian) and half American. The American half can be of any racial extraction. A *Eurasian* technically is someone who is half native European and half native Asian, although the term is often used to describe someone who is half European American and half Asian American.

As the Asian American community goes, so go the expressions of its playwrights. The community is changing. The high outmarriage rate promises an increasingly multiracial and multicultural Asian America in the future. This change began to take root during the U.S. occupation of Japan, during which the first large number of Asian interracial marriages occurred; these were between native Japanese women and American soldiers. Contrary to the belief of Misha Berson, European American San Francisco theater critic who edited *Between Worlds,* a volume of Asian American theater pieces and plays (by men and women writers), these marriages were not solely with European Americans. Berson, speaking about the Asian American experience and how it affected the growth of Asian American theater, noted the shift in attitude toward Asian Americans after U.S. soldiers returned with native Asian international brides. She reflects the limitations of the European American perspective by noting only that "intermarriages and social interactions between Asians and Caucasians increased."[9] She gives credit solely to these marriages for changing America's perception of Asian (or

[9] Misha Berson, ed., *Between Worlds* (Theatre Communications Group, Inc., 1990), ix–xiv.

what she refers to as "Asiatic") America.[10] Numerous post–World War II Asian intermarriages also occurred with African American, Mexican American, and Asian American soldiers who brought home their international brides and forever changed the face of Asian America. (Intermarriages also resulted from the Korean conflict and the Vietnam War.) In addition, in America, marriages between Asian Americans and Americans of other races occurred. These interracial marriages continue at a rapid rate today.

Slowly, out of necessity, Asian American values and outlooks are shifting according to these dynamics. Even more slowly, Asian American artists have begun to reflect the diversity of the community. After years of silence and perceived docile cultural invisibility, their voices have begun whispering, projecting, and (when necessary) shouting. Writing for the theater is an important aspect of this expression.

The dynamics of change often reveal people who fall between the categories: immigrants who are Asian by blood and birth, but who are transplanted by some means to America and begin their American socialization journey late, or the binational and bicultural children to whom they give birth. My Japanese mother, being a newcomer to this country, a Shin-Issei (new first generation), falls into the former category. If you ask her what she is (despite the fact that she holds an American passport), she will tell you with clarity and centeredness that she is Japanese. My American friends often balk when they hear me say that I am not American. But it is a simple truth. I am an American citizen, but I am not American. I am Amerasian—half American and half native Japanese. In the past, political activists have said that I glorify my Japanese heritage. That is not the case. I glorify my deserving mother for the strength and grace she has exuded throughout difficult years of struggling to survive in America and managing all the external pressures that society foists upon interracial, intercultural marriages. That she happens to be Japanese merely must have been part of some greater plan. She knew how to raise me and my sister, Rika, in only one way—the Japanese way—and I make no apologies for that conditioning. It is hers; it is mine; it is I.

Traditional Asian American ethnicities usually are considered

[10] Ibid.

to be Japanese Americans, Chinese Americans, Filipino Americans, Korean Americans, and Vietnamese Americans. Nontraditionals include Amerasians, Pacific Islander Americans, indigenous Hawaiian Americans (one percent of the population of Hawai'i, according to the *Honolulu Advertiser*), East Indian cultures, and others. The U.S. government's one-eighth ancestry definition (as noted in Executive Order 9066) is the generally accepted guideline for defining an Asian/Pacific American.

What is an Asian American playwright? Easy answer: an Asian American playwright is a playwright is a playwright is a playwright. To be more specific, he or she is a playwright who is at least in part of Asian descent.

What is an Asian American play? It is a play written by an American citizen of Asian ancestry. Because, however, the subject matter of Asian American playwrights is not limited to Asian American topics, subject matter also may become a consideration (from a theater's point of view) in labeling a play an "Asian American" play. Often, plays authored by people who are neither Asian nor Asian American but who use Asian or Asian American subject matter are labeled Asian American plays. Is the play *Rich Relations,* written by David Henry Hwang, an Asian American play? It focuses not on issues of ethnicity but on the matters of a European American family, yet it is authored by Hwang. Is my play *Necessities* an Asian American play? It is about a European American woman and deals head-on with issues of race and culture, which are but two of many that are important to the enlightenment of the central character. Her Japanese American best friend and a multiracial Afro-Sicilian woman figure importantly in the character's dramatic journey. So what is it? An African American play? An Asian American play? (Is it not interesting that we never hear comments such as "Oh, that's a white play"?) It is parochial, then, to think that Asian American women can write only about Asian American female topics. Putting such a limitation on our subject matter "ghettoizes" the scope of Asian American women playwrights' views of the world and becomes another form of oppression. As Julia Miles, artistic director of the Women's Project and Productions in New York, notes in her book *Five New Plays from the Women's Project,* regarding plays developed by her organization, "These plays put an end to the old question, 'What should a woman write about?' Everything she knows or dreams about. All of it. Amen." [11] The same can be said for Asian American women in the theater. We must write about what we know or dream. But I add that we also should write about what we think and about subjects for which we feel passion.

What is Asian American theater?   It is theater that is either by or about Asians, Amerasians, or Asian Americans, usually presented in an Asian American theater (one that produces primarily Asian American plays). Again, the question of subject matter arises.

What is feminism?   The feminism that reveals itself in this volume is more than political ideology, more than a stereotypical label bandied about by the media in an attempt to make the women's movement appear to be obsolete. It is self-empowerment, self-definition, and self-determination for women as they try to bring the scales of economic, professional, domestic, and educational justice into balance.

Lim decries the label of *feminism* because she feels that, like *multiculturalism,* it has lost its usefulness. "The label tends to get absolutist and people create all these dichotomies that cause 'feminism' to appear to be so simplistic," she said. "Feminism, however, is very complex. It shouldn't be reduced to just a gender issue. It is also a race, class, and culture issue." Yamauchi does not like the label either, although she believes she is a feminist. "I like to think of myself as an individualist," she said. "I believe in every woman standing up for her rights. Does that make you a feminist? If it does, then my mother must have been a feminist, too, because she certainly stood up for herself." Yamauchi described her mother as "not the silent, complying Japanese woman, but very strong, independent, and outspoken." She feels that feminism as a categorical label becomes confining, stating that it is "unfair to limit the perspective of what feminism stands for." "It stands for more than economic rights," Yamauchi said. "Feminism is concerned with the humanity of women." [12]

As women, we produce art—in essence, *give life.* I see feminism as referring to the gifts of patience, resilience, fortitude (that is,

[11] Julia Miles, ed., *Five New Plays from the Women's Project* (Applause Theatre Book Publishers, 1989), v.
[12] Wakako Yamauchi, conversation with the editor, 3 August 1989.

nurturance), and a hunger for truth that allow us not only to give life but also to try to teach survival. In Shirley Geok-lin Lim's critique of my plays, she defined my feminism as "not a party-line feminism" but a concern about women's spirit, intellect, and lives.[13] I think her perception fits the other writers in this volume as well. To enlarge upon that definition, feminism is a compassionate, sensitive, and *active* concern for the spirit, intellect, politics, sociology, economic health, ethnocultural identities, and emotional and physiological complexities of women; indeed, for our very lives and fates.

The feminism in these plays explores the souls of Asian and Asian American women whose personal and public politics marry for life. It is feminism without a loss of femininity or individuality. And to limit an understanding of femininity to the colloquial connotation of beauteous and decorative behavior that subordinates women to men is simply more stereotype. I equate being feminine with being strong and powerful *because* we are women and not *in spite* of it. The truth is, individual women are so unique that the mind boggles at the wide range of what can be defined as feminine or feminist. Journalist Nina J. Easton writing in *Los Angeles Times Magazine* noted that life in today's America demands that feminism become more pragmatic, a brand that "helps women muddle through the daily conflicts of work and family, not one that constructs 'politically correct' road maps of how women should live their lives."[14] The playwrights in this volume do not draw politically correct road maps either. They struggle to balance perspectives on family, work, and art with the pressures and challenges of culture and ethnicity. There can be no road maps or narrow views.

Lim noted the dangers of lumping women under a singular banner. "Each woman is so different," she said. "Right now, there's a subtle backlash going on in our society in terms of people seeing feminism as a threat. We simply aren't a monolithic group, and it is unfair for society to treat us in that way. When working-class

---

[13] Shirley Geok-lin Lim, unpublished critique offered at Asian American Cultural Transformations Conference, University of California at Santa Barbara, California, April 1991.

[14] Nina J. Easton, "I'm Not a Feminist But . . .: Can the Women's Movement March into the Mainstream?" *Los Angeles Times Magazine, Los Angeles Times,* 2 February 1992, 14.

women are seen as a collective enemy then we become more op-
pressed than before. Toni Morrison calls herself a womanist instead
of a feminist. I won't call myself either."[15] Modern feminism cannot
ask us to wear a uniform, or the peculiar personal colors blend into
the background and are never seen, and subsequently we are cursed
by society's narrow perspectives of our complex realities.

THROUGH OUR OWN EYES

This is one of two anthologies of plays by Asian American women
that are coming to market concurrently. The other book, *Unbroken
Thread,* is edited by my colleague and sister in art Roberta Uno.
Artistic oppression kept the voices of Asian American women playwrights behind closed doors for many years.

   The need for *Unbroken Thread* and *The Politics of Life* became
obvious from the numerous requests to help individuals, organizations, and educational institutions locate plays written by Asian
American women. In 1990, for instance, the International Women
Playwrights Center contacted me because they had virtually no
information about Asian American women playwrights. The de-
mand has remained strong and consistent, especially from women's
studies' programs at colleges and universities. Inundated with requests, I could no longer act as an information clearinghouse for
myself or my fellow playwrights. For several years, Uno has been uti-
lizing manuscripts of *Tea* and several other plays by women of color
in her theater classes at the University of Massachusetts at Amherst.
At the University of Southern California, I have used Yamauchi's
And the Soul Shall Dance in my dramatic literature class, while
Dr. Herbert Shore has assigned *Tea* and *Asa Ga Kimashita* in history and literature courses. Although the dramatic literature in the
academic world remains virtually monochromatic, incorporating
almost no plays by Asian American women in particular, I continue
to get requests from universities around the country for information. In order for Uno, Shore, and I to teach these plays, we have had
to take a grass-roots approach. In my efforts to encourage universities to use these plays in traditional dramatic literature courses, I am

[15] Genny Lim, conversation with the editor, 4 February 1992.

astonished at the inability of some academics to grasp even conceptually the reality of Asian American theater. I say "Asian American" and many say "Asian," as in Kabuki, Noh, or Bunraku theater. Even many who understand the legitimacy of an African American or Hispanic American theater tradition do not see the distinction I am making. Only some who teach women's studies, ethnic studies, and Asian American studies seem to recognize the value of teaching diverse dramatic literature. The changing ethno-racial demographics of our country (especially of California) mandate broadening the knowledge base by offering a wider spectrum. I am not suggesting that we replace European and European American dramatic literature, but rather that plays created by Asian American women be allowed to coexist with them with integrity and fairness. In order to coexist, however, we must first exist. We must exercise our voice and have it available in print in order to widen its exposure.

When I first began teaching at the University of Southern California, the syllabus long in use for a class in modern dramatic literature included twelve plays by European and European American men, ten of them deceased. But modern drama did not stop being modern in the 1940s. The very definition of modern drama as plays that break with the past and strive to create a future that is discontinuous with it incorporates an evolving dynamic. We define today's modernism as "contemporary" dramatic literature, but, for today, it is indeed as modern as *Ghosts* was when it appeared in the 1880s. American playwrights are continuing to push the edge of the envelope and dynamically are redefining what is "modern" about dramatic literature. The U.S.C. syllabus now includes the works of both women and people of color while maintaining at least one play by each of the deceased playwrights: Henrik Ibsen, August Strindberg, Anton Chekhov, Eugene O'Neill, and so forth. One of the plays added was Lorraine Hansberry's *A Raisin in the Sun,* a selection that met with a surprising response. In my first semester of teaching the play, it was chosen as the favorite play in a class whose students were 99 percent upper-class European American. So much for relevancy or generic prescriptions of what the people want to read or see.

In desiring cultural and gender diversity in theater, I am not asking for political correctness. Rather, I am asking people to challenge their minds and broaden their perspectives. I consider "political correctness" to be a term created by the European American far right in order to maintain its position of power and privilege in this society, a position achieved by a long legacy of racial and sexual oppression. The right presents political correctness as a demon created by the liberal left, when in reality it is mere camouflage for their own self-defense. Let us not forget: once upon a time, African American slavery was politically correct; once upon a time, the incarceration of Japanese Americans was politically correct. Last year, while discussing the issue of diversity with several European American professors, I noted the concerns of an Asian American female student who felt that most European American professors saw her as "only an Asian face and not as a human being." Several took umbrage at this remark, stating with great emotion that they were insulted. I was awestruck by their outcry. As women and people of color ask America to let us come to the table as equal partners, we are asking that the men and European Americans of our society find it in their hearts and intellects to listen and to ask, "How can we work together to insure everyone has the opportunity to learn and contribute as an individual?" How can we, as a community of theater artists, work together to begin to reflect an even richer palette of our increasingly diversified society in our theater art? What good are we as an American theater of the future if our theater does not reflect the experiences of a broader range of cultures and races? What good are we as a society if we are growing in racial and cultural diversity, but the structures of power and learning do little to reflect the contributions of women and of non-European races and cultures?

The other problematic element of raising the profile of dramatic literature by Asian Americans is that, like other writers of color in this country, our work often cannot be published unless a European American chooses to analyze, edit, and present us. In effect, we must have a chaperone or it is difficult to come to the party. In illuminating this reality, I do not mean to diminish the importance of works that have traveled that necessary path (indeed, better to go chaperoned than not at all) or that will travel that path with integrity in the future. I simply am pointing to the need for self-determination.

Many people share a feeling of resentment and sometimes

anger that the legacy of racism has limited the access of people of color to both publication and production. Two-time Pulitzer Prize–winning playwright August Wilson succinctly expressed his feelings about this with regard to African Americans: "The history of blacks in America has not been written by blacks. And whites, of course, have a different attitude, a different relationship to the history. Writing our own history has been a very valuable tool, because if we're going to be pointed toward a future, we must know our past." [16] And our present, I might add. This is so basic and simple. While I encourage everyone to explore their areas of interest—no matter how foreign—Asian American women are stepping to the fore and realizing the value of examining our lives and our work ourselves. Doing so is a human and artistic right and a cultural necessity.

People of color too often are examined, labeled, and defined through the historical legitimacy of a European American perspective (because we live in a society that is unabashedly Eurocentric, that diminishes all other perspectives as secondary or inferior). Michael S. Berliner, writing for the *Los Angeles Times* service, stated that Western civilization should be honored because "it is the objectively superior culture" that "stands for man at his best." [17] In condescending to all other cultures, such narcissism seeks only to diminish the genuine concerns of multicultural diversity (which *includes* Western cultures along with others) and perpetuate the racism that limits the opportunities of people of color and women. A feeling exists among many people of color that European Americans believe they understand us better than we can understand ourselves because they have studied us. At the Interaction Amerasian Resettlement Conference held in Los Angeles in 1991, I gave a presentation on the historical aspects of the Amerasian experience to a mostly European American audience. Most of them were accustomed to working with Vietnamese refugee Amerasians and had never been confronted with the reality of a university-educated Amerasian. One couple, a European American man and woman, continually disrupted the session with their snickering. When I challenged the disruption, the

---

[16] August Wilson in *In Their Own Words*, 295.

[17] Michael S. Berliner, "It's 'Politically Correct' to Denigrate Columbus and Seriously in Error," *Honolulu Advertiser*, 1 January 1992, A13.

man said to me with disdain and condescension, "You're being too sensitive. You're *all* too sensitive."

What he meant, of course, was that Amerasians are sensitive. I am all too familiar with his emotions. It is the anger that is born in the rescuer when the victim develops a voice and walks on her own two feet. He could not absorb me as an authority when my face appeared to him as the mask of a victim. Because I am Amerasian, I understand the cultural and racial plight of the refugee Amerasian, especially what they face in their efforts to survive in America as multiracial and multicultural beings. This is a kind of insight that education, research, study, and third-party perspective can never own. As Japanese poet Junko Nishi says,

> I am
> forced to live by your images,
> I am always living like that,
> [and] so
> I understand revolution.[18]

Take, for example, *Between Worlds,* the very first anthology ever published of Asian American theatrical works (except for *Broken Promises,* an anthology solely of plays by David Henry Hwang). Although Berson, the book's editor, shows a caring attitude toward the development of Asian American theater, certain elements of her introduction reflect what August Wilson calls (as mentioned above) the "different attitude" and "different relationship" of European Americans to the history of people of color in America. Berson herself, noting the works of American plays and movies written by "non-Asian writers" (meaning non-Asian or non–Asian American), says of the ethnic stereotypes rife in these pieces: "Conceived by non-Asian writers, [they] had little to do with actual human behavior, and nothing at all to do with Asian self-definition."[19]

Berson understands the importance of self-definition for the Asian American writer, but her use of the terms *Asian* and *Asiatic* interchangeably for *Asian American* is discomfiting and empha-

---

[18] Junko Nishi, "Revolution," in *Women Poets of Japan,* ed. Kenneth Rexroth and Ikuko Atsumi (New Directions Books, 1977), 132. Reprinted with permission of New Directions Publishing Corporation.

[19] Berson, *Between Worlds,* ix–xiv.

sizes an inherent insensitivity toward people of Asian descent.[20] For example, I doubt Berson would confuse German Americans with Germans, using the terms interchangeably or referring to them as *Germanic*.

Berson also completely disregards an entire element of Asian American theater that has contributed an otherwise unheard voice to the scene, making no mention of Kumu Kahua, the second Asian American theater after East West Players, established in 1970 by several University of Hawai'i students and Dennis Carroll, a University of Hawai'i professor. She is not alone. This error of omission often also is committed by mainland Asian Americans in their conceptualization of the composition of Asian American theater. In omitting Kumu Kahua, they may be including Asian Americans or multiracial Asian Americans who label themselves *Hawaiian* because they were born in Hawai'i, but they dismiss the true indigenous Hawaiian culture and the Pacific Islander American cultures—both of which are significant parts of the tapestry of Asian American theater. Kumu Kahua is the only Asian American theater company that produces a wide range of plays that either explore those cultures or are created by persons who are of those cultures. The people at Kumu Kahua should be doubly commended for bringing to Asian American theater something that very few Asian American theater artists have brought—an inclusion of the experiences of Polynesians, indigenous Hawaiians, and contemporary multiracial people who live in the state of Hawai'i. Nontraditional cultures such as Pacific Islander Americans and Amerasians are often either overtly or inadvertently excluded from the definition of "Asian American experience."

Many European Americans have brought a clear and sensitive perception to the works of people of color and probably will continue to do so. In my own experience, several directors, artistic directors, and others who happen to be European American have enriched my work and brought illuminating perspectives to bear upon it, most notably my friends at the Old Globe Theatre and at Manhattan Theatre Club. Both are artistic homes at which I have experienced genuine nurturance of my theater art, based not on the fact that I am Amerasian or female but on my plays. This is because we connect as human beings and because they see me as an

[20]Ibid.

artist—not a person of color and a woman—first. As Jack O'Brien said, "The obvious thing is that here is also a woman of remarkable history and parentage. It begs the question, 'Did you take this playwright because of the area she covers?' No. It's a popular subject right now [referring to the themes of spiritual defoliation and private adoption in my play *Necessities*]. We're up to our hip boots in sensitive issues. But that's not why we selected [her play]. It's elegant, stunning writing."[21]

I use this quote in particular for the conservatives who think that if a playwright of color is desirable or successful today, it is because of his or her color and not because of artistic merit. A director with whom I worked told me about a young European American male playwright who complained that he cannot obtain any grants or fellowships because he is white. It is my belief that such a complaint is defensive euphemism. If anything, today his chances to be produced, published, or receive awards remain better than those of women and people of color. Grants and fellowships largely are awarded on the basis of the quality of one's writing and the subject matter of the material as it relates to the vision of the granting institution. The goal is not to be invited to the party because of our race or culture or gender but because of our artistic merit. It is the definitions of what is meritorious or good in quality or appropriate or relevant that need to be brought up to date. Playwrights of color must begin to be perceived as *playwrights* rather than as people of color who happen to have written plays.

The first two anthologies of Asian American plays written by women are collected and edited by Uno, a Japanese American whose children are half Jamaican, and by me—an Amerasian woman. This is important, not because others cannot or should not care about us, examine us, and comment upon us, but because it represents a challenge to members of our community to take part ourselves in the documentation of our history and to enlarge the outlook on our future by creating in our own voices. As Berson aptly reflected, it is "self-definition," self-determination. We have grown up now. We are old enough to be welcomed to the party without chaperones and to move forward with resolve. Of course, all are invited to enjoy the

---

[21] Jan Breslauer quoting Jack O'Brien, "Hues and Cries," *Los Angeles Times' Calendar*, 7 July 1991, 3.

festivities with us side by side, ever welcome in our efforts to coexist and enrich crosscultural understanding.

HISTORICAL PERSPECTIVES

In setting the context for the plays in this volume, I want to point out that Asian American dramatic literature is of relatively recent origin. In 1928, an Asian American woman, Gladys Li, wrote what may well be the first Asian American play, *The Submission of Rosie Moy*. In 1932 she wrote a second play, *The White Serpent*. The next known play by an Asian American woman dates back to the 1940s, in the years following World War II and the internment of Japanese American citizens by the U.S. government. The play is *Reunion* by Bessie Toishigawa Inouye, written in 1947.[22] For many years after Toishigawa Inouye, the female voice of Asian America in the American theater was silent.

In 1965, East West Players, the first Asian American theater company, was established in Los Angeles. Under the artistic direction of accomplished actor Mako, it became a vital force. In 1968, prompted by news of a national Asian American playwriting contest sponsored by East West Players, Momoko Iko, a fiction writer living in Chicago, decided to rework her novel about the internment experience into a play. The result was *Gold Watch*, produced in 1972 at Inner City Cultural Center, Los Angeles, making it the first professional production of an Asian American play. The play's 1976 PBS television production under the direction of Lloyd Richards signified mainstream recognition for the work of an Asian American woman playwright. Interestingly, literary expression in Asian American theater began with women, echoing the ancient historical patterns of culture and mythology in many native Asian societies. Soon, almost simultaneously, Chinese American playwright Frank Chin emerged on the scene with his play *Chickencoop Chinaman*. Clearly, the pace of Asian American dramatic production had quickened. By 1974, another important play by an Asian American woman was presented at the Asian Exclusion Act, an Asian American company

---

[22]This is mentioned by Roberta Uno in her forthcoming book *Unbroken Thread*, planned for 1994 publication by the University of Massachusetts Press.

in Seattle. The workshop production of Wakako Yamauchi's *And the Soul Shall Dance,* adapted from her short story of the same title, led to the play's professional premiere at East West Players in 1977; that same year, the play also was produced for television by PBS. As with Yamauchi's play, Genny Lim's *Paper Angels* also found mainstream recognition; first produced in 1980 at the Asian American Theater Company, San Francisco, it subsequently was produced in New York in 1982 at the New Federal Theatre and was produced for television by PBS in 1985. In 1981, my play *Asa Ga Kimashita* was produced at the University of California at Los Angeles. In 1984, *Asa Ga Kimashita* premiered at East West Players, and its sequel, *American Dreams,* simultaneously premiered Off Broadway at the Negro Ensemble Company. The following year, my play *Tea* began its theatrical life in a workshop production at the Asian American Theater Company. In 1986, the play had its professional premiere Off Broadway at Manhattan Theatre Club and currently is one of the most produced plays about the experience of Asians in America.

In addition to East West Players, Kumu Kahua, the Asian American Theatre Workshop, and the Asian Exclusion Act (now called the Northwest Asian American Theatre Company), other theaters also emerged. These included Pan Asian Repertory, founded in New York by Tisa Chang; the Asian American Actors Ensemble, founded in San Diego; the Asian American Theater Company, founded in San Francisco; the Theatre of Yugen, established by Yuriko Doi in San Francisco; and the Canadian Artists Group, founded in Toronto, Canada. These theaters produced the works of Asian American playwrights; they also produced European and/or European American plays cast with Asian American actors and usually directed by Asian Americans. Of late, a new company, Mako Productions, has been founded by Mako and former East West Players producer Keone Young. Chicago has spawned two Asian American companies, Angel's Island Theatre Company and Mina-sama-no.

Today, the works of the women included in this anthology continue to flourish, both in Asian American theaters and mainstream theaters. *Tea* was the first play by an Asian American woman to be produced at major Off Broadway and regional mainstream theaters, including Manhattan Theatre Club, the Old Globe Theatre, and Whole Theatre, the last produced by Academy Award–winning actress Olympia Dukakis. These productions opened the door for the consideration of plays by other Asian American women. Clearly, Asian American feminist expression in the theater had made its mark. As persons of Asian descent compose an increasingly larger segment of American society and non–Asian American society extends its interests into new areas, the works of these women may take on even greater significance, and, we hope, the artistic vision of mainstream theaters will expand in kind. From the now sixty-four-year-old legacy of Asian American women writing for the theater, I hope an abundance of works by new generations will spring forth. Speaking about the works of playwrights of color and of women, playwright David Henry Hwang noted, "These are more than merely fads or splinter movements. They are attempts by the American theater to come to grips with the multicultural character of our society, to portray it truthfully. As such, they represent simply the artistic face of what is essentially a political transformation." [23]

The writers included in this anthology span two generations, two countries, and two cultures. Iko and Yamauchi (along with Li and Toishigawa Inouye) represent the first wave of Asian American women playwrights. Lim and I are the early part of a second wave that also includes Akemi Kikumura, Karen Yamashita, Linda Kalayaan Faigao, Rosanna Yamagiwa Alfaro, and Karen Huie. While Iko and Yamauchi were influenced and catalyzed by the existence of Asian American theater, Lim and I arrived at our playwriting in unique ways that had nothing to do with the existence of such theaters. Lim, for instance, wrote *Paper Angels,* her first play, after exploring poetry that was discovered to be carved on the walls of Chinese immigrant detention centers on Angel Island in San Francisco Bay. When I began writing plays in Kansas, I had no idea what Asian American theater was, much less what an Asian American was (being part of a native Asian immigrant community where there were no Asian Americans). My desire to write for the theater was born purely out of literary instinct and the rather peculiar stimuli in my environment—stimuli related to ethnicity, race, culture, gender, and politics. I first heard about East West Players in 1983, several years after I had penned the first draft of *Asa Ga Kimashita.* My initial encounters with Asian Americans produced

[23] Hwang, *Broken Promises,* xi.

culture shock because they were and are so different from native Asians and Amerasians, in terms of aculturation and assimilation. The first and second waves, along with a fresh third wave, of Asian American women playwrights are all part of a tidal wave of literary feminist expression in America.

SOCIOPOLITICAL REALITIES

"Bein alive & bein a woman & bein colored is a metaphysical dilemma/do you see the point my spirit is too ancient to understand the separation of soul and gender," says the Lady in Yellow from Ntozake Shange's *for colored girls who have considered suicide when the rainbow is enuf.*[24]

The inability to separate the politics of living and one's ethnocultural identity and gender is a commonality among women of color writing for the American theater. In her book *Nine Plays by Black Women,* Margaret B. Wilkerson discusses this reality with regard to African American women playwrights' works: "Their characters embody a world in which the personal is political, in which something as intimate as one's hair may indeed declare one's politics."[25] We can never escape politics. I often say that if being who I am takes some explanation because it is something new, then I am bound and determined to explain it. Journalist Janice Arkatov once asked me if this gets tiring. In her *Los Angeles Times* interview I noted, "It does. But the need to solidify and create consciousness about who we are goes on. You can say, 'All right, enough. Let's get on with it.' But the reality is, in the getting on with it, experiences come up that need to be challenged, addressed. It's not like I go around with a sign saying, 'I'm Amerasian and let's have a political discussion about it.' I just go about my life—writing, teaching, being a mother—then I walk into a bank and somebody says something."[26] At moments when a racist remark cuts into the gut of my

[24]Ntozake Shange, *for colored girls who have considered suicide when the rainbow is enuf* (Bantam Books, 1976), 48.

[25]Margaret B. Wilkerson, ed., *Nine Plays by Black Women* (Mentor, New American Library, 1986), xiii.

[26]Janice Arkatov quoted in "Playwright Draws on Experience of Growing Up in an Interracial Household," *Los Angeles Times' Calendar,* 27 January 1991, 68.

being, personal life is uncontrollably transformed into the political. There is no sidestepping it and living peacefully with yourself. As a multiracial woman, I encounter racism not only from the European American majority but also from African Americans, Asian Americans, and Native Americans. Survival of spirit and the preservation of personal dignity become constant challenges.

Balancing the political nature of one's existence with one's artistic expression is not new. Women playwrights of color have been struggling with it for some time and always seemed to have exhibited the courage of one of our pioneers, Lorraine Hansberry, who should be an inspiration to anyone writing for the theater, but especially to women playwrights and women playwrights of color. For Margaret Wilkerson, the works of African American women writers "integrated the social and political with the private and personal self." Hansberry's "insistence on the social nature of art, the implicit criticism of American society in her plays, and her uncompromising views on the pervasiveness of prejudice and oppression made her work unpopular in some critical circles."[27] August Wilson does not dress the truth with euphemism or avoid it out of fear when he proclaims, "All art is political. It serves a purpose. All of my plays are political, but . . . not . . . didactic or polemical."[28] The same is true for Asian American women writers. The playwrights in this anthology peer into the lives of Asians and Asian Americans who are ensconced soul-deep in this never-ending struggle to balance the presence of the political in their lives with their personal humanity.

In *The Chairman's Wife,* Yamauchi examines the life of Madame Mao, wife of People's Republic of China Chairman Mao Tse Tung. Yamauchi follows Madame Mao from her childhood and days as a stage actress through her reign as the most powerful woman in China. The journey ends with Madame Mao as a political relic languishing in a prison hospital, suffering from throat cancer. Yamauchi's portrait depicts not only the realities of Madame Mao's life in China but also the political reality that her power created and the distortion of it in the European American media. Yamauchi approaches this subject matter with compassion and insight to draw

---

[27] Wilkerson, *Nine Plays by Black Women,* xxi.
[28] August Wilson in *In Their Own Words,* 304.

a meticulous portrait of an Asian woman's rise and fall. Madame Mao's journey is riddled with passion, politics, deceit, seduction, and desperation for power. The play's style is expressionistic, but the setting and other characters offer a harsh reality that one cannot avoid: a prison cell, a guard who is symbolic of the post-Mao government, and a young soldier who leaves us with an unnerving and unforgettable reverberative moment as he reveals the Tiananmen Square massacre. The play is set on the day of that massacre in June 1989.

In *12-1-A*, Yamauchi delves into subject matter that is tied into her personal history. The family at the center of this play, like Yamauchi's, is Japanese American and is sent to an incarceration camp in Poston, Arizona, by the U.S. government during World War II. *12-1-A* is a personal and political play about the Japanese American World War II incarceration experience. The story is seen through the eyes of Mrs. Tanaka, her son Mitch, and her daughter Koko, but it touches on myriad political elements of camp life. The play was called a "stirring account of those bitter years" by the *Los Angeles Herald Examiner* when it was produced by East West Players in 1982.[29] Focusing on the uprooted Tanaka family, we are taken to their new quarters (block 12, barrack 1, unit A), barely fit for animals. The Tanakas arrive emotionally unprepared for the reality of three people living in a tiny barrack. And, as if having your U.S. citizenship blatantly disregarded and being forced to live under unsatisfactory conditions were not enough, the Tanakas experience their first dust storm. They are blowing in the wind just like the Muratas and Okas, Issei families struggling to eke out an existence in *And the Soul Shall Dance*. The howl of the wind, however, echoes the Tanakas' fear, their unspoken rage, and the angst in their souls as they contemplate their situation and their uncertain futures. The characters feel distrust and anger toward America for, in effect, withholding the promise of the American dream from first-generation Japanese Americans on the basis of their race. Nisei, who are American by birth, are indignant that all the promises of democracy are no longer theirs because their face looks too much like the enemy. The young are torn by confusion as they sort out their emotions and politics amid a hostile America and families who

[29] Jay Reiner, *Los Angeles Herald Examiner*, 18 March 1982, C5.

are frustrated by grave losses, shame, and dishonor. The land of the free and the brave has been falsely advertised. Yamauchi takes us on this journey with gentle acuity that allows us, if we are open, to see through every character's eyes and understand the human frailty of government and the injustice done to Japanese Americans.

This play reverberates deeply for me today because of the changing political climate toward Japan (and, consequently, toward Americans of Japanese ancestry). A teenager in Kansas calls my mother a "Jap" and European American citizens of Detroit are quick to use the same epithet. A Japanese American in Pasadena receives an anonymous phone call saying "Go home, Jap!" At a ceremony marking the fiftieth anniversary of the incarceration of Japanese Americans, popular Los Angeles newscaster Tritia Toyota noted that, after she presented a news segment about the camps, the television station received anti–Japanese American hate mail. Yamauchi calls the political mood scary. "This is the way it happens," she shared in a personal interview. "The climate and all the words we are hearing are just like it was before World War II." She feels that the Asian-bashing has been going on for a long time but that America's current economic problems have intensified the Japan-bashing. Although she has not experienced overt racism, she said she has experienced the subtle modern kind that "you can't put your finger on." She said that she can visit stores in European American sections of Los Angeles and "never get waited on until every last customer has been waited on." Recently, in a Los Angeles restaurant, a European American man pointed at an Asian American family and asked, "Are you all Japs?" The father smiled, shook his head, and exclaimed with relief that they were from the Philippines.

Hysteria based on race fuels the political and racist rhetoric we now are hearing in America against Japan. It hides behind the generous euphemism of "nationalist sentiment" or, when America really wants to be critical of itself, Japan-bashing. It is the same hysteria that led to the incarceration of Japanese Americans during World War II. Though 12-1-A is about events that happened more than forty years ago, the play reminds us that history must not repeat itself, that we must learn from these mistakes, or, once again, past will be prologue.

In Bitter Cane, Genny Lim focuses on the political and socio-economic exploitation of immigrant Chinese who are recruited to labor on sugar cane plantations in Hawai'i. The play also focuses on the politics of love and the politics of family—in terms of a broken nuclear family and a family of human beings bound by the fact that they all are Chinese. The politics of love are examined through the relationship of protagonist Wing and the beautiful prostitute Li-Tai. Wing is running from the oppression of the plantation owners, but he also is running from the ghosts of history as he becomes privy to answers that he did not necessarily seek: he discovers that Li-Tai was the lover of his deceased father Lau Hing. She gives birth to Wing's manhood, not merely by being his first lover, but also by forcing him to face the truths of his own and his father's history. A soulful and poetic axis in the play, she serves as an important link for many of the Chinese cane laborers. She links them to their memories of the women of their homeland, helps them realize their sexual needs, and, even if only in the dreams of the men, links them to a future—the future when their contracts with the plantation have been fulfilled, when they will be free men again ready to build a future with a woman. In some respects, Li-Tai becomes all women for these Chinese laborers. Lim does not succumb to the cliche of painting Li-Tai as the prostitute with a heart of gold. Instead, Li-Tai is an intelligent, spiritual, maternal woman-child who lost her dreams and was so scarred by domestic and cultural oppression that she chose sexual slavery over freedom because the uncertainties and risks of freedom were too frightening.

In *Asa Ga Kimashita,* I examine the life of a Japanese patriarch (modeled after my maternal grandfather) who loses his estate in the face of the U.S. occupation's land reclamation regulations that were enforced after World War II. The loss of assets degrades his economic status, manhood, and dignity. This, coupled with his youngest daughter's love for an African American soldier, leads to his suicide. The play focuses on the position of Japanese women in terms of both Japanese postwar society and American men as represented by the U.S. Army in Japan, and it provides a prophetic preview of Japanese and American perceptions of Japanese Amerasians. It examines the controlling power and influence of patriarchy foisted upon the Japanese female and how the legacy of this patriarchy shaped women's lives.

Above and beyond the inescapable sociopolitical realities of living as women of color, these writers are dealing with the added element of culture. Their characters are Asian and Asian American women who are faced with and must challenge the cultural and sexual stereotypes of the Asian female within the worlds of the plays in which they exist. The stereotypes include the Asian woman as decorative accessory, model minority, dragon lady, exotic, the tragic butterfly, the prostitute, or the docile and deferential woman-child. In developing these characters and endowing them with the ability to challenge the status quo, the playwrights break down the stereotypes and create honest understandings of the varied intellects, emotional realities, cultural truths, and peculiar visions of Asian and Asian American women.

It is not enough, then, simply to write about ordinary life in ordinary ways because life can never be ordinary for the female of color. Asian American women playwrights are faced with the task of creating meaningful theater and expressing themselves artistically while sustaining a sensitivity toward culture and gender. These women are doing it with determination, as are a host of other Asian American women playwrights. The politics of living as women of color in this society and in the global village must continue to be examined.

OPPORTUNITIES

In 1987, I participated in a U.S.–Soviet theater arts exchange round-table. I was the only playwright with American citizenship. The Soviet artists charged that much of what was being produced in mainstream American theaters was "fluff," or superficial examinations of an elitist culture. Their complaint was that the soul had vanished from the American theater, that American writers were no longer writing for a "theater of meaning." According to these Soviet artists, only American playwrights of color and women playwrights were writing plays that delved into the social and political consciousness and provided some enlightenment with which to push forward in an increasingly culturally complex society such as America. Perhaps they were right.

In 1989, twenty thousand people attended a Broadway play

each night. Only a thousand attended a play written by a woman (Wendy Wasserstein's *The Heidi Chronicles*).[30] None saw a play written by a woman of color.

Thank God for theaters that provide opportunities for women writers and writers of color. A playwright and her play should never be commodities. There was a time when a playwright had an artistic home, a necessity that allowed the work to grow and refine over a period of years. This kind of nurturance is rare for playwrights in the American theater today. There are too many playwrights, theaters continue to be largely patriarchal and Eurocentric, and theaters are in economic trouble as they continue to feel the reverberations of the Reagan era arts cutbacks. Playwrights require not only the opportunity to be produced but also the all-important opportunity to fail. By this I mean that playwrights need an artistic home in which they can work on plays-in-progress and nurture them until they are ready to fly. This supportive development environment is still a rarity for the woman playwright and even more of a rarity for the Asian American woman playwright. Theaters have a long way to go in learning to be more imaginative and to stretch beyond the standard production slate into new ethnocultural territories. Playwrights of Italian, German, Irish, Polish, Russian, Norwegian, or British descent are not the only ethnicities whose plays may interest a subscription audience. David Henry Hwang spoke frankly about the tendency of theaters to focus on only white ethnic groups: "By focusing on the smallest thing, we expose the design of the whole. If we neglect some of the communities which make up our society, our perception of the whole becomes a lie. America has traditionally denied the importance of its minorities, and this denial has been reflected in its theater."[31] It is not the ethnicity or gender; it is the story and the execution of that story that ultimately matter.

August Wilson argues for an active commitment to new work: "If every regional theatre would select a playwright and commit themselves to doing a play of his or hers every year, by the third year you're going to have a better playwright. A theater will do its fifth Shaw in five years on the mainstage without even considering whether a new play deserves more attention than a staged reading or

[30] Miles, *Five New Plays*, v.
[31] Hwang, *Broken Promises*, xi.

second-stage production. Theaters should be encouraging and nur-
turing, providing a home for playwrights and providing audiences
with an alternative." [32]

All the more reason, then, to enjoy the voices in this volume, invisible to the masses for far too long. Any study of Asian American—
or, for that matter, *American*—dramatic literature is incomplete
without them. These women are members of a growing community
of women of color—Latina, African American, Native American,
and others—who are giving birth to a new dramatic literature for a
new America.

---

[32] August Wilson in *In Their Own Words*, 303.

Wakako Yamauchi

BORN IN CALIFORNIA'S IMPERIAL VALLEY in 1924 to Issei (first-generation Japanese American) parents, Wakako Yamauchi was one of four siblings, sharing her life with two sisters and a brother. Her father, Yasaku Nakamura, had come to the United States from Shimizu, Japan, where his family specialized in the making of kamaboko (a Japanese fish cake). The playwright's mother, Hamako Machida, came from Shizuoka, Japan, where her family was engaged in the packaging of tea. Both parents are deceased.

Yamauchi's family sustained itself by farming but had to move every two or three years due to the Alien Land Law. As a result, she grew up in the cities of Westmorland, Brawley, and Imperial—California desert communities near the Mexican border. Yamauchi's mother assisted the father in the fields and taught Japanese on Sundays at the Buddhist church. Yamauchi, who is a gifted painter, says of her mother, "[She] taught me all I know about morality, empathy, and compassion, and also about longing and love. She had a feeling for color and design, which I like to think I inherited." Of her father, Yamauchi says, "[He] was a quiet man and suffered his pain in silence. I did not inherit these traits."[1]

Yamauchi is undeniably a trailblazer for Asian American women writing in the American theater but seems unaware of the significance of her role. When I first contacted her about this anthology, she kidded that only her age qualified her as a "pioneer." Presuming that her parents continue to guard and guide her spirit, an Eastern view that I certainly uphold, Yamauchi believes that they are proud of her decision to be involved in the theater art. She bases this belief upon the fact that, in her parents' day, particularly when she was growing up in the Imperial Valley, racism was so overt that the chances of a young Japanese American girl becoming a playwright were slim, if not altogether nonexistent. Yamauchi says of her parents and her writing, "My mother smiles, drawing down the corners of her mouth. She knows she is reflected in every story I write. My father watches me grow old year by year, looking more and more like him. He smiles, too."

Yamauchi says that she writes by "trial and error and instinct" and that she chose playwriting because she enjoys watching the audi-

[1] This and following quotes from Yamauchi are from personal conversations with the editor, 3 August 1989.

ence respond to art. She studied briefly with the Writers Guild of America's Open Door Project in screenwriting and completed a correspondence course in short story writing. But her interest in writing began in her youth from stories her mother told her and stories in twenty volumes of *The Book of Knowledge,* which her father purchased from a traveling salesman. Yamauchi remembers cutting her fingers on the pages of those volumes in her zeal to absorb their stories. She shares that she "wished I knew all the words I read. [I] dreamed one day of painting pastoral pictures like Corot and writing poems like Tennyson." The stories that her mother shared with her were about Japanese people and unrequited love that often ended in tragedy or fables about loyalty in human relationships. One such story of loyalty that her mother told her is one that my mother also shared with me: that of Hachi-ko, the Akita dog who, until his death, faithfully returned to Shinjuku Station in Tokyo to wait for his master, who had passed away. A statue of the dog stands at Shinjuku Station today, forever a reminder of the importance of loyalty and faith in Japanese relationships of old.

When Yamauchi was released from a Japanese American internment camp (Poston 1 in Arizona) at the end of World War II, she went to Chicago and spent her hard-earned money, made working at a candy factory, to see plays for the first time in her life. She recalls seeing *Porgy and Bess, The Glass Menagerie, The Voice of the Turtle* (with Hugh Marlowe), and Diana Barrymore in a play called *Rebecca.* But Yamauchi says she did not dare think of becoming a playwright until after her short story "And the Soul Shall Dance" was published in an anthology and Mako, founder and then artistic director of East West Players, encouraged her to adapt it into a play. Says the playwright, "I was sort of pushed into playwriting—blind and unaware."

In 1955, Yamauchi gave birth to her only child, Joy, who today is editor of the Asian American newspaper the *Tozai Times.* Joy is married to dentist Victor Matsushita. All live in Gardena, California. They gave Yamauchi her first grandchild, Alyctra, in 1990. Threads of Yamauchi's mother and Yamauchi herself appear to have been reborn in Alyctra Matsushita. Yamauchi describes her as "very independent and strong" and says "she knows what she wants and expresses herself." Yamauchi feels this is necessary in today's world:

"Joy says that a girl *has* to be strong in order to survive and be a success."

Yamauchi struggled to pass on the Japanese culture of her mother to her daughter, but she feels that the anti-Japanese mood before and after World War II diminished the ability for Japanese Americans openly to adhere to their cultural practices, and beyond that, it was difficult to speak two languages in one household. "My husband and I tried to keep the culture and language alive but couldn't do it," she said. "We tried to talk Japanese once a week, but Joy would overhear us and it was like we were talking secrets. I decided then that English would be the first language in our home."

In reflecting on her life, Yamauchi said that, if she could change anything, she would have liked to have been "a little kinder." Because I think of her as kind, I asked her to elaborate and she laughed. "Well," she said, "I like my privacy. I'm pretty selfish about that. I don't mind giving what I have at all, but not my personal time and privacy." Most of all, Yamauchi said she wishes that she would have given more time to her daughter while Joy was growing up. "I often wonder how she's forgiven me for that," Yamauchi mused. Even if Yamauchi could not pass on Japanese language to Joy, what she did maintain with her daughter was the closeness that she also had shared with her own mother. "I feel that by writing, Joy can come to understand who I was and am by reading my words and seeing my plays," Yamauchi said. She also passed on a love of literature to her daughter, who writes and loves to read. Today, Yamauchi, who has been divorced for several years, said she feels "pretty good" about her life. Her family is the most important thing, and when it comes to writing, she prefers to write plays because they offer the opportunity to connect with human beings in the theater. Currently, Yamauchi is not writing anything new for the theater, but she said she still has a lot to say, and like Alyctra, I am certain she will express herself when the time comes.

Yamauchi's plays are about simple, but certainly never simple-minded, people. Indeed, the portraits she draws are of people—educated or otherwise—who examine their existence in complex ways, sometimes not even realizing the depths to which they are exploring. This is true of Emiko Oka in *And the Soul Shall Dance*. In fighting to keep alive her dreams of returning to Japan and reuniting with a lover whom she was forced to leave ten years earlier, Emiko dreams too hard and eventually succumbs to a death of the spirit because of an inability to cope with the hopelessness of the reality of her life in America. Emiko calls her ten years in America a "temporary exile." The characters that Yamauchi creates struggle with passions, racism, economic depression, the incarceration of American citizens of Japanese descent in America in concentration camps, and, as Yamauchi adds, "with all the wars from Pearl Harbor to Iraq." Yamauchi believes that "like it or not, all our lives—big and small—are influenced by those in power. It's an uphill battle to hang on to principles and basic truths."

Two of Yamauchi's important early works, *And the Soul Shall Dance* and *12-1-A*, illustrate her themes. *And the Soul Shall Dance* is about two Japanese American families, the Muratas and the Okas, farming in the Imperial Valley in 1935. The various members of these families are magnetically drawn to their homeland for diverse reasons and yet are struggling to eke out an existence from the soil while at the mercy of the environment—not only the weather but also the climate of racism and the personal angst engendered by dreams that become less and less possible in the face of the bleakness of their reality. The playwright includes several interesting portraits of Issei and Nisei women in the play. There is the teenaged Masako, a Nisei, who is torn between her Japanese and American values as she struggles through her coming of age. She is balancing the obligations placed upon her by her parents' dreams with her personal desires for adventure and independence. A second portrait is that of the aforementioned Emiko, the wife of Murata. Emiko serves as Masako's window to a world of dreams, sensuality, beauty, abuse, and loneliness that teach Masako about the ways of the world in ways that Masako's mother cannot. Emiko is a beautiful woman who is fighting to keep her dreams alive. If they die, Emiko feels that she must perish with them because life on a desolate California farm and life with her abusive husband is too much to bear anymore. Ultimately, it is Emiko's soul that "dances," her body nothing more than a shell, the woman who once lived in it having dehydrated in the uncomfortable climate and turned to powder that is picked up by the dry winds and scattered to the clouds—just like the dust storms that plague the local farmers. And there is Hana Oka, the mother of Masako, a stalwart Issei who preserves her dream of making enough money and returning home to Japan in style to live out the rest of their lives. But, as each year passes, the ability to realize that dream fades and Hana sinks into the drudgery of maintaining an existence in a place that is also exile for her, but it is an exile that she will not admit. She, too, is trying to keep her dream alive, lest its death place too much emphasis on the bleakness of the world that surrounds her.

As I note in the introduction, *12-1-A* is about the Japanese American World War II incarceration experience and focuses on the uprooted Tanaka family, who is assigned to a camp in Poston, Arizona (where Yamauchi herself was interned). The Tanakas and the other Japanese American detainees in the camp are trapped in what easily could be termed a political nightmare, especially if one is an American citizen with certain inalienable rights. They do not know how long they will be there. Indeed, they do not know if they will ever leave the dismal camp alive. The hysteria of the media, the American government, and the American people has stripped them of their citizenship and dignity, and they are living in fear of very uncertain, undefined, perhaps nonexistent futures. The storm blows in Yo to the Tanakas' tiny quarters. Yo is alone because her father was sent to another detention camp. Her manner, her politics, and her fortitude send different messages to each of the Tanakas about what two short weeks in a prison camp can do to a Japanese American. Yo is one of the strong female presences in the play. On the surface, she is cynical and manages to laugh at the utter impossibilities of her existence. When she talks about the barrack for single women in which she lives, she says the women are lined up on narrow beds like inmates in a prison and Mitch Tanaka, a young Nisei, laughs at her, saying it is what she gets for being a woman. With bitter humor, Yo agrees: "Yeah, for being a woman. For being single. For being Japanese. I think someone up there dealt a stacked deck." The wind also blows in two young Nisei, Ken Ichioka and Harry Yamane. They all wonder how long the war will go on and how it will affect their lives. Mrs. Tanaka, mother of Mitch and Koko, is told that the outcome of the war will determine their fates, but as Yo points out, there will be no liberation for Japanese Americans. "In a war, Obasan, one country wins; the other loses. . . . We all look the same to them. We lose both ways." Mrs. Tanaka's concern is amplified by the senselessness of unlawful imprisonment and the fear of death.

Yo counsels her not to worry: "What is there to fear? Life? Death? Just roll with the punches."

The survival of the women in the camp is of particular interest. The politics of their lives are in turmoil. The older generation represented by Mrs. Tanaka was learning to be American and trying to aculturate the children. Then the U.S. government put them in camps, and the ideals, customs, and behavior of the country seemed ludicrous in the face of such destructive racism. Yo survives her political and personal losses by hiding behind a tough exterior. Still, Yo remains the optimist. When Koko wonders if she will ever have the kind of love Yo once had, Yo hopes the best for her, and we glimpse the sentiment underneath the cynicism. Koko, on the other hand, is a teenager who feels the world has disappeared. She cannot afford to have hope, nor can she afford to bend to convention and leap into the routine of life in the camps. She was a bud in bloom, nipped in mid-furl. She may be fated to live out her life in this stage of aborted womanhood, looking for answers with the utter, quiet belief that there simply are none for a Japanese American woman in the United States. Koko can never treat the camp world as normal and firmly believes that normalcy is a thing of the past, left to the ignorant, obedient, or complacent. She holds on to this belief to keep her dreams alive. Like Emiko in *And the Soul Shall Dance,* she must keep her soul dancing even if her exterior self is emptying bed pans and experiencing a longing [for Ken], which she cannot confess to its catalyst. While all this emotion takes its toll, there is a visual symbol: a guard tower that slowly encroaches upon the environs of the play, looming larger and larger and representing a sense of the characters' realization of their plight, which leads to politicization, challenges, and political imprisonment. How Koko matures through the course of the play and how political actions—those of the U.S. government incarcerating citizens and those of the no-no boys (who answered no to two questions on the camp questionnaire referring to service in the U.S. Army and renunciation of loyalties to Japan)—affect her life and that of her family are apparent in the touching conclusion to this play that explores the politics of the Japanese American incarceration without sacrificing the personal.

The Chairman's Wife is, according to Yamauchi, a departure in theme for her because it focuses on a Chinese public figure, Madame Mao, and on sociopolitical incidents in historical and present-day

China. At the same time, however, the play richly explores terrain that Yamauchi has mined before. Madame Mao, as depicted in *The Chairman's Wife,* also struggles with her passions, economic rise and fall, incarceration of mind, spirit, and finally body, and civil wars in her country. Madame Mao's life also is influenced by those in power: Chairman Mao, the opposing revolutionary forces, and, perhaps most important, herself.

Yamauchi's work looks at the past and tries to separate the illusion from the reality to find that delicate balance between the sustaining of dreams and coping with reality that allows human beings to survive and endure. In *The Chairman's Wife,* we travel back in time guided by Yamauchi, who does not confront, challenge, or celebrate the past. Ray Loynd quoted the powerful last words of Yamauchi's *The Chairman's Wife* in his *Los Angeles Times'* review of an East West Players production: "Politics is like fashion. Yesterday, me. Today, you. Tomorrow . . ."[2] In *12-1-A,* we remember with fear, regret, embarrassment, and rage how easily a country can dishonor its citizens, strip them of their civil rights, and break all laws in the name of power and racist paranoia. But we remember it through a very personal view of several lives caught up in the whirlwind and dust storms of the politics of the camps and how those politics altered the lives of all Japanese Americans. In her plays, Yamauchi explores the past probingly and brings it into context with the present, which is hauntingly appropriate in the case of the political life of Madame Mao and the incidents at Tiananmen Square in 1989, as well as in regard to the U.S. government finally apologizing to interned Japanese Americans and offering redress and reparations.

Plays

And the Soul Shall Dance

Production History

Asian Exclusion Act (1974, workshop), East West Players (1977, world premiere), University of Hawai'i (1977), Kauai Community Theatre (1977), Pan

---

[2]Ray Loynd, "*The Chairman's Wife:* A Great Rise and Fall in China," *Los Angeles Times' Calendar,* 23 January 1990.

	Asian Repertory Theatre (1979 and 1990), Asian American Theatre Company (1980), Cal State Asian American Theatre (1985)
12-1-A	East West Players (1982, world premiere), Asian American Theatre Company (1982), Kumu Kahua (1990), University of Southern California's Massman Theatre (1992), University of California at Los Angeles (1992)
The Music Lessons	New York Public Theatre (1980), Cal State Asian American Theatre (1982), Asian American Theatre Company (1982), East West Players (1983)
The Memento	Pan Asian Repertory Theatre (1984, under the original title of *The Facebox*), East West Players (1986), Yale Repertory Theatre Winterfest (1987)
The Chairman's Wife	East West Players (1990, world premiere), Kumu Kahua (1990)
Not a Through Street	East West Players (1991, world premiere)
Shirley Temple, Hot-Cha-Cha	The Mark Taper Forum (staged reading)
Songs That Made the Hit Parade	East West Players (staged reading)
A Fine Day (one-act play)	
The Trip (one-act play)	
Stereoscope (one-act play)	

Teleplays

And the Soul Shall Dance   Hollywood Television Theatre
(1977), PBS (1978–79), Arts and
Entertainment Channel (1987)

Poetry and Prose

And the Soul Shall Dance   (short story and play versions)

Boatmen on Toneh River

The Poetry of the Issei

Songs My Mother Taught Me

Sensei

The Handkerchief

In Heaven and Earth

Awards and Honors

The Brody Art Fund Fellowship (1988), two Rockefeller Foundation playwriting fellowships (1985 and 1979), Human Relations Commission of Los Angeles Bicentennial Salute (1981), Rockefeller Playwright-in-Residence at the Mark Taper Forum (1979), American Theater Critics Regional Award for Outstanding Play (1977), and Rockefeller Playwright-in-Residence at East West Players (1976).

12–1–A

Wakako Yamauchi

CAST OF CHARACTERS

Harry Yamane, 25, retarded Nisei
Mitch (Michio Tanaka), 20, Nisei son
Mrs. Tanaka, 40, Issei widow and mother
Koko Tanaka, 17, Nisei daughter
Yo (Yoshiko Yoshida), 25, Nisei woman
Ken (Kenji Ichioka), 19, Nisei son
Mrs. Ichioka, 45, Issei wife of invalid, mother of Ken
Sam (Isamu), 19, Nisei
Bill, 19, Nisei
Mr. Endo, 45, Issei
Yama (Yamasaki), 35, tall husky man
Fuji-san's Daughter, 16

Issei: Immigrants from Japan
Nisei: Second-generation Japanese Americans, born in
       America, American citizens
Obasan: Lady, older woman, also aunt

Act One
Scene One   May 1942
Scene Two   A few months later
Scene Three   September 1942

Act Two
Scene One   November 1942
Scene Two   Early December 1942
Scene Three   February 1943
Scene Four   July 1943

ACT ONE

Scene One

(Time: May 1942. Wind sounds. The tar-papered interior of a barrack faces downstage. There are two workable glass-paned windows [sliding sideways] facing upstage. Three army cots stand in an otherwise empty room. A naked light bulb hangs from the rafter. The barrack has a double door and a small wooden porch. 12-1-A is stenciled in white. The door faces stage right. In the background the silhouette of a guard tower looms ominously. A sentry is on duty at all times. This tower is barely visible in the first scene and grows more prominent as the play progresses. A wind blows. HARRY YAMANE, 25, walks slowly and anxiously on stage. He wears a battered felt hat and old-man clothes. He is somewhat stooped. HARRY has a twelve-year-old mentality and has spent many years working on his father's farm. He hums a tuneless rendition of "Yes sir, that's my baby" when he is anxious. He is lost and bewildered. He hums as he enters from stage left. HARRY takes out a scrap of paper, looks at the number on the barrack, shakes his head as though to clear it, and takes off his hat and spins it with his two hands. He hums louder. He sits on the porch for a while, his head down. He hears voices and steps downstage, trying to be inconspicuous. MRS. TANAKA, 40, Issei widow in traveling clothes for middle-aged women of the period, carries a suitcase and a cardboard carton. MITCH, 20, her Nisei son, in jeans and plaid shirt carries two duffel bags. KOKO, 17, her Nisei daughter, wearing a short dirndl skirt, white socks, and saddle shoes, carries two suitcases. They enter from stage left and walk in wordlessly—as though in a dream. MITCH leads the way. They open the barrack door, enter, and stare at each other in silence.)

MITCH *(tiredly):* Did you see the baggage some people brought? They said only as much as your arms can carry.

KOKO *(sitting on her suitcase):* Some people must have arms like octopuses.

(MITCH opens the windows.)

KOKO *(continuing):* Octopi? Octopedes?

MITCH: What?

KOKO: That's obscure. Rarely used.

MITCH: What's wrong with you, Koko?

KOKO: It's an archaic form of the plural of octopus.

(Outside, HARRY *moves downstage and sits unseen by the family.)*

MITCH: Octopedes! Here we are in this goddamn place and you talking about fish! You act like nothing's happened.

KOKO: I'm trying to get my bearings!

MRS. TANAKA: Shhh! Don't fight.

(She opens her shopping bag and brings out a tube of salami and begins slicing. MITCH *takes a bowling trophy from his suitcase and sets it on a rib of the barrack frame. He pulls out a letter-man's sweater and puts it on a wooden hanger and hangs it from the same frame rib.)*

KOKO: It's unreal. Rows and rows, miles and miles of barracks . . . and people like us . . . zombies in the desert . . . with two duffel bags, suitcases . . . cartons.

(The light behind the upstage window is yellowing.)

MRS. TANAKA *(passing the salami as she scolds):* Not fighting like you. This is not time for fighting. Time for taking care of each other.

KOKO: I'm just trying to get my bearings.

MITCH: I'm sorry. *(looks carefully at* KOKO) What's the matter? You crying?

(The light grows murky and ominous. Wind sounds increase. Outside, HARRY *looks at the sky and turns his hat anxiously.)*

KOKO: I'm not crying. The meat is . . . is spicy.

(HARRY acts like a cornered animal as the storm approaches. He finally hides behind the barrack. KOKO *is attracted to the strange light. Her eyes turn to the window.)*

KOKO: Look at that yellow cloud. Like in Kansas maybe. Like in the movies . . .

(MRS. TANAKA *follows her gaze. The wind roars.*)

MRS. TANAKA: Michio!

MITCH: Holy Mac! It's a tornado!

(*The three run around closing the door and windows.* MRS. TANAKA *rewraps her salami and puts it away. She finds handkerchiefs for* KOKO *and* MITCH, *who put them over their mouths. She pulls* KOKO *to the duffel bags and they huddle together.* MITCH *remembers his trophy and sweater and returns them to his suitcase. The wind howls, dust swirls, and the door flies open. The* TANAKAS *react to the wind, covering their noses and hunching up.* YO YOSHIDA, *25, a Nisei woman, staggers in. She is dressed like a boy—in jeans and a work shirt. Her hair is tucked into a snow cap, and a red bandanna covers the lower half of her face. She carries a small sketch pad and pencil. She curses and mutters.*)

YO (*startled to see* MITCH): What are you doing here? (*sees* MRS. TANAKA *and* KOKO) Shit! I'm in the wrong barrack. Where is this?

MITCH (*drily*): Poston, Arizona.

YO: I know that. I mean what barrack? What block?

MRS. TANAKA: Twelve-one-A. What you looking for?

YO: Block eleven.

MITCH (*pointing right*): I think eleven is out that way. Eleven what?

YO: No number. I live in the spinsters' quarters there. (*dusts herself off*) Been sketching and got caught in the storm. You just get here?

MITCH: Yeah, just now. We're from Fallbrook. Where're you from?

YO: Originally? Terminal Island.

MRS. TANAKA: Ah, the fishing village.

MITCH: Does this kind of thing happen often? (*meaning the dust storm*)

YO: Often enough. Mind if I stay awhile? I mean 'til the dust . . .

MRS. TANAKA: Please. Please sit down. *(offers the edge of a cot)*

KOKO: Do you ever get used to it?

YO: The dust?

MITCH: Dust . . . everything.

YO: Don't know. Just been here two weeks myself. Two weeks and three days. You do or you don't, I guess. What is, is. *(looks at the three cots)* Just the three of you here?

MITCH: Yep. Pop died long time ago.

MRS. TANAKA: Long time 'go. Maybe lucky he not here.

YO: You're lucky you don't have another family in here. They still might do it. Throw in another family.

KOKO: You mean strangers living together?

YO: Sure. Oh, say, I'm Yo. Yo Yoshida.

MRS. TANAKA: We're Tanaka. This is Michio and Koko. You here all by yourself, Yo-chan?

YO: Yeah. My father's in another detention center. They took him early. They took all the fishermen who owned boats.

MRS. TANAKA: Yo-chan lonely without family, ne?

YO: Well, there're ten, twelve of us girls—bachelor women—in the barrack. We're sort of kin, I guess. We have one thing in common: we're alone. *(laughs)* You know, they give us just this much room . . . *(indicates the bed space)* . . . like single people need less space than others. You should see us at night—all line up in a row on these narrow beds—like whores in a whore-house . . .

(MRS. TANAKA gives her a look.)

YO: . . . inmates in a prison. Orphans in an orphanage.

MITCH *(laughs)*: That's what you get for being a woman.

YO: Yeah, for being a woman. For being single. For being Japanese. I think someone up there dealt a stacked deck.

(KOKO opens her suitcase and brings out a deck of cards.)

KOKO: All of us. Why don't you live with us? *(shuffles the cards)*

(Outside, HARRY *moves to the door and huddles against it.)*

MRS. TANAKA: Ah-oh. Koko . . . Michio, somebody at the door.

YO *(laughing):* Live with you? Why, I hardly know you.

MITCH: Naw, just the wind, Ma.

KOKO *(to* YO): But you're all alone.

YO: Those are the breaks. *(indicating the cards)* What's your game?

KOKO: What do you want to play?

MITCH *(incredulously):* You're not going to play cards, are you?

*(*KOKO *makes a table with the suitcase.)*

MRS. TANAKA: You people crazy!

KOKO: Maybe we *are* crazy. Maybe this is really a bobby hatch and we're the lunatics.

YO: No, there're thousands of us. There can't be that many boobies. *(takes the cards from* KOKO)

(The noises outside grow louder.)

MITCH: Hey! There *is* someone out there!

*(*KEN ICHIOKA, *19, bangs on the door.)*

KEN: Open up!! Let us in!

*(*MITCH *opens the door.* KOKO, YO, *and* MRS. TANAKA *protect themselves from the wind.* KEN *and* HARRY *stumble in. They have a difficult time closing the door.* MITCH *helps them.)*

KEN *(brushing himself off):* Boy! The dust out there . . . Thanks . . . *(peers around)* Ken. Not much better inside. *(looks at* MITCH) Hey! I know you!

MITCH: You know me?

KEN: Sure! Fallbrook High! Class of '40. Mitch Tanaka, right? Varsity football?

MITCH *(eagerly):* No kidding! You were on the team, too?

KEN: No no. I was a couple classes below.

KOKO: Hi, Ken.

KEN: Oh! Hi.

KOKO: Koko. Remember? Latin II, room twenty-three?

KEN: Oh yeah, yeah. Mr. Nelson, right?

KOKO: Yes. Right.

YO: Looks like a class reunion. Hi. I'm Yo. Who's your friend?

(HARRY *spins his hat.*)

KEN *(turns to* HARRY): I don't know. He was huddled against the door when I came by. I thought he lived here.

MRS. TANAKA: No. We just came.

KEN *(loudly):* What's your name, friend?

(HARRY *shrinks.*)

MITCH *(loudly):* What's your name?

KOKO: You're scaring him, Mitch.

HARRY *(turns his hat rapidly):* Ah . . . ah . . . Harry.

MRS. TANAKA: Ah, Harry-san.

YO *(counts heads and shuffles the cards):* Good! Just enough. Five.

KEN: No kidding! You really playing cards?

YO: Why not? What else is there to do?

KEN: Crazy.

MRS. TANAKA: That's what I said.

KEN *(to* Yo): Are you related or something?

MITCH *(overlaps with* Yo): No!

YO: No, sir! I'm just like you. I blew in with the wind.

(MITCH *brings his trophy out of the suitcase.* HARRY *watches.*)

HARRY: Whazzat?

MITCH *(looks at* KEN): It's a bowling trophy. *(polishes it with his sleeve before setting it against the wall)*

(HARRY *picks up the trophy and examines it.*)

MITCH *(to* KEN): You bowl?

HARRY: Naw . . .

MRS. TANAKA: Michio was champion bowler . . . outside . . . before.

KEN: Yeah?

MRS. TANAKA: Michio win fifty dollars with that. *(indicates the trophy)*

KOKO: For the team's most valuable bowler.

MITCH: We tore that championship right from Sweetwater's mouth. Man-o-man! They were already tasting it! *(takes the trophy from HARRY and sets it back on the wall)*

HARRY: Fifty dollars?

KEN: Fifty dollars, eh?

MITCH: Yep. It was a regional. You bowl?

KEN: No, not me. *(looks at YO)* I don't even play cards.

YO: No problem.

KOKO: We'll teach you.

YO: You'll be an expert by the time we get out of here.

(They look at each other and turn silent.)

YO: Well, what'd you want to play? *(looks from face to face)*

HARRY: I don't wanta play.

KEN *(overlaps HARRY)*: Not me.

MITCH *(to KEN)*: How long you figure we'll be here?

KEN *(shrugs)*: Probably 'til the end of the war.

MRS. TANAKA: Whaa . . .

KOKO *(overlaps)*: Do you think they'll do anything to us?

YO: They already have.

KOKO: I mean, you know . . .

MRS. TANAKA: 'Til end of war?

KOKO: Then what?

KEN: That'll probably depend on the outcome.

MRS. TANAKA: Outcome?

YO: In a war, Obasan, one country wins; the other loses.

MRS. TANAKA: What if Japan wins? *(fearfully)* What happen if Japan lose?

YO: We all look the same to them. We lose both ways. *(points to* MITCH's *bags)* Got anything to drink in there?

MITCH: Firewater is contraband here.

YO: Hell.

KOKO: Oh, that's right. That's right. This is a . . .

HARRY *(imitating* KOKO): That's right—that's right.

KOKO: This is an Indian reservation.

HARRY *(snaps his fingers as though exasperated for having forgotten)*: Oh yeah! That's right!

YO: Now we know how they feel.

MITCH *(to* KEN): How long you figure the war's going to last?

KEN *(shrugs)*: Who knows? One, two . . . maybe four years? I don't know.

MITCH *(suddenly yelling)*: Four years! I'm not staying here no four years!

(MRS. ICHIOKA, *45, occupant of the next barrack, bangs on the wall.)*

MRS. ICHIOKA *(offstage)*: Shhh! I got sick man here!

(HARRY *lifts his fist to bang back.* KEN *stops him.)*

KEN: HARRY, don't do that. *(clears his throat)* That's my mom.

KOKO: Oh! Do you live next door?

MRS. ICHIOKA *(offstage)*: Kenji! You over there?

KEN: Yeah, Mom. I'll be right home. *(to the others)* My dad's been sick ever since we got here. I think it's the water.

MRS. TANAKA: I'm sorry.

KEN: Well, I better go.

(KEN *opens the door, sees the storm is over, and exits.* KOKO *follows him out after a beat.)*

KOKO: Storm's over!

MRS. TANAKA; Michio, you better get mattress filled. Man said we fill our own mattresses. He said straw is at block manager.

MITCH: Where do you live, Harry? I'll take you home . . . I mean, to your barrack.

(HARRY *shuffles through his pockets and finds the paper with his address. He gives it to* MITCH.)

YO: I'm going, too.

MRS. TANAKA: Yo-chan, what you think is going to happen?

YO: Who knows? Maybe they got us all together to drop a bomb on us. Phhht! *(snaps her fingers)*

(There is a stunned silence from all.)

YO: Just kidding.

KOKO: It's not funny. How can you joke about it?

YO: I make it a point not to worry about things I can't help.

HARRY: I don' . . . I don't wanta die.

MITCH: You're not going to die. She's just kidding. Come on.

MRS. TANAKA: Get mattresses, too, Michio.

MITCH: Right.

(They exit. MRS. TANAKA *sits on a cot and looks depressed.)*

YO: Obasan, don't worry so much. What is there to fear? Life? Death? Just roll with the punches.

*(*KOKO *picks up the cards and plays solitaire.* MRS. TANAKA *takes off her identification tag. Fade out.)*

Scene Two

(Time: A few months later. The silhouette of the guard tower is visible. In 12-1-A, one upstage window is covered with a curtain. There is a hand-sewn curtain dividing the sleeping area from the living space. A table and a crude bench face the audience downstage. Outside, there is another bench. It is midday. KOKO *plays solitaire on the table.* MRS. TANAKA *hand sews a curtain.* MITCH *is at work. A radio plays "Don't Sit Under*

the Apple Tree" from another barrack. The bowling trophy is visible throughout the play. KOKO's *shoes are under the table.* HARRY *enters from stage left carrying lumber he has stolen from a construction site. He hums when he hears* MRS. TANAKA. *He leaves the lumber and exits to the left.)*

MRS. TANAKA: Most girls like you find jobs already.

KOKO *(continuing her solitaire):* I know.

MRS. TANAKA *(pretending to be involved in her sewing):* No use to stay home all the time.

*(*KOKO *shuffles the cards.)*

MRS. TANAKA: Ichioka-san says many jobs open in camp office now. Jobs in hospital, too. You work there . . . nurse's aide or something.

KOKO *(drily):* And meet a nice young doctor maybe?

MRS. TANAKA: Nothing wrong with that.

KOKO: No. Not for you.

MRS. TANAKA *(hanging the curtain on the window):* I wish I didn't sell my sewing machine. Man only gave me five dollars for it.

KOKO: That's what I mean. What good is money here?

MRS. TANAKA: You need money here, too.

KOKO: For what?

MRS. TANAKA *(exasperated):* You tryna give me hard time, Koko? You know what I mean . . . cold cream, magazines . . . *(inspired)* Lipstick?

KOKO: They're going to give us a clothing allowance. I'll use that for what I need.

MRS. TANAKA: That three dollars a month? You need that for shoes. Pretty soon it will be cold and you will need coat.

KOKO: No I won't.

MRS. TANAKA: You going stay naked in the barrack? You not going to come out of barrack? *(reconsiders)* Ne, Koko. Michio got nice job in motor pool. Twelve dollars a month. Pretty soon he's going to get raise.

(MR. ENDO, 45, *enters from stage right with a tenugui [thin cotton towel] around his neck. He walks leisurely across, swabbing at his face.*)

KOKO: Ma, I told you I don't want to work here.

MRS. TANAKA: Who likes here? You think Mama put you here?

(KOKO *is silent, still concentrating on her cards.*)

MRS. TANAKA *(muttering):* Hunh! She thinks Mama put her here. *(more reasonably)* Koko . . . Mama don't want you to be alone all time. Go out, have good time, make nice friends.

KOKO: I have friends.

MRS. TANAKA: Oh? Who your friends? You sit home all time, play cards all . . .

KOKO *(irritated):* I have friends. Yo says all you need is one . . .

MRS. TANAKA: "Yo says, Yo says." Yo-chan crazy girl! Don't you know that?

KOKO: Yo is not crazy!

MRS. TANAKA: People laughing at you. They say Koko got funny friends: one crazy girl and one funny man. They think maybe Koko's funny, too. *(taps her head)*

KOKO: So what? Who needs them? I don't care what they think.

MRS. TANAKA *(lowering her voice and giving KOKO a warning look toward the ICHIOKA barrack):* Koko, if you don't make nice friends, how you going to find good husband?

KOKO: Oh, please!

MRS. TANAKA: Never mind, "Oh, please." One day you going be all alone. Then you say . . .

KOKO *(under her breath):* Good God!

MRS. TANAKA: Koko's going be just like Mama. Alone. Going to work in restaurant every night; every night come home, soak feet, count tip money . . .

KOKO: Pa died! He couldn't help what happened to you!

MRS. TANAKA: All same. Same! This is first time I don't work ten hours a day. First vacation.

KOKO: Don't call this a vacation, Ma!

MRS. TANAKA: You know what I mean. This is first time I don't worry about shoes, clothes . . . If Koko . . .

KOKO: Oh, for crying out loud! *(picks up her cards and storms out of the barrack)*

MRS. TANAKA *(calling after her)*: What'sa matter you! You listen to Mama! *(sees* KOKO's *shoes)* Put your shoes away!

*(*MRS. TANAKA *picks up the shoes and sets them in the bedroom area.)*

MRS. TANAKA: Lazy girl!

*(*MITCH *enters from stage left. He glances at the sullen* KOKO, *who plays solitaire on the bench. He enters the barrack to hear* MAMA *fuming.)*

MITCH: Aw . . . simmer down, Ma. Don't get your blood pressure up. Leave her alone.

(He looks in his suitcase for his catcher's mitt.)

MRS. TANAKA: Michio. Koko is going have hard time like that.

MITCH: She'll be all right.

MRS. TANAKA: What's going happen to her? Mama can't be all time with Koko, you know.

MITCH: Don't worry, Ma. Give her a chance to grow up. She's only seventeen. When we get out of here, well, things will . . .

MRS. TANAKA: How? How we getting out? We can't get out. We got no friends to help us and we got no money.

MITCH *(examining his mitt)*: I don't know yet, but I'll find a way. We're not going to stay here forever. And don't worry. I'm going to take care of you and Koko.

MRS. TANAKA: Ah, Mitch-chan. You're a good boy, but you . . . you one day going marry, too. You and Koko.

MITCH *(glancing at his watch)*: Yeah. Gotta go now.

MRS. TANAKA: Talk to Koko, Michio.

*(*MITCH *leaves his mother, passes* KOKO, *and taps the top of her head.)*

MITCH: Take it easy, kiddo. *(notices the lumber)* Hey, where'd that come from?

KOKO: I don't know. Santa Claus, I guess. *(continues her solitaire)*

MITCH: Say, couple more pieces and I can make a bench with this. Maybe a chair for you and you can sit here in style and watch the world go by.

KOKO: What world?

(SAM [Isamu], 19, walks in swinging a baseball bat.)

MITCH: You know what I mean.

SAM: Come on, Mitch. We'll be late!

MITCH: Wait up, Sam! *(to KOKO)* Don't cheat now.

KOKO *(overlaps)* Mitch . . .

(MITCH bumps into YO. They exchange friendly curses and MITCH exits.)

YO *(to KOKO)*: Whew! Ho already!

(YO removes her cap. MR. ENDO walks left to right downstage. He carries a bucket.)

KOKO: Hi . . .

YO: How are you?

KOKO: Everyone's yelling at our house.

YO: Nowhere to go but up, hunh? *(helps KOKO with a card)* You really like this game?

KOKO: No . . .

YO: Why d'you play it then? I think it's a sheer waste of time.

KOKO: It's the only thing I have to waste.

YO: That's perverse. *(moves a card for KOKO; KOKO affectionately slaps her hand)* I quit my job again, Koko.

KOKO: How many does that make?

(MR. ENDO walks right to left with a full bucket of water. He nods to KOKO and YO. They nod back.)

YO: Let's see . . . intake, mess hall, block office. Three. Who he?

KOKO: Mr. Endo. Well, what will you do next?

YO: Get another job, I guess. I don't know. I can't get along with these people.

KOKO: Well, "these" are us. Too bad. You're stuck with us. You're surrounded.

YO: Yep. They're us, all right. *(makes another move)* I just don't fit in.

(MR. ENDO *walks from left to right again with his bucket.)*

KOKO: Let's face it. You're an oddball.

YO: It takes one to know one.

(MR. ENDO *walks right to left, his bucket full of water.)*

YO: What's he do with all that water?

KOKO: Talk is, his wife won't go to the showers. Too shy, I guess.

YO: She must have one hell of a time when she has to line up at the toilets with the rest of us peasants.

KOKO: Who doesn't?

YO: Yeah, it's enough to constipate a body.

(MR. ENDO *walks by with a chamber pot.)*

YO: Oh-oh. A Japanese toting a chamber pot for his wife? Koko, there's hope for our men yet.

KOKO: How the mighty have fallen.

YO: War is hell.

(They *giggle and* MR. ENDO *gives them his middle finger.* HARRY *appears with another piece of lumber.)*

Yo *(referring to* MR. ENDO): Must habla Ingles.

MR. ENDO: Si. Y Espanol tambien. *(pretends to throw the contents of the pot at them)*

YO: Euuuhhh! *(pulls her hat over her face)*

KOKO *(to* HARRY): Oh, *you're* the Santa Claus.

HARRY: Heh-heh-heh. I brought this. *(sets the lumber down)*

KOKO: Did you get it at the construction site?

HARRY: Yeah.

KOKO *(concerned):* You shouldn't be pilfering in broad daylight. It's dangerous.

YO: Yeah, you'll get a butt full of lead. You should do your appropriating at night.

HARRY: I didn' do that. I stole it.

(They laugh affectionately.)

KOKO: It's funny how we . . . how we met here. I mean you and I . . .

HARRY: And me.

KOKO: Yes, and you. And Ken. I knew Ken in school, but I never spoke to him. We never . . .

YO: You got it bad, eh, kid?

KOKO: Well, I don't know about that. But it's true, Yo, we *are* oddballs. Birds of a feather.

YO: Yeah.

HARRY: Yeah.

KOKO: You know, you're my first *real* friend. Oh, I've had friends before, but . . . not *real*, do you know what I mean? I think we should stick together. We should make a pact to always be together.

YO: *Real* friends don't need pacts. When one has to go, the other releases. That's the whole ball game.

KOKO: I guess you're right. Still, while we're here, we can . . .

YO *(singing):* That's friendship/Just a perfect friendship/When other friendship's been forgot . . .

KOKO: I'm trying to say something important! *(grows angry)* You never take anything seriously!

YO: Whoa! I'm your friend, remember? Jesus, you're edgy!

KOKO: Yeah. I'll probably die friendless and alone.

YO: Is that your ambition?

KOKO: There you go again.

YO: I'm sorry, Koko. I guess I'm really a cynic. Too many things go wrong. I just don't want to expect anything from anyone anymore. I just want to laugh. I don't want to cry anymore.

KOKO: Was it a man?

YO: Man, sister, father, country . . . it doesn't matter. You bank too much on any one thing and . . .

KOKO: Did he leave you?

YO *(laughing):* I wish it were as simple as that.

KOKO: I wonder if I'll ever feel like that for someone.

YO: Hell, I hope so.

KOKO: Gosh, you're not a cynic. You're an optimist.

YO: Golly-gee.

(KEN *appears, carefully carrying three paper cups of punch.)*

KEN: Are you ready? Here I come . . .

KOKO *(delighted):* What 'cha got there?

KEN: Punch! The canteen's selling punch. You should see the mob out there! One for you, Koko-nut, and one for you Yo . . . I thought you might be here and . . . *(he hadn't counted on* HARRY*)* . . . for Harry.

KOKO: We'll share this, Ken.

YO: Thanks. Ken, I do believe the Dixie cup has replaced the bouquet. Well, we just have to move along with the times.

KEN: Ha ha. Well, ah . . . how are you, Koko?

(FUJI-SAN'S YOUNGEST DAUGHTER, *16, enters. She passes the group slowly and smiles at* KEN.)

KOKO: Okay, all things considered. Thanks for the treat. It's really nice of you.

FUJI-SAN'S YOUNGEST: Hi, Ken.

KEN: Oh, hi.

(She throws another smile and exits.)

YO *(in reference to* FUJI-SAN'S DAUGHTER): Angh!

KEN: What's the matter? Don't you like it?

YO: It's okay if you like hemlock.

HARRY *(happily):* Yeah.

KOKO (*overlaps*): It tastes all right, Yo. (*gives her cup to* KEN; *he sips from it*)

HARRY: I like it. It's good. I drank this at home.

KOKO: Oh, Harry, it's no use to remember that anymore.

(MRS. ICHIOKA, 56, KEN'S *mother and wife of invalid Ichioka, enters carrying her laundry. She nods to the girls and they smile back.*)

MRS. ICHIOKA: Kenji, how come you're here?

KEN: Oh, Mom, yeah. I was on my lunch break . . . I saw this crowd at the canteen. They're selling punch. I brought some back for . . . I brought some back.

MRS. ICHIOKA: Government give you twelve dollars a month. You spend money in canteen and give all back to government. Government take all your money away again. That's baka.

KEN: Just three cups of punch, Mom.

MRS. ICHIOKA: Papa feel bad today again.

YO: Here, Obasan, take this to him. (*gives her cup to* MRS. ICHIOKA)

MRS. ICHIOKA: Maybe not so good for him.

YO: It won't hurt him. He'll like it, Obasan. Hurry, while it's still cold.

MRS. ICHIOKA: You come home pretty soon now, nah, Kenji? (*takes the punch and leaves*)

KEN (*embarrassed, but with a certain bravado*): Well, do you like it, Koko? Can I get you some more?

KOKO: No, Ken, I don't want anymore.

HARRY: No use to remember anymore.

(*Fade out.*)

Scene Three

(*Time: September 1942. The barrack is considerably more habitable. A tablecloth, pitcher, and glasses are on the table. It's another hot day. The door is open and a radio from another*

barrack plays, "I Got a Gal in Kalamazoo." KOKO *and* HARRY
play cards. HARRY *keeps his hat on his lap.)*

HARRY *(setting down his hand):* Gin!

KOKO *(checking his hand):* No, Harry. Every trick has to have at
least three cards. See, you have only two here. *(shows him her
hand)* You have to have three cards of the same suit.

HARRY: Oh yeah. I forgot.

KOKO: We'll play something else. How about . . .

HARRY: I don' wanta play cards.

KOKO: Okay. Well . . . you want me to read to you?

HARRY: I can read. *(spins his hat)*

KOKO: You want to talk?

HARRY: Okay.

KOKO: Well . . . Tell me about your mother.

HARRY: She's dead.

KOKO: Well, shall we talk about your father, then? What's your
father like? Is he . . .

*(*HARRY *moves from the table to the upstage bench.)*

KOKO: Is he tall? Is he short? Is he . . .

HARRY: He's not very nice.

KOKO: How come? Does he hit you?

HARRY: He don' talk to me.

KOKO: No, that's not very nice.

HARRY: He always say, "Baka, baka . . ." Baka means stupid. Make
me feel bad. He don' like me.

KOKO: Harry. He likes you. He's like my mom. She keeps nagging,
"Find a job, go to work, find a nice man." Sometimes I think
just because she tells me to, I won't. Funny, hunh?

*(*HARRY *laughs.)*

KOKO: I don't know why I feel so . . . I don't know. Maybe it's the
weather. It's so hot here. Maybe it's this place. Maybe it's the
world . . . the war.

HARRY: Yeah . . .

KOKO: Maybe everyone feels like this. This place is like . . . like a vacuum . . . You're shut out from the outside and inside everyone pretends like nothing's wrong.

HARRY: Yeah.

KOKO: Like this is normal. But it's not normal. What are people really feeling?

HARRY: I don' know.

KOKO: Maybe we shouldn't worry about things we have no power to change. Maybe we should go to work every day, smile hello, say good-bye . . . spread small joys . . . inflict little hurts . . . skirt around this whole crazy situation. Maybe this is the way it's supposed to be.

HARRY *(depressed):* Yeah . . .

KOKO *(realizing she's depressing* HARRY*):* Yo's got another job. She's so strong . . . all alone here. I'd probably fall apart. But, of course, I have my mom and Mitch . . .

HARRY: Yeah . . .

KOKO: And Yo and Ken . . .

HARRY: And me, too.

KOKO: Harry?

HARRY: Hunh?

KOKO: Do you . . . do you think he likes me?

HARRY: Who?

KOKO: You know who.

(HARRY *shrugs and turns inward.)*

KOKO: I suppose I'd know it if he did . . . wouldn't have to ask anyone.

(KEN *enters and peeks through the door.* KOKO *is surprised and embarrassed.)*

KEN: Hi!

KOKO: Oh! Hi! Ah . . . aren't you working today?

KEN: I'm out in the field today. Hot enough for you? Hi, Harry. *(enters and sits at the table with them)*

KOKO: What a cushy job. What do you do?

KEN: Oh . . . I just . . . I just walk around. See what's going on.

(KEN holds out a candy bar for KOKO. He gives HARRY the one he brought for himself.)

KEN: And for Harry. They're selling them at the canteen today.

KOKO *(her eyes grow wide)*: Candy bar! I haven't had one of these since . . . I'll save mine for later. *(breaks the bar in half and gives one half back to KEN)*

HARRY *(overlaps)*: Thanks. *(eats carefully)*

KEN *(to KOKO)*: Eat it now. Otherwise it'll melt.

(MRS. ICHIOKA enters from upstage right. She hears KEN's voice and is tempted to look in the window.)

KOKO *(eating her candy)*: So you walk around, see what's going on. Are you a reporter?

(MRS. TANAKA enters from stage left and catches MRS. ICHIOKA.)

MRS. TANAKA: Ichioka-san, come to my house. I want to give you something.

MRS. ICHIOKA: Give me something?

MRS. TANAKA: Yes, yes.

KEN *(overlaps, hastily)*: I'd better get back to work. I'll see if I can get another one for you. There's such a crowd, I'll have to hurry.

KOKO: That's all right, Ken.

KEN: See you around.

MRS. TANAKA *(to MRS. ICHIOKA)*: Shhh . . . come with me.

(KEN hurries off, successfully avoiding his mother. MRS. TANAKA and MRS. ICHIOKA enter the barrack.)

KOKO: Hi, Obasan . . . Ma . . .

MRS. ICHIOKA: Hallo, Koko-chan.

MRS. TANAKA *(to* MRS. ICHIOKA): Harry-san's here. All the time, here.

KOKO: Oh, Ma!

MRS. ICHIOKA *(to* MRS. TANAKA): Boyfriend?

MRS. TANAKA: No-no-no! Just friend. *(taps her head; takes from her apron four eggs, one at a time)* Look, look! *(gives one to* MRS. ICHIOKA)

MRS. ICHIOKA: Oh! Where did you get?

MRS. TANAKA: Kitchen. Kitchen.

MRS. ICHIOKA: Thank you. Thank you. This's treat for Ichioka. He can't eat the greasy food from the mess hall. Hurts stomach too much. Outside, cook-san was shoemaker.

MRS. TANAKA: Lucky I work in the kitchen. Get good chance . . . to bring home . . .

KOKO: "Appropriate," Ma. The word is "appropriate."

MRS. TANAKA: That's okay. Leave to Mama, everything. That food no good for people. We going get sick with it. I know. I work in the mess hall.

MRS. ICHIOKA: That's all right, Miss Koko-san. They take from us; we take from them. Only they take more. We never catch up to what they took from us. We never catch up to that.

KOKO *(to* HARRY): Here we go again.

MRS. ICHIOKA: Sick people here don't get no help. They want sick people to die.

MRS. TANAKA: I'm going order hot plate from Sears Roebuck.

HARRY: That's illegal.

MRS. TANAKA *(waving him away):* Going cook nice at home. Michio getting too skinny now. We going eat good again and Koko going say, "Thank you, Mama." *(to* MRS. ICHIOKA) Getting too smart. Just like Yo-chan. Smart mouth.

MRS. ICHIOKA: Smart girl, smart mouth. Ha ha. Thank you, Tanaka-san. Ichioka likes eggs. Favorite.

(MRS. TANAKA gives her another egg.)

MRS. ICHIOKA: Thank you very much. Bye-bye, Koko-chan.

(ICHIOKA *leaves.*)

KOKO *(to HARRY)*: We're getting to be a bunch of petty thieves.

HARRY: Yeah.

MRS. TANAKA: You all time playing cards with Harry-san. No good.

KOKO: People have feelings, you know. He's not deaf.

MRS. TANAKA: Not good for Harry-san, too. Not good for anybody.

KOKO: If I went to work, would I feel more real?

MRS. TANAKA: Real? Sure, make you feel real all 'round.

KOKO: Would you guarantee that?

MRS. TANAKA: Sure.

KOKO: Put it in writing?

MRS. TANAKA: Okay. Then you have no time to think. Think too much make people crazy. No good.

(MITCH *enters. He's in great spirits.*)

MITCH: Hello-hello-hello! What're you doing? Hi, Harry!

KOKO: Something good happen?

MRS. TANAKA: Michio! Look. *(shows MITCH the eggs)*

MITCH: That's nice. Guess what I heard today! They're recruiting volunteers to harvest sugar beets.

KOKO: Sugar beets? Here?

MITCH: Not here, silly. Outside! Yeah! Looks like our white citizens are all doing defense work and making a pile of money, so the farms are short of help. All you gotta do is get a clearance and you can get out of here! Ain't that something?

KOKO *(jumping up and down)*: I can't believe it! Ma! We're getting out!

MRS. TANAKA *(almost screaming)*: That's good!

MITCH: No-no. Just me. Just men. We go on a seasonal leave and we come back after the harvest.

MRS. TANAKA: That's no good, Michio. No good. We stay together. We are a family. We stay together.

MITCH: It's just for a short time, Ma.

KOKO: You mean you'd leave us? You'd leave us here? You'd go without us?

MRS. TANAKA: Michio is not going.

MITCH: It's a short-term leave. A month or two and I'll be back. It's a chance to make a little money, buy a few things . . . *(gently)* What do you want, Koko?

KOKO: I don't want anything. I don't want you to go. You can't do that, Mitch.

MITCH: Aw . . . don't be like that.

MRS. TANAKA *(firmly):* No, you don't go, Michio. We stay together.

MITCH *(very patiently):* It's a chance to be free for a little while, Ma. I'll look around. Maybe I'll find a little place where we can settle. I'll make a little money. It'll be a start. Later we can get out of here—all of us together. Just think, Ma—free!

(HARRY spins his hat.)

KOKO: What will happen to us while you're away? What if you don't come back?

MITCH: Don't be silly. What can happen?

KOKO: Don't leave us, Mitch. Don't go. Yo says blood is only thing you can count on. She really misses her dad.

MITCH: I know, Koko. But I can't stay here just because of that. We got to start doing something. We can't grow old here. You know that, don't you?

MRS. TANAKA: No good! Don't like! Ichioka-san says people spit you!

MITCH: Don't worry, Ma. I can take care of myself. And I'll come back. By then, I'll have a plan. Everything will be all right.

MRS. TANAKA: Maybe just a rumor, Michio. Lots of talk 'round here, you know.

MITCH: It's not just a rumor! Guys are signing up already.

MRS. TANAKA: Don't make up mind yet. We talk some more.

KOKO: What if . . .

MITCH: "What if, what if . . ." What can happen? Don't you think I can take care of myself?

KOKO: Anything can happen! You can't tell. Did you think you'd be *here* last year? Oh, MITCH, don't go.

MITCH: I gotta, Koko.

MRS. TANAKA: You head of family, Michio. Don't forget that. You don't go and leave Koko and . . .

MITCH: Ma! I'm not leaving her. I'm not leaving you. If I'm the head of this family, I gotta get out and make plans for us. Don't you see? You gotta trust me. You gotta let me try it!

MRS. TANAKA: See, Koko? You going be all alone. You see what Mama was talking 'bout? You see? We going be all alone.

MITCH: Cripes! I come rushing home with the best news since . . . since they put us here and . . . and . . . Jesus Christ!

MRS. TANAKA: We talk 'bout it. We talk first!

KOKO: Listen to Ma!

MITCH: I'm going back to work, goddamnit! *(stamps out, slamming the door behind him)*

MRS. TANAKA: Michio! Come back! *(almost goes after him but stops at the door, looks at KOKO helplessly, takes a moment, and goes back to her eggs)* Michio is talking back to Mama. *(peels an egg)* Ah, Koko. Michio is mad.

KOKO *(gently):* That's okay, Mama.

MRS. TANAKA: Sure. Michio will be all right. *(waves KOKO and HARRY to the table)* Come on. We eat eggs, ne, Koko? Harry-san, too.

(They sit without enthusiasm.)

KOKO: Ma?

MRS. TANAKA: Hmm?

KOKO: Tomorrow I'll look for a job, okay?

(MRS. TANAKA smiles sadly. HARRY spins his hat. MITCH returns from stage right. He almost opens the door, then sits on the outside bench brooding. YO enters.)

YO: Hey, hello! It's me, Yo. Hey, what's the matter?

MITCH: Yeah? Oh, nothing.

YO: Nothing? Hate to see you when you're really upset.

MITCH: Shit. I finally find a way to do something . . . Screw it! The whole world's against me.

YO: You know what they say. "Where there's a will, there's a way. While there's life, there's hope," and all that stuff.

MITCH: That's what they say, but it ain't true.

YO: Use your brains, man. You'll think of something.

MITCH: It don't take brains. Just guts and balls. *(exits)*

YO *(calling after him):* So? *(raps on the door and enters the barrack)* Hello!

HARRY and KOKO *(glumly):* Hi.

YO: Brought you something, Obasan.

MRS. TANAKA: Yo-chan, come eat eggs.

> (YO *pulls out an egg from under her cap.* KOKO *and* MRS. TANAKA *laugh briefly and a pall settles over the group.)*

YO: What is this? The Last Supper?

KOKO: Almost.

MRS. TANAKA: Michio is going to pick sugar beets outside.

YO: He's getting out? Where do I sign up?

MRS. TANAKA: Only men, Yo-chan.

YO: Balls! Always only men. Who said it's a free country?

KOKO: Free?

MRS. TANAKA *(to* KOKO): Daijobu, daijobu. *(meaning "everything will be all right")*

> (Fade out.)

End of Act One

ACT TWO

Scene One

> (*Time: A November afternoon, 1942. Outside 12-1-A,* MRS. TANAKA *and* MRS. ICHIOKA *fold clothes and gossip on the downstage bench.* SAM *and* FUJI-SAN'S YOUNGEST DAUGHTER, *dressed in winter army clothes, walk arm in arm.*)

MRS. ICHIOKA: Fuji-san's youngest girl. Every time with 'nother boy. Pretty soon . . . (*indicates pregnancy*) Only way that kind get married.

> (YAMA [*Yamasaki*], *35, enters from upstage right. He is tall and husky. He carries a tablet and pencil.* MRS. TANAKA *nods to him.* HARRY *enters carrying a handmade chair covered with an army blanket. The chair has one short leg.*)

MRS. TANAKA: Hallo, Harry-san. What you got there?

> (HARRY *sets the chair down and pulls off the blanket.*)

MRS. ICHIOKA: Two hundred people in Fresno camp; one whole block sick.

MRS. TANAKA: How come? That's purty, Harry-san.

> (HARRY *beams.*)

MRS. ICHIOKA: Food poisoning. They going kill us all. Two hundred people at a time. Manzanar got big trouble, too. M.P. stealing food from Manzanar people. People saying . . .

MRS. TANAKA: Ichioka-san, don't listen to everything. Can't help those things. Don't listen. Too scary. (*to* HARRY) You made it?

HARRY: Yeah.

MRS. ICHIOKA: Tanaka-san, no good to hide head all the time.

MRS. TANAKA (*to* HARRY): That's nice. Your papa be proud, ne? (*starts to sit on* HARRY's *chair*)

HARRY (*stops her midway*): No! It's for Koko.

MRS. TANAKA: Koko?

MRS. ICHIOKA: You made chair for Koko-chan! (*suspiciously*) Very nice chair, Harry-san.

HARRY (*troubled*): Yeah.

MRS. ICHIOKA *(to* TANAKA): Koko-chan is working now. Harry-san got lots of time now. *(exchanges significant nods with* MRS. TANAKA)

MRS. TANAKA: Ah-ah . . . Harry-san. You know . . . ah . . . Koko is not good for you. Koko is not nice girl friend for you.

HARRY: I don' care.

MRS. TANAKA: Koko's going hurt you, Harry-san.

HARRY: I don't care.

MRS. ICHIOKA: Better find 'nother girl friend. Koko-chan is too smart for you.

HARRY: I don' care.

MRS. TANAKA: You going one day cry, Harry-san. Koko going make you cry.

HARRY: I don' care.

MRS. TANAKA: Ah . . . Harry-san.

(HARRY *wipes the seat of the chair and hastily recovers it.* KOKO *and* KEN *enter.* KOKO *wears a white uniform under her seater.* KEN *wears a pea coat and jeans.)*

KOKO: Hi, Ma . . .

MRS. ICHIOKA: Koko-chan looks like real nurse now.

MRS. TANAKA: Just nurse's aide.

(KOKO *and* KEN *retreat to stage right near the barrack door.)*

KOKO: I think they save their excreting for my shift. I've been washing bedpans all day. If I see just one more . . .

KEN: Look at it this way: they're giving you all they got. My work gets me down, too.

KOKO: What exactly do you do? I never knew what you did.

KEN: Ah . . . I just shuffle papers.

KOKO: What kind of papers?

KEN: Surveys. You know. Sociological surveys.

KOKO: Sociological?

KEN: Yeah. You hear from Mitch?

KOKO: Not very often. He says it's back-breaking work . . . you know, bending over, topping sugar beets . . .

MRS. TANAKA *(to* Ichioka): Michio says Nebraska is too cold. He's too tired to write. Just only postcards.

MRS. ICHIOKA: That so?

KEN *(overlapping):* What else does he say?

KOKO: Not much else.

KEN: Well, say hello for me.

MRS. ICHIOKA *(to* TANAKA): Big crowd at police station people say.

MRS. TANAKA: Oh yeah?

MRS. ICHIOKA: They put in jail two people who beat up informers.

*(*KEN *listens from stage right.)*

MRS. TANAKA: Informers?

MRS. ICHIOKA: Yeah. Informing on *own people.* Inu! Dogs! They deserve beating.

KEN *(moving in):* Now wait, Mom. Wait a minute. The informing hasn't been proven yet. And, even if they did inform, those two guys have no business beating on people. They're thugs! How would you like to be dragged out in the middle of the night and beaten? No one would be safe. It's lawless!

MRS. ICHIOKA: Law? Don't talk law. You going make lots of people mad, talking law here.

KEN: Mom . . .

MRS. ICHIOKA: Mo . . . *(meaning "already")* . . . enough! We already talk over and over. You never listen.

KEN *(patiently):* The law, Mom. You're innocent until proven guilty.

MRS. ICHIOKA: If there is law like that, then why you here? You been proven already? And Koko-chan and Harry-san, too?

*(*HARRY *spins his hat.)*

KEN: That's different, Mom. We're talking about people who beat up other people . . .

MRS. ICHIOKA: Nobody says Joe DiMaggio is guilty. He's enemy alien, too. How come you and Koko guilty? How come *we* guilty?

MRS. TANAKA *(very concerned):* That's all right, Ichioka-san. No use. We only leaves in the wind.

MRS. ICHIOKA: That's all right. Kenji will understand when Japan wins the war.

KEN: Mom, there's no way Japan can win this war.

MRS. ICHIOKA: Japan will win!

KEN: Already they're being slaughtered in Guadacanal. What kind of resources do you think they have? Just look at it logically. You think planes and . . . you think the Sun God supplies the oil and ammunition and ships and . . .

KOKO: Just read the papers, Obasan.

MRS. ICHIOKA: Papers? You reading *American* papers! You better think these Japanese people as your brothers. When they die, you die, too! *(to* MRS. TANAKA*)* Young people, baka. Don't understand. Don't know Yamato Damashi, nah, Tanaka-san? *(to* Ken*)* Spirit of Japan can beat bigger, richer countries. Look Russia. *Big* Russia! Read your history book! Americans—heh —call Japanese "Little Yellow Men." They will show you. You watch!

MRS. TANAKA *(picking up her laundry):* Ichioka-san, come on. I will make tea for you. No use fighting with own son. Better, more better families stick together. No good to fight.

(She pulls MRS. ICHIOKA *with her and the two enter the barrack and prepare the tea.)*

MRS. ICHIOKA: Young people empty head. Freedom only for white people. When they going learn that. Baka . . .

*(*HARRY *grows uncomfortable and spins his hat.)*

MRS. TANAKA: Can't help. Young people learn from American books and we learn from Japanese books. Michio and me . . . we fight, too. Now Michio is far away. Now we don't fight no more.

*(*SAM *and* BILL, *19, enter from upstage right.* SAM *waves to* KEN.*)*

SAM: Let's go to the police station!

KEN: What's going on?

BILL: Where you been, man? Ain't you heard? We're forming a mass protest!

SAM: They're tryna take the guys to Tucson!

KEN: The ones who were arrested?

SAM: Yeah! We got to stop them! They'll never get a fair trial in Tucson!

BILL: Come on! It's a mass assembly—ho ho—against all those camp regulations!

(SAM *cocks his ear and hears faint strains of Japanese martial music.*)

SAM: You hear that? That's the old "Gunkan Maachi." I hear they hooked up loud speakers and they're playing all those old military songs. Boy!

(MRS. TANAKA *and* MRS. ICHIOKA *come from the barrack and* MR. ENDO *appears from stage right. He carries an army blanket.* BILL *exits left.*)

MRS. ICHIOKA (*listening and smiling*): Ah . . . Japanese music. Let's go, Tanaka-san. Come on, let's go.

MRS. TANAKA (*looking at* KOKO): Too cold out there.

SAM: No worry, Obasan! They got bonfires and everything!

(MR. ENDO *exits upstage left.*)

SAM: You coming, Ken?

MRS. ICHIOKA: We just go hear music. Iko ya, Tanaka-san. (*meaning "let's go"*)

KEN: Wait, Mom . . .

MRS. ICHIOKA: You come, too. Papa be all right.

HARRY: KOKO, I made . . .

KOKO: Let's go, Ken.

(*Everyone leaves but* KEN, KOKO, *and* HARRY.)

KEN: Wait. This is . . . this is mob action.

KOKO: Just see what's going on.

KEN: I can't take part in this sort of thing.

KOKO: We don't have to participate. Come on. My mom went. She's not going to get in trouble. She's a coward.

KEN: No telling what *my* mom will do.

KOKO: Well, we better go keep an eye on her then.

HARRY: Koko . . .

KEN: Until this war, she's always said, "Study hard; be a good citizen." She was the most American of us all. Now she's trying to erase everything she's taught me.

KOKO: She's hurt.

KEN: Well, who isn't? *(moves away from* KOKO*)* I wish my dad were well. He'd straighten her out. He's so sick, he doesn't care what happens. He used to be so strong. Now look. Doesn't care about anything. *(looks away)* When I was a kid, I wondered if I'd ever be the man he was.

*(*HARRY *takes his chair and enters the barrack. He sits on it dejectedly.)*

KOKO: I used to feel like that, too. I wondered if I could get up in the morning and cook breakfast and make lunch for my kids and go off to work, hurry home at night and make dinner and go off to work again. I thought I'd have to do all those things. We never had a man around, you know.

KEN: Sounds like a dream: settling down with someone . . . marrying . . .

*(*MR. ENDO *enters from stage left. He wears a pea coat.)*

MR. ENDO: Come on. Everybody. Station, station. *(gestures downstage left and exits)*

KEN: I wonder if it will ever happen. I mean to us.

KOKO: Of course it will. It always happens.

KEN: You grow up thinking life will continue forever . . . night following day, people marrying, having children . . .

KOKO: Night always follows day. People will always marry and have children.

KEN: But things are so changeable. Suddenly there's a war and all your values shift and change. You're torn between countries . . . between families . . *(shakes his head)* Look at my dad . . . fallen so low.

KOKO: Those things happen, war or no war.

KEN: But there *is* a war. And things are *not* the same.

KOKO: I know that. I feel it, too.

KEN: We're in limbo, Koko. One day, this; another day, that. We can't make plans. We can't make promises.

KOKO: But people do.

KEN: You may be unable to keep those promises.

KOKO: You keep them as long as you're able. That's all.

KEN: What about "till death do us part"?

KOKO: Only as long as you're able. That's all you can do. That's what Yo says.

KEN: I wish I could say what I feel . . . or be sure of what I feel. I don't even know that. I feel so . . .

KOKO: Me, too, Ken. Let's go inside.

KEN: Wait just a minute.

(YAMA enters from stage right. He walks with purpose, sees KEN and KOKO, and passes out flyers.)

YAMA: Oi, Yangu! You wa striku senno ka?

KEN: Strike?

YAMA: Yeah! Strike! You don't like administration? Strike! Don't like hotshot block council? Food bad? Don't get enough? Fight! Strike! Everybody gotta work together this time.

KEN: I thought the issue was the prisoners.

YAMA: Yeah! We're gonna take care of that, too. We gotta stick together this time, man. This time we gotta do something!

KEN: Well . . .

YAMA *(overlaps):* Hey, you Ichioka?

KEN: Yeah.

YAMA: You work at administration, yeah?

KEN: Yeah?

YAMA: Well, you better watch your step, brother. More better you quit the job. People start to talk, you know. Nights get plenty dark here. Plenty hotheads 'round, you know.

KEN: What are you saying? You threatening me?

YAMA: That's no threat, brother. That's a promise. It's assholes like you put us here in the first place. Buncha shitheads like you!

KEN: Who you calling "shithead"?

KOKO *(overlaps)*: Don't pay attention, Ken.

YAMA: You. I'm calling you shithead. Why? You wanta fight? Inu? Dog?

(YAMA pushes KEN. KEN lunges at him, but YAMA punches him in the belly. KEN collapses. There is confusion as MRS. ICHIOKA enters from the left.)

KOKO *(clawing at YAMA)*: You bastard!

MRS. ICHIOKA *(overlaps)*: Kenji! *(to YAMA)* He's not inu!

(YAMA, surprised from behind, puts up his hands as MRS. ICHIOKA pummels him.)

YAMA *(incredulously)*: I'll be a son of a bitch.

MRS. ICHIOKA: What'sa matter you? You crazy? My son is not inu!

YAMA: Don't be too sure, lady.

MRS. ICHIOKA: You crazy! Get outta here! Kenji works in office. He's not inu. Nah, Kenji?

KEN: I am not an informer.

MRS. ICHIOKA: See? Get outta here!

YAMA *(leaving to the left)*: I wasn't going to hurt him. Just give him warning.

MRS. ICHIOKA: You crazy! Go!

YAMA *(laughing)*: Wish *I* had a mama to help me out. *(exits)*

KOKO *(brushing KEN off)*: Are you hurt?

KEN *(angry, pushes KOKO's hands away)*: I'm okay.

MRS. ICHIOKA: You . . . you not inu, nah, Kenji?

KEN: No! I just write reports.

MRS. ICHIOKA: Reports? You make reports?

KEN: Yes! That's *all* I do.

MRS. ICHIOKA *(sadly):* Ah . . . Kenji . . .

KEN: I don't do anything wrong, Mom. I just write observations. Reactions. That's all I do.

MRS. ICHIOKA *(bewildered):* Reports . . .

KEN: *After* they happen, Mom. It's going to be important one day.

MRS. ICHIOKA: Then, Kenji, you make report of man shot in back for getting too close to the fence? You write that, too, nah? Sick people dying, no medicine, son turn against mother—you write all that, nah?

KEN: Oh, Mom . . .

(KEN *exits upstage left.* MRS. ICHIOKA *looks helplessly at* KOKO *and manages a smile. After a moment, she leaves.* KOKO *and* HARRY *are alone.)*

KOKO *(with an empty laugh):* It's you and me again, Harry.

HARRY: Yeah.

KOKO: Let's go in.

HARRY: Okay.

(They enter the barrack. HARRY *goes to his chair.)*

HARRY: Koko, Koko . . . *(pulls off the blanket with a flourish)* Ta-daaa!

*(*KOKO *stares dumbly.)*

HARRY: I made it for you.

*(*KOKO *utters a small cry and runs to the bedroom area and sits on the bed.* HARRY *watches her, puzzled. He spins his hat and, after a moment, he leaves, humming tunelessly. He closes the door carefully and shambles off. Fade out.)*

Scene Two

(Time: An early December evening, 1942. Interior of 12-1-A. The table is spread for a small party: crackers, three apples, chips. Small glasses are on a covered table. HARRY's chair is in the room. The bowling trophy is still visible. MITCH has returned from his farm stint earlier in the day. His suitcase is open on the bench. KOKO and MRS. TANAKA are behind the screen, trying on the dresses that MITCH has brought them. MITCH is sitting at the table, wearing his pea coat. It is cold in the barrack. MITCH pares an apple. He listens to the happy woman-talk.)

MRS. TANAKA *(behind the curtain):* That's pretty, Koko.

MITCH: You like it?

KOKO *(behind the curtain):* Oh, I like it. Ma likes hers, too, don't you, Ma?

MRS. TANAKA: Yes, yes. You spent too much money. You shouldn't spend so much when you work so hard for it.

(KOKO comes out like a model, holding the skirt of a pinafore outward, humming "A Pretty Girl Is Like a Melody." MRS. TANAKA also parades in a drab new old-lady dress, a size too large, another gift from MITCH.)

MRS. TANAKA *(continuing; pinching in the excess of her dress):* Michio, you think Mama's an old lady and Koko's still a little girl, ne?

MITCH: There wasn't enough to save. I couldn't bring anything home, Ma.

MRS. TANAKA: That's all right.

KOKO: You're home . . . I mean, here with us. That's the main thing.

MITCH: We had to buy our own groceries and pay for that lousy cabin we slept in, too. There wasn't much left after that.

(MRS. TANAKA sneaks into the bedroom area to get a "Welcome Back, MITCH" poster while KOKO holds MITCH's attention.)

KOKO: Did you . . . ah, look around? Was it a nice place to move to . . .?

MITCH: We worked six days a week. Didn't have much time after that. No, it's not a "nice" place to move to. It's cold there.

(KOKO stands by her mother by the sign and simultaneously they speak)

KOKO and MRS. TANAKA: Ta-daaa!

MITCH *(trying to look happy):* That's nice. Real nice. *(moves downstage)* Well, what's new here? Anything good happen?

KOKO: Like what?

(KOKO and MRS. TANAKA start to decorate the bleak barrack walls with crepe paper streamers.)

MITCH: Like I thought Ma would have found a nice doctor for you—ha ha—by now.

MRS. TANAKA: Not yet. But Koko got a nice job.

KOKO: If you call cleaning bedpans nice.

MITCH: Bedpans?

KOKO *(engrossed in decorating):* We had a strike not long ago.

MITCH: No kidding. What d'you strike for?

KOKO: Well, it started with two men being jailed for beating an informer and ended up a strike against general policy.

MRS. TANAKA: Everybody out in firebreak, day and night. Two weeks. Singing songs, making speeches . . . music going all the time . . .

MITCH: Did you get what you struck for?

KOKO: Not much change here. But the men who were arrested . . . they were scheduled to be tried in Tucson . . . you know they wouldn't have gotten a fair trial there . . . well, we stopped that.

MITCH: So they'll be tried here?

KOKO: No no.

MITCH: Well, where then?

KOKO: They disappeared. Talk is, they were sent to Tule Lake.

MITCH: Tule Lake! That's the camp up north where they send all the troublemakers.

KOKO: Yes, the dissidents, incorrigibles, recalcitrants, repatriates . . .

MITCH: A buncha fancy names for "shit list." I hear it's maximum security camp . . . tear gas, riot guns, curfew . . . the whole thing. Why the hell you let 'em do that?

KOKO: It's still better than being tried in Tucson. At least they'd be with their own. *(helps* MITCH *unpack)* They say it's a deportation center. It's from there and on to Japan. The last stop before Japan.

MRS. TANAKA: Last stop before Nihon.

MITCH: Must be a holy hellhole.

*(*KOKO *finds a bottle of whiskey in* MITCH'S *bag.)*

KOKO: What's this?

MITCH *(tries to hide it from* MRS. TANAKA *and grabs the bottle):* Careful! I took a lot of trouble to smuggle that in.

MRS. TANAKA: Michio, you drink osake now?

MITCH: Not much. Don't worry, Ma. I don't drink much. Sometimes I'd get so tired, I couldn't sleep. I just take a drink now and then, Ma.

MRS. TANAKA *(setting the bottle on the table):* Good. Now we have something special for the party.

MITCH: Oh, the party. God, I don't feel like no party tonight. Let's call it off. Let's just us have a drink and go on to bed.

MRS. TANAKA: Can't do that. People already coming.

MITCH: Hell . . .

KOKO: Just our friends. Yo, Ken . . . Harry . . .

MITCH: Oh, yeah, Harry. Sometimes I wish I were like Harry . . .

KOKO: Something else, Mitch. They're asking for volunteers for a separate . . . a segregated unit of Nisei soldiers.

*(*MITCH *takes out his letter-man's sweater and stops.)*

MITCH: Segregated? Hell, ain't nobody going for that! Nisei boys got kicked out of the army when the war broke out. They don't want us. We're Japs to them. They won't get two people to

WAKAKO YAMAUCHI

volunteer for that shit! *(returns his sweater to the bag and snaps it shut)*

KOKO: No, Mitch. They already got it started in Hawai'i. They're setting up a recruitment center here right now.

MITCH: Hawai'i's different. They didn't get rounded up like us. With all those Japanese on the island, they didn't . . .

KOKO: No, Mitch, it's true.

MRS. TANAKA: You not going volunteer, ne?

MITCH: Hell no! What d'you take me for? I'd be a fool to do that.

MRS. TANAKA *(breathing easier)*: Good. Get ready now for the party.

(YO raps on the door and enters. She wears high heels and a coat over a party dress. KOKO and MRS. TANAKA admire her as she removes her coat and she in turn admires their new clothes.)

KOKO: Oh, Yo, you look so . . . sophisticated!

MRS. TANAKA: Oh, yes.

YO: You both look great, too!

MRS. TANAKA: Michio's presents.

YO *(to MITCH)*: So you did come back. I thought you'd find a way to stay out for good. Hey! You look great!

MITCH: Hello, Yo.

YO: "Hello Yo"? Is that all I get? How's about a big hug? *(hugs MITCH)*

MITCH: Good to see you, Yo. Really good. Like coming home again.

YO: Ain't that something? He's calling this place home!

KOKO: Home is where the loved ones are.

YO: Don't make me puke, Koko. This is supposed to be a party. *(sees the bottle)* Hey, do I see something? Now it's a *real* party. *(starts pouring the drinks)*

(HARRY and KEN rap on the door and enter.)

KEN: So you made it back! Good to see you. How's everything?

MITCH: Yeah yeah. Okay. I'm okay. Hi, Harry, how's the world treating you?

HARRY *(grinning broadly):* Okay. *(shakes* MITCH's *hand)*

MRS. TANAKA: Come sit down, everybody.

KOKO: This reminds me of the first day we met.

YO *(passing out the drinks):* A toast!

KOKO: Remember that terrible dust storm, Yo?

YO: Do I ever. I thought this was my barrack.

MITCH: Hell, she wanted to know what *I* was doing here.

YO: A toast to the return of the prodigal!

> *(They toast* MITCH: *"To Mitch!" "Bottoms up!" "To the future!")*

KOKO *(to* KEN*):* And you came in with Harry. Just like tonight.

KEN: He was huddled by the door. I don't know how long he was there before I came along.

MRS. TANAKA: Yo-chan playing cards. I remember.

MITCH *(quietly):* Seems a long time ago. And we're still in the same place. Nothing's changed.

KOKO: But it has! Look, you went outside . . . and we're good friends now.

YO: Hear, hear! Our own Miss Goody Two Shoes!

KEN *(turning inward):* Everything's changed.

YO: Aw, come now. Stop this serious talk. This is a party! *(to* MRS. TANAKA*)* Obasan, you should have planned a program.

MRS. TANAKA: Program? But Ichioka-san's not here yet.

> *(*YO *pours another round for everyone.* KEN *drinks morosely.)*

YO: Well, let's rehearse then. Who wants to sing?

MITCH: Naw, we don't want to sing. I can't even carry a tune.

YO *(slightly drunk):* Harry, you wanta start it?

HARRY *(grinning foolishly):* I know only one song.

YO: Well, hit it, baby!

KOKO: Sing, Harry!

MRS. TANAKA: Ichioka-san's not here yet.

HARRY *(standing):* Yes, sir, that's my baby/No, sir, don't mean maybe/Yes, sir, that's my baby now . . .

MRS. TANAKA: Ichioka-san's . . .

YO *(with* HARRY): And by the way/And by the way . . .

(Everyone joins in. MRS. TANAKA *reluctantly keeps time on the table.)*

EVERYONE: When we reach that preacher/I will say/Yes, sir, that's my baby/No, sir, don't mean maybe . . .

(There is a loud banging on the door. YO, *still singing, opens it.* MRS. ICHIOKA *enters.)*

MRS. ICHIOKA: Too much noise!

(One by one, people stop singing. HARRY *is the last to stop.)*

MRS. TANAKA: Sorry, sorry. Sit down, Ichioka-san. We expected you . . .

YO *(inebriated):* Come in, come in. Bring Papa, Mama. Join the party. *(pushes* MRS. ICHIOKA *to a chair)*

MRS. ICHIOKA: Can't sit down. Papa pretty sick, Kenji.

KEN: I'd better go.

*(*KEN *gets up and leaves quickly with his mother. Everyone is surprised.)*

YO *(to* HARRY): 'Smatter with him?

HARRY: I don' know.

MRS. TANAKA: I'm going to bed. I think I'm a little bit drunk. *(turns back)* Be quiet now.

KOKO: 'Night, Ma. *(to* YO) Ken's . . . something's wrong with him.

YO: Aw . . . he's no fun. He's been like that ever since . . . ever since . . . what?

KOKO: He's changed. That's what he said.

YO: Well, someone ought to change mama's little boy. His diapers, that's what.

MITCH: Every man's got a right to piss in his pants sometime.

*(*HARRY *laughs hard.)*

YO: Oh, is that so, Mr. . . . Mr. Guts and Balls. Oh, hey, did you get your bowling done outside? Bet you just parked your butt right in that ol' bowling alley, hunh?

MITCH *(turning grim):* No.

KOKO: Didn't you bowl, Mitch?

MITCH: I said no!

YO: Temper, temper. *(to* HARRY*)* 'Smatter with him?

HARRY: He's mad.

MITCH: You goddamn right, I'm mad. They wouldn't let us *in* the alleys, let alone bowl. Or the barber shops . . . or the restaurants. Can you believe it? And us breaking our fucking balls for their harvest—for *their* sugar—for *their* army! And for peanuts. Peanuts! That's one town I'll never go back to. You can't *give* me enough money to go back there.

YO: Well, you see, you've learned something.

MITCH: Damned right, I learned. I learned good. You're going to learn, too. It's mean out there. A hanging party on every good ol' main street, USA.

YO: Come on, kid. You just had some bad luck. It's not like that in *every* town.

MITCH: Wanta bet?

YO: You can't start thinking like that, Mitch. We're going to get out pretty soon and . . . *(pours another drink)*

MITCH: Go easy on that stuff. That's gotta last me 'til the end of the war. Or forever. Whichever comes first.

YO: Don't worry. We're going to get out purty damn soon and . . . I'll tell you what. I'll buy you the next bottle. Okay? We're getting out purty soon now.

MITCH: Sez who?

YO: Sez me. I happen to know something.

MITCH: Yeah? What's 'at?

YO: We're all going to get out of here. All of us. We-are-getting-out-of-here. You hear 'at? All we do is . . .

MITCH: Yeah, hang yourself.

YO: No no no. We fill out a questionnaire and get a clearance 'n voila! We're free!

KOKO: That's all? Fill out a questionnaire?

MITCH *(suspiciously):* What kind of questions?

YO: Easy ones. You know: Where're you born, what schools, what organizations . . . were you ever arrested and why . . . those kinds.

MITCH: How come so easy? What's the catch?

YO: They wanna get rid of us. It's getting kind of embarrassing to 'em, you know, corbeas hab . . . due process and all that stuff. *(takes a drink)* Know where I'm going?

KOKO: Where?

YO: I'm agoin' to Montana. Missoula, Montana, look out!

MRS. TANAKA *(offstage):* Shhh!

YO: I'm going get my daddy out of that prison.'N I'm gonna find a vine-covered cottage an' get me a job 'n take care of my little ol' daddy. He's my family. All I got.

KOKO: That makes me sad. Mitch, can we go to Montana, too?

MITCH: We'll see if it's true first.

YO: Sure, it's true. You'll see.

KOKO: Let's go to Montana, Mitch.

MITCH: We'll see. We'll find a place.

YO: Know any Montana songs?

HARRY: Not me.

YO: Let's hear it for good ol' Montana! *(sings to "Oh Susanna")* I'ma goin' to ol' Montana/Oh, my daddy for to see . . .

KOKO: Gonna find a . . . vine-covered cottage/For my daddy and for me . . .

YO and KOKO: Oh! Montana! Oh, don't you cry for me . . . *(dance together)* Gonna find a . . .

MRS. TANAKA: Be quiet!

YO *(whispering)*: Hooray for freedom!

(HARRY spins his hat nervously. Fade out.)

Scene Three

(Time: A February night, 1943. Inside 12-1-A. HARRY's chair is in the corner. The bowling trophy remains visible. It is bitter cold. MITCH sits at the table in a bathrobe, pajama tops, shoes, and socks. MRS. TANAKA, in a robe, crochets a muffler. MITCH fills out a questionnaire, squinting over the forms in the weak overhead light. There is quarreling in the ICHIOKA barrack. MRS. TANAKA looks at MITCH.)

MRS. ICHIOKA *(offstage)*: You writing again? *(no response)* More better you write to President Roosevelt. Give him report of camp.

(KOKO enters. She wears a pea coat over her uniform. She shivers from the cold.)

MITCH: Working overtime?

MRS. ICHIOKA *(offstage)*: Tell him come live with us. Sell everything for five dollars a piece and come live with us.

KOKO *(overlapping)*: There was an emergency. Are those the questionnaires?

MR. ICHIOKA *(offstage)*: Mo ii yo! *("Enough!")*

MITCH: You ought to come home after eight hours.

KOKO: Can't. Patients get sick regardless of the time. Well, I guess the experience will come in handy outside. I could get a job in a hospital. I guess they'll be paying more than sixteen dollars.

MITCH *(reading the form)*: I should hope so. Ma, are we registered with the Japanese consul?

MRS. TANAKA: I don't think so. No. Papa died before. *(reminisces)* I told him every year, every year, "Register the kids; register the kids . . ." But he never did.

MITCH: Lucky for us now.

KOKO: Have we decided where to go?

MITCH: Lot of guys at the motor pool are talking 'bout Chicago. You wanta go there?

KOKO: I want to go back home.

MITCH: Forget that. They won't let us back there. *(reading the form)* Was Pa ever in the Japanese army? *(to* KOKO*)* Plenty of bedpans in Chicago, Koko.

KOKO: Funny.

MRS. TANAKA: Papa don't like army. That's why he came to America . . . so he won't have to go to army. He was peaceful man. He was eighteen then. Younger than you, Michio.

KOKO: There's a lot of army people . . . suddenly you see so many soldiers around. They're stepping up the recruiting.

MITCH *(contemptuously)*: Fat chance they got! You'd have to have rocks in your head to volunteer. No one I know is . . . They'd have to sneak out in the middle of the night . . . *(still reading the questionnaire)* Look here. It says, "List all the addresses you have ever lived in for the period of as much as three months during the last twenty years." For crying out loud!

MRS. TANAKA: We moved lots . . . lots. Mama had to live near work. Ah . . . can't remember addresses.

MITCH: I'll just put down some that I remember.

KOKO: Do them right, Mitch. You're filling out ours, too, aren't you? They should be consistent. Otherwise, they might not release us. *(removes her coat and quickly puts it back on after realizing the cold)* Or, worse yet, they might let us out one at a time.

*(*MITCH *stretches, yawns, and rubs his eyes.)*

MITCH: They'll be the same. They'll be perfect. We'll get out together or we won't go at all. Don't worry.

KOKO: Have we decided where to go?

MITCH: Let's get free first.

KOKO: We ought to go with friends. Yo or Ken. It'll be so lonely without friends. I wonder where the Ichiokas are planning to go.

MRS. TANAKA: I don't know.

KOKO: Since I started working nights, I hardly see Ken anymore. I wonder if he's all right.

MITCH: I saw him in the mess hall tonight. He looks bad. Maybe he's sick. God, I hope he's not cracking up. Those types sometimes do, you know.

MRS. TANAKA: Lots of fighting over there. *(meaning the* ICHIOKA *barrack)*

KOKO: Poor Ken.

MRS. TANAKA: Maybe sometimes better to be like Harry-san. Don't care 'bout nothing.

KOKO: Oh, he cares, Ma. he cares about a lot of things. He's very sensitive. He feels a lot of pain.

MRS. TANAKA: Yo-chan still going Montana?

KOKO: That's what she says. Gosh, I'm going to miss her.

MRS. TANAKA: Can't go with everybody, Koko. When we make nice home, she will visit, ne?

(MITCH returns to the questionnaire and suddenly springs to life.)

MITCH: Holy mack! It says here . . . Boy, what a nerve!

KOKO: What? What?

MITCH: It says here: "Are you willing to serve in the armed forces of the United States on combat duty wherever ordered?" That means . . .

(MITCH stops. No one speaks. He slams the paper on the table.)

MITCH: So that's why they're here.

KOKO: Who?

MITCH *(grimly):* That's why they're here. The goddamn recruiters. It's a frame-up . . . it's a trap! They need cannon fodder! *(slams his fist on the table)* They got us again. They got us again! What does it take for us to wise up? *(he grows stony)* Well, I'm not falling for it. No. I'll stay right here. I'll stay here 'til I rot.

(KOKO takes the paper and reads it.)

KOKO: But, Mitch, if you don't say yes, they might put you in jail!

MRS. TANAKA: Jail!

MITCH: I don't care. If I say yes, they'll put me in the front line. They take away every right we have except the right to be shot at. No. I'll rot here first. I'll rot.

MRS. TANAKA: What it say, Michio?

(MITCH *walks away from the table and pours himself a drink from the bottle and swallows it. He pours another and drinks.)*

KOKO: It says if he says yes to the question, he goes to combat. If he says no, he's a traitor, Ma. A traitor is . . . Ma, Mitch might have to go jail or they might . . . Mitch! You can't say no!

MITCH: Hell, I'm not scared of no firing squad. I'm not afraid to die . . . not for what I believe in. I believe in freedom . . . equal rights for all men! I'm the real patriot! *(jumps on the table)* Look at me, Koko . . . I'm the true patriot! I'm acting in the grand tradition of Patrick Henry. Remember the guy? "Give me liberty or give me death!" *(makes a trumpet with his hands)* Ta-da-da-dum-ta-da!

KOKO: Mitch, don't . . .

MRS. TANAKA: Come down, Michio.

(*In his bathrobe,* MITCH *marches in place on the table.)*

MITCH: Mine eyes have seen the glory of the coming of the Lord/ He has trampled out the vintage where the grapes of wrath are stored . . .

(KOKO *puts her hands on* MITCH's *legs.)*

KOKO: Stop . . . Shhh . . . Mitch. Make him stop, Mama.

MRS. TANAKA: Shhh! Ichioka-san's sick. Be quiet! Stop right now, Michio!

MITCH: Glory, glory hallelujah!/Glory, glory, hallelujah!/Glory, glory . . .

MRS. TANAKA: Michio! No more! Koko is crying now!

(MITCH *jumps down.)*

MRS. TANAKA *(trying to calm herself):* Calm down.

MITCH: It's okay, Koko. I'm not going crazy. But I'm not going to say yes. You have to understand that. You'll have to shoot me on the spot before I say yes.

KOKO: But, Mitch, I don't want to say no. I don't want to go to prison. I want to stay right here. I want to stay here!

MITCH: You can answer yes. There's no reason for you to say no. Hell, they can't take women for combat duty. It's all right. You and Ma, you'll be free. You can make it together.

MRS. TANAKA: We stay together, Michio.

MITCH: I've made up my mind, Ma. You can't change it.

MRS. TANAKA: If we separate now, we maybe never see each other again. We stay together.

MITCH: I made up my mind.

MRS. TANAKA: Mama make up mind, too. *(more calmly)* Now. All questions same for everybody?

MITCH: The same for everybody. Everyone over seventeen.

MRS. TANAKA: We say no then. Koko and Mama, too.

KOKO: No!

MITCH: No? But Ma, it won't hurt to say yes. You'll be free.

MRS. TANAKA: We say no together.

MITCH: I'd rather do this alone, Ma. It might get pretty rough and . . . I can do it alone better. You can't tell what will happen.

MRS. TANAKA: If they shoot, they shoot us together.

MITCH: I don't think they'll do that. They'll probably deport us. Send us to Tule Lake and then . . .

KOKO: Tule Lake!

MRS. TANAKA: Tule Lake, this camp, that camp, all the same. Camp is camp, ne, Koko?

KOKO *(in protest)*: We'll be leaving all our friends!

MRS. TANAKA *(firmly)*: We stand by Michio, ne, Koko? Together. One family. We live together or die together. We be together.

MITCH: It might get rough, Ma. We may starve out there.

MRS. TANAKA: Then we be hungry together. Ne, Koko? Papa be proud of us.

(KOKO straightens up.)

MITCH: You really mean it, don't you?

MRS. TANAKA: We mean it, Michio.

MITCH: I'm proud of you, too. I'm proud of our little family. Eh, Koko?

KOKO: Yes. *(reads the rest of the questionnaire)* Question twenty-eight: "Will you swear unqualified allegiance to . . ."

MITCH: "Unqualified . . ."

KOKO: "To the United States of America and faithfully defend the United States from any or all attack . . ." *(skims over a couple of sentences)* "and foreswear any form of allegiance or obedience to the Japanese emperor, to any . . ."

MRS. TANAKA: That's okay, Koko. We go to Tule Lake. No-no to both questions. Michio, we go to Tule.

(The door opens and KEN enters.)

MRS. TANAKA: Oh, Papa can't sleep, ne? We make so much . . .

KEN: I think you're wrong, Mitch. I heard you and I . . .

MITCH *(surprised):* Wrong? Where am I wrong?

KEN: The questionnaire. I think . . .

MITCH: You want me to say yes to that goddamn thing?

KEN: I don't "want" you to say anything . . .

MITCH: You want me to say yes, right?

KEN: No! I just say . . .

MITCH: Yeah! "My country, right or wrong," eh?

KEN: I didn't say that.

MITCH *(patiently):* Look, fella. You ain't never been outside. I ain't told you half what happened to me out there. They think I bombed Pearl Harbor, you know that? Me, Mitch Tanaka, all-American bowler! They think I'm going to blow up those bowling alleys, so they won't let me in. *(gets excited)* "Japs!

Keep out!" Okay, top the sugar beets, but don't come in. I'm the Jap! And you want me to fight for this country? If I fight for freedom, I want that good stuff, too!

KEN: All right! You're entitled to your opinion, but . . .

MITCH: You goddamn right.

KEN: But you shouldn't take everyone with you. You can't take Koko and your mother . . .

MITCH: Hey! They're going because they want to. They made up their own minds. They believe in me. That's more than I can say for . . .

KEN: Let Koko talk then. Let her say what she feels . . .

MITCH: She talked! She talked!

KEN *(stubbornly pursuing)*: Koko, do you really want to go . . .

MITCH: Hey, wait a minute! Who the hell you think you are come busting in here like you owned the place . . .

MRS. TANAKA: Michio, iikagen ni shinasai. *("That's enough now")*

MITCH: Hey, Mr. USA. You sit up there in your cozy barrack writing your little reports . . . calling it your patriotic duty . . . while your Ma's eating her heart out and your Pa's dying.

MRS. TANAKA *(overlaps)*: Michio . . .

MITCH *(waving MAMA way)*: Yeah, he's been lying on that straw mattress from the day he got here and you say it's the water that makes him sick. His heart is breaking, man, don't you know? Asshole! When you going to be man enough to say "Enough! Enough! I had enough!"?

KOKO *(overlaps)*: Mitch, don't.

MRS. TANAKA *(overlaps)*: Michio, yoshinasai. *("Stop now")*

MITCH *(pushing KEN)*: Look at you, Mr. Home of the Brave. Hiding behind mama's skirts! Yeah, I heard about it . . .

(MRS. TANAKA steps up to MITCH and slaps him.)

MRS. TANAKA: Baka!

(Without further word, KEN stalks out, slamming the door behind him. KOKO looks at MRS. TANAKA, waits a moment, and

follows KEN. KEN *moves downstage left, stops, and looks back toward* KOKO. KOKO *stops.* KEN *then moves toward his barrack, upstage left. The night is cold and dark.* KOKO *slowly returns to her barrack. Fade out.)*

Scene Four

(Time: A July day, 1943. The guard tower is clearly seen. Inside 12-1-A, the room is empty; only the benches and table are scattered around. The tablecloth is gone. The curtain that separated the living area is gone. Curtains have been stripped from the windows. The iron cots have only the lumpy mattresses on them and seem to have been shoved around. The bowling trophy and deck of cards are on the wall frame. HARRY'S *chair is downstage. Outside, two duffel bags, two suitcases, and a cardboard carton lean against the wall.* MRS. TANAKA *puts the last of her items in her handbag: a couple of postcards (from* MITCH*), a photo of her husband.* KOKO *takes a comb from her purse and runs it through her hair. They are dressed for travel, as is* MITCH. HARRY *sits on a cot.* SAM *helps* MITCH.*)*

SAM: All this stuff goes, Mitch?

MITCH: Yeah. That stuff there. *(to* MAMA*)* Ma, I'm going ahead and see the baggage off. I'll be back.

MRS. TANAKA: All right. *(to* KOKO*)* Mama going say good-bye to Ichioka-san, Koko.

*(*YO *enters from the right, just before* MITCH *leaves.)*

YO: You leaving now?

MITCH: Gotta see this luggage gets on. I'll be back.

*(*YO *stops* MRS. TANAKA *as she goes toward the* ICHIOKA *barrack.)*

YO: Obasan, you look nice.

MRS. TANAKA: Thank you. Going now to say good-bye to Ichioka-san.

YO: What? She's not going, too? I thought she would be on the first boat to Japan.

MRS. TANAKA *(sadly):* She talk like that, ne? But she don't want to move. She says Tule Lake too mean. She says husband going die there. He is so sick.

YO: I'm going to miss you, Obasan. Maybe we'll see each other again. Never can tell.

MRS. TANAKA: Maybe in 'nother life. Tule Lake is long way away. *(laughs weakly)* Japan is far away, too.

YO: I'll miss you.

(MRS. TANAKA *puts her hand on* YO's *head.*)

MRS. TANAKA: Be good girl now. *(laughs softly and exits)*

YO: Okay, Obasan. *(enters the barrack)* Well, kiddo, how you doing?

(KOKO *simply smiles.*)

YO: I guess this is it. Don't think it ain't been charming . . . *(sees* KOKO *holding back tears)* Don't cry, Koko.

KOKO: I won't. It would be a good time to say good-bye right now.

YO: Now?

KOKO: Before we make fools of ourselves. So long, Yo.

(YO *embraces* KOKO *for a moment.* HARRY *spins his hat.*)

KOKO: At least I know it can't get much worse. It can't, can it?

YO: Jesus, I hope not. Well . . . say good-bye to Mitch for me. I've loved you a lot, Koko. *(leaves)*

KOKO: I can't take the chair with me, Harry. I'll leave it for you. Funny how things turn out. Your present to me is now my present for you.

HARRY: Funny, hanh? *(tries to smile)*

KOKO: Harry?

HARRY: Hunh?

KOKO: You've been a good friend to me. I thank you for that. You'd better leave now, okay?

HARRY: Hunh?

KOKO: You'd better go.

HARRY: Not yet.

KOKO: We're not going to cry, are we?

HARRY: No.

KOKO: Ma says, "Time passes; tears dry . . ." But what happens to tears we can't let go?

HARRY: I don' know.

KOKO: I wonder if we'll remember today when we grow old? Will we remember how we met . . . how we said good-bye . . . and how we wouldn't let ourselves cry? Maybe those tears stay with us until we're old. And maybe one day, a little punch in a Dixie cup, half a candy bar, or maybe one of those orange sunsets will open up the memory. Maybe we will cry then.

(HARRY *shrugs. They are silent a moment and* KOKO *picks up her suitcase and walks downstage.* KEN, *who has been waiting outside, comes forward.*)

KEN *(seriously):* Hi, Koko.

KOKO: Hi. *(turns her back to him so he can't see her face)*

KEN: I'm joining the army tomorrow.

KOKO: No!

KEN: I have to do it.

KOKO: Why didn't you tell me?

KEN: I've been thinking about it for a long time and . . .

KOKO: But your mother . . . your mother will die!

KEN: Shhh . . . She doesn't know yet. I'll tell her just before I leave.

KOKO: Ken, how can you do such a thing?

KEN: I can't help it.

KOKO: And your dad. He's so sick.

KEN: I know, I know. Christ, I know. But I just got to do this. I just got to.

KOKO: God forgive you, Ken.

KEN: Koko, don't blame me. I have to make a decision and this is what I choose . . . in spite of everything. If all that talk about freedom and democracy is a lie, then I have to try to change it. That's all. I have to try. Do you understand, Koko?

KOKO: No, I don't understand. Who knows what's right or what's wrong? Who cares? And what good does it do to care? I don't care about freedom or democracy or countries or nations anymore. I don't care who wins or who loses. I only care for myself.

KEN: I'm really sorry how things turned out.

KOKO: You got to care for yourself. Who else will do it for you?

KEN: I wanted to tell you . . . so often . . . how I felt about you . . .

KOKO: It's too late. I may never see you again. It's too late now.

KEN: I'm sorry. What can I say?

KOKO: You can say good-bye. That's all there's left to say.

(KOKO *picks up her suitcase and starts to go.* KEN *takes it from her and leads her to the bench.*)

KEN: Koko, not like this. Don't say good-bye like this. Let me know you'll think of me now and then. Help me. Tell me something . . . anything . . . that will make me want to live through this. Tell me when the war is over, you'll . . . you'll . . .

KOKO: How can I say such things? How do we know what will happen to us? You're going one way, and I'm going another.

KEN: But you can say, "I promise to think of you," can't you?

MITCH (*offstage*): Ma! Koko! Let's go! Come on, let's go!

KEN: Koko, can you say that?

KOKO: Yes, I promise to think of you.

KEN: Will you write me?

KOKO: I will. As long as I am able. Will you write me?

KEN: As long as I am able. That's my promise.

KOKO: And let's promise to live a long, long time, so that one day we may meet again . . . okay?

KEN: That's our promise.

MITCH (*entering*): Koko? Ma? (*sees* KEN *and* KOKO) What say? Take it easy, pal. (*shakes hands with* KEN *and turns to* KOKO) Get a move on, Koko. *(goes to the barrack door and sees* HARRY*)* So long, Harry. Don't take any wooden nickels. *(calls to the* ICHIOKA *barrack)* Come on, Ma! Bus leaves in ten minutes! *(nods to* KEN *and leaves)*

*(*KEN *touches* KOKO *on the shoulder as she follows* MITCH *out.* MRS. TANAKA *enters upstage, looks at* KEN, *and smiles.)*

MRS. TANAKA: Ken-chan . . . *(takes a last look around and exits)*

*(*KEN *exits slowly. Inside the barrack,* HARRY *walks to the iron cots, goes to the wall, and touches the trophy. He picks up the cards and lets them flutter to the floor. He sings, softly at first, then loudly)*

HARRY: Yes, sir, that's my baby/No, sir, don't mean maybe/Yes, sir, that's my baby now.

(The guard tower is strongly visible. Wind sounds grow and turn into the music of a flute playing "She's My Baby" in minor key.)

End of Play

The
Chairman's
Wife

Wakako Yamauchi

CAST OF CHARACTERS

Chiang Ching, 75, female
Guard, 41, male
Male Actors:
Papa (Li Dewen)/Tang Na
Communist Recruiter/Stage Manager/Shansi
Nationalist Soldier 1/Judge
Nationalist Soldier 2/Judge
Yu Chi-wei/ Chou En-lai
Female Actors:
Mama/ Zhang Yufeng
Woman Spy/Wang Guangmei

Playwright's note: This play was inspired by events in the life of Chiang Ching, the widow of Mao Tsetung.

ACT ONE

(Time: June 4, 1989, late afternoon. On rise: Upstage is a stage plastered with peeling posters. Covering the stage is a scrim painted with an open curtain. Slides can be projected on it, and much of the past takes place there. The stage is dark. Distant sounds of sirens grow and fade, overlap, then fade again. Muffled confusion prevails. Whispers—distorted, toneless, surreal, overlapping—start softly, grow louder, then fade again, repeating the growing and fading. Downstage is set with a hospital cot [doubles as a platform], a chair for CHIANG CHING, *and upstage is a chair and desk for the* GUARD.*)*

VOICES: Tiananmen ... *(overlapping)* Tiananmen ... Tiananmen ... Tiananmen ...

(Lights fade in. CHIANG CHING, *75, sits on a chair in a prison hospital. Stark shadows of bars cross the stage. She nods over a small red book. She is in a recurring dream.)*

CHIANG CHING *(muttering):* Un-un-un. Tiananmen?

(Lights throb as though in a nightmare.)

VOICES *(overlapping, distorted):* Tiananmen ... Deng Xiaoping ... Tiananmen ... Deng Xiaoping ...

CHIANG CHING: Angh? Deng? Deng Xiaoping?

VOICES *(overlapping, softly):* Tiananmen ... beat-her-up ... Tiananmen ... beat-her-up ...

CHIANG CHING: What's going on?

(Voices fade gradually as CHIANG CHING *awakens.)*

CHIANG CHING *(continuing):* I know, I know. On trial again, anh? You'll get nothing more from me. Nothing more. I was not responsible for that ... that Tiananmen.

VOICES *(fading):* Tiananmen ... Tiananmen ...

CHIANG CHING *(continuing):* I had nothing to do with it. Deng Xiaoping was at the bottom of it. The Red Guards ... the Red Guards did it. THEY fired into the crowd. Not me.

(Moans overlap CHIANG CHING'S *dialogue.)*

CHIANG CHING *(continuing):* Listen to that. Is there nothing they won't do? *(loudly)* You can stop that now. I know what you're up to. *(pause)* Guard! Guard!

(The area of light widens and grows brighter. The GUARD, 41, enters fastening his belt.)

GUARD: What do you want?

CHIANG CHING: Tell them to stop that infernal racket. I can't concentrate. *(strokes her red book)*

GUARD: What racket?

CHIANG CHING *(a little embarrassed):* I need water.

GUARD: I don't fetch water. That's the orderly's job.

CHIANG CHING: Orderly?

GUARD: Orderly. Where do you think you are? Confused, anh?

CHIANG CHING: You. You're the guard from prison, aren't you? Beijing prison?

GUARD: This is the prison hospital. Don't pretend you don't know.

CHIANG CHING: What are *you* doing here?

GUARD: I got a transfer.

CHIANG CHING: Is that all you do? Follow me around?

GUARD: That's right.

CHIANG CHING: Then you can bring me water. Where are my dolls?

GUARD: It's not my job to cart your dolls around. You want the Occupational Therapy Department.

CHIANG CHING: Not my job, not my job. Is this the new breed of Chinese?

GUARD: I'm only here to guard you. No more, no less.

CHIANG CHING: And it's *my* job to sew dolls. If I don't, you'll be accusing me of dereliction of duty. Get my dolls. I've already lost valuable time.

GUARD: Don't stress yourself. So we'll add a few more years to your sentence. Life without parole is life without parole.

(She looks into a small box and finds scraps of red cloth.)

CHIANG CHING: Get some red silk too. Three yards.

GUARD: Silk? For dolls?

CHIANG CHING: Red. Red is good luck. Red is everything: the color of passion, the color of our flag, the color of . . . of patriots.

(She presses the cloth to herself.)

GUARD *(sarcastically)*: Yeah, patriots. Blood is red, too.

CHIANG CHING: Her cheong-sam will be red. She'll never take it off . . . wear it always. Like I wear China. The history of China.

GUARD: I don't want to hear that today, you understand?

CHIANG CHING: Why, the facts are there.

GUARD: The facts—yeah—*your* facts.

CHIANG CHING: Millions crawled out of their dismal lives . . . out of villages and factories . . . dark streets . . . to raise one voice: "Re-vo-lu-tion!"

GUARD: You think you did it all by yourself, anh? Well, your glory days are gone.

CHIANG CHING: Gone. Who remembers now? Who remembers how we freed them? They starved while the rich stuffed their bellies . . . squandering . . . killing . . .

GUARD: You did your share too. Don't forget that.

CHIANG CHING: You'll never believe this now, but in our village executions were gala affairs. Swords flashing . . . heads rolling in the dust. We sat on the walls to watch.

GUARD: Don't forget.

CHIANG CHING: Hunh?

GUARD: Don't forget the killing and torturing *you* did.

CHIANG CHING: Ridiculous! I saved millions . . . educated them on what could be done with their collective power. History will prove it one day. That's what Mao wanted to do and—

GUARD: Leave the Chairman out of it! Let him rest in peace.

CHIANG CHING: How can he, unh? Rest in peace. All those two-faced people who licked his boots while he lived: "Oh, Chairman, Oh, Chairman . . ." doing this to *me*. How can he rest?

GUARD: Wait a minute. You did it to yourself. You—

CHIANG CHING: I laid the groundwork . . .

GUARD: Groundwork paved with bones.

CHIANG CHING: . . . groundwork for a smooth transition and one month—one month after he dies . . .

GUARD: . . .paved with bones and mortared with blood.

CHIANG CHING: . . . they arrest me. Confess!? Chiang Ching confess? Ha ha.

GUARD: Hardly anyone lives today to tell . . . Well, I remember. I'll never forget.

CHIANG CHING: Everyone knows certain measures must be taken during a revolution. It's called revolutionary behavior.

GUARD: That's why you're here now. For your "revolutionary behavior."

CHIANG CHING: I've been in jail before. You can't break me.

GUARD *(laughing):* Life without parole?

CHIANG CHING: There are ways. There are ways.

GUARD: Sewing dolls?

CHIANG CHING: Sewing dolls is like Tai Chi. It frees the mind for important thoughts. Bring me my work.

GUARD: Cheh.

CHIANG CHING: Oh, the dolls I've made in these years! The thoughts I've put in their little cloth heads. Sometimes I'd feel like a mother again. Li Na . . . Li Na . . .

(CHIANG CHING *holds the blanket like her child. The distraught, white, schizophrenic face of* LI NA *appears behind the scrim.)*

CHIANG CHING *(continuing):* What have they done to you?

GUARD: It's you. You abandoned her.

CHIANG CHING: I didn't! I *had* to send her away. For safety. You don't know. Sometimes mothers have hard choices to make. Ah! My mother . . . it was a different time for women. She was a thistle seed blown about by the breath of men. When

106

you're number two wife, you pay a price. Hardly more than a concubine. No will. No sense of destiny.

GUARD *(sarcastically):* And that's something you always had.

CHIANG CHING: Oh, yes. That's why I joined the theater. Oh, I loved theater. Even in dusty Chucheng, there were troops of dancers and actors . . . traveling troops on makeshift stages. My mother loved them too.

(As she speaks, lights change and we hear faint music. Behind the scrim in pale light, overlaid with a slide of a village, a ribbon dance starts. CHIANG CHING *imitates with her red cloth. At once she is a five-year-old.* PAPA *[Li Dewen], in whiteface, magically appears from stage right in peasant clothes, drunk.)*

CHIANG CHING: Papa!

PAPA: Lai! Lai-lai-lai. ("Come-come-come.")

CHIANG CHING *(rushing to him):* Can I go to the square, Papa?

PAPA: What's at the square?

CHIANG CHING: You know, Papa. The festival. Everyone's there. Puppets and dancers and everything. I want to dance, too.

PAPA: Look at your big feet. You want to dance with those big feet? Everybody's going to laugh at you. *(drunken laugh)* You going to like that? Everybody laughing at you? *(pause)* Where's Mama?

CHIANG CHING: Lantern show's starting.

PAPA: Where is she, enh? Where's supper? *(pause)* She's there, anh?

CHIANG CHING: There's food at the square, Papa. Roast pig, *bao* . . .

PAPA: Go get her. *(muttering)* Making up to those landlords again. I'll give her a thrashing she won't forget. Not for a long time.

*(*MAMA *enters carrying [mime] a plate of food. She smiles and puts something in* CHIANG CHING'S *mouth.)*

CHIANG CHING: Mama . . .

PAPA: Where you been?

MAMA: I brought supper, Papa.

PAPA: What'd you pay for it?

MAMA: It's a festival. Everything is free.

PAPA *(mocking):* "Everything is free, everything is free." Nothing is free. Who you think pays for it?

MAMA: The landlords, of course. You know that.

CHIANG CHING: The landlords, Papa.

MAMA: They pay for everything on Festival. You *know* that. Look. He even gave me a special piece of pork . . .

PAPA: I know nothing! I only know they rob me all year long, then give me this shit on "Festival." I only know that the whole village laughs about the landlord who comes here while Li Dewen *(points to himself)* works. I only know you're a piece of dog shit that clings to any man's pants.

(*He knocks the food from* MAMA's *hands and walks menacingly to* MAMA. CHIANG CHING *runs to protect her.* PAPA *strikes* CHIANG CHING *instead. The two collapse to the floor, crying.*)

PAPA *(continuing):* Shut up! Stop that sniveling!

(PAPA *covers his ears and disappears into the shadows. Lights dim.* MAMA *comforts* CHIANG CHING, *examining her bruise.*)

MAMA: Does it hurt? Does it hurt?

(CHIANG CHING *feels her tooth.*)

MAMA *(continuing, snarling):* Beast. We don't have to take this. We . . . we won't stay here. We'll . . .

CHIANG CHING: But you say that every time. We always come back.

MAMA: This time . . . this time . . . *(pause)* Who am I fooling? *(pause)* It's hard to be a woman. You work like a servant and take abuse. I want to tell you life will be better for you but I can't. I can't. Things will not change. It was like this for my mother, and it will be so with you. It will not change.

CHIANG CHING: But if we run away and don't come back.

MAMA: There's no place we can go.

CHIANG CHING: Grandma's.

MAMA: That's just as bad. You know how Grandpa is.

CHIANG CHING: We can live under the bridge, Mama. Lots of people live under the bridge.

MAMA: We can't be beggars. *(pause)* The landlord knew Papa would rage. He said, "I'd like to give you more, but your husband . . ." We can't go to the landlord's. Only tonight he said, "Why do you stay with that brute?" He said, "Come to my house."

CHIANG CHING: But isn't he married?

MAMA: Not as his wife. To work. To work for him.

CHIANG CHING: Will he give us food?

MAMA: You'll have to be a good little girl . . . not fight with the other children. Do you understand?

CHIANG CHING: Will we have a place to sleep?

MAMA: Maybe he'll give us a room.

CHIANG CHING: Our own room?

MAMA: You'll wait for me while I work, Yunhe. No fighting, you understand?

CHIANG CHING: I fight because they tease me, Mama. They laugh at my clothes; they call me "Rags, Yunhe." They say my heels stick out of my shoes like duck eggs. They pull my hair. That's why I fight, Mama. *(angry)* Why are we so poor?

MAMA: Everyone is poor.

CHIANG CHING: Not the landlords.

MAMA: No, not them.

CHIANG CHING: One day, Mama, I'll be the empress of China, and you will have a hut of your own.

(MAMA *laughs. She moves away from* CHIANG CHING *in pain.*)

CHIANG CHING *(continuing):* You'll never be hungry when I am empress, Mama.

MAMA *(not turning):* The children, Yunhe. No fighting . . . remember?

CHIANG CHING: They're mean, but I'll give them food too. First, I'll make them wear rags and torn shoes. Then I'll give them food.

First . . . *(her voice becomes a low threatening growl)* . . .they must be punished.

(MAMA disappears, her small laugh remaining and fading. Lights return to normal, shadows of the cell bars very pronounced. CHIANG CHING *appears to look for* MAMA.*)*

GUARD: Your mother. They say she worked nights.

CHIANG CHING: So many nights I lay awake, hungry. So many nights.

GUARD: Nights, anh? *(he laughs obscenely)* She worked nights?

CHIANG CHING: You dog.

GUARD *(laughing)*: Woof woof.

(Simultaneously, a pack of dogs barks in the distance.)

CHIANG CHING: Never mind. I've fought dogs before.

(The barking grows louder.)

CHIANG CHING *(continuing)*: Chucheng was full of dogs. Dogs like you and . . . and real dogs. Hungry as me. Woke up one night— my stomach hurting—went out looking for her.

(Behind the scrim, black shadows of dogs snarl and attack. Immersed in her dream, CHIANG CHING *flails at them downstage. She screams.* MAMA *runs [behind the scrim], screaming. She buttons her blouse hurriedly.)*

MAMA: I told you to stay inside!

(CHIANG CHING whimpers and rubs her leg.)

MAMA *(continuing, screaming above the dogs)*: We'll leave this awful place!

CHIANG CHING: You say that all the time, Mama.

MAMA: We'll move. I promise. I promise. Come . . . come . . .

(MAMA reaches out to CHIANG CHING, but her image fades from behind the scrim.)

CHIANG CHING *(continuing)*: Mama! *(she glances at the GUARD and returns to reality)* We moved then. We moved to Tsinan.

GUARD: Maybe more business there, anh?

CHIANG CHING: That's where I went into the theater. Did I tell you?

GUARD: Dozens . . . hundreds of times. Twice a day. Five days a week. You were fifteen. They let you in because there weren't enough female actors and the director wanted real girls to play women roles. Did I get that right?

CHIANG CHING: You know about that?

GUARD: I know everything. University of Tsinan. Actors! Dancers! Opened the world for you.

CHIANG CHING: The world! Strindberg, Chekov, Ibsen.

GUARD: But the Japanese invaded Tsinan, right? 1931?

CHIANG CHING: Murder! Rape!

(The GUARD *leaves.* CHIANG CHING *calls after him.)*

CHIANG CHING *(continuing):* I saw it all! *(muttering)* I saw it all. Our own people collaborating with the Japanese. Spies everywhere. Dangerous to open your mouth. We just tried to keep alive, keep out of trouble . . . mind our own business . . . keep out of trouble.

(A COMMUNIST RECRUITER *in whiteface, disguised as a beggar, materializes from the shadows passing out leaflets. He comes downstage and surprises* CHIANG CHING.*)*

COMMUNIST *(softly):* How are you tonight, little sister?

CHIANG CHING *(startled):* Unn!

COMMUNIST *(giving her a flyer):* Here. Take this home and read it.

CHIANG CHING: What is it? I don't want it. Get it away from me.

COMMUNIST: Don't be afraid. I just want to ask you something.

CHIANG CHING: Well, ask me.

COMMUNIST: Ever been to a Shanghai factory?

CHIANG CHING: No.

COMMUNIST: Know what they're like? Know what they earn?

CHIANG CHING: What?

COMMUNIST: The girls earn twelve yuan a month. That's not much, is it?

CHIANG CHING: Well, no.

COMMUNIST: And they pay one yuan for every needle they break. Some end up with nothing at all. Is that fair?

CHIANG CHING: Well, they don't *have* to work there, do they?

COMMUNIST: No, they don't *have* to. They can live under a bridge; they can beg on the streets . . . they can sell their bodies. But if they work, don't you think they should be paid?

CHIANG CHING: Well . . .

COMMUNIST: Ever been hungry?

CHIANG CHING: Of course. I'm hungry now.

COMMUNIST: Well then, you want to see a change, don't you?

CHIANG CHING: Nnnn . . .

COMMUNIST: Come with me, little sister. *(he takes her hand)*

CHIANG CHING: I'm not going anywhere with you. You're trying to trap me. I'm not falling for that. Oh, no, you collaborators will try anything. I've been warned about you.

COMMUNIST: We're not collaborators. We're not Nationalists. They're the ones we're fighting.

CHIANG CHING: We?

(A WOMAN SPY, dressed in 1930s' clothes, walks slowly by, pausing to light a cigarette close to them.)

COMMUNIST *(loudly):* And how's your old auntie? Still sick, is she?

CHIANG CHING: Hanh?

COMMUNIST: I'm going to see her soon. Take her some oranges. She likes oranges, anh? I'll take her some oranges.

(The WOMAN SPY walks away.)

COMMUNIST *(continuing):* Shhh . . . A group of us. We're guerrillas. You know: strike and disappear. Strike and disappear.

(He seems to enjoy the theatrics.)

CHIANG CHING: Aren't you afraid I'll report you?

COMMUNIST: Listen, I trust you. And you gotta trust me. There're millions of us waiting . . . praying for a change. You too, unh? But who will start it? Who will risk the first step?

COMMUNIST *(continuing):* It's you and me, sister. And our chief.

CHIANG CHING: Your chief?

COMMUNIST *(delighted at the interest):* Can't tell you his name, but it'll soon be known. We call him the Maverick Warrior.

CHIANG CHING: The Maverick . . . *(she laughs)*

COMMUNIST *(laughing along with her):* When you meet him, you'll see why we follow him. You'll see why he's our leader. He has vision, sister, and courage and . . .

CHIANG CHING: Well, I'm an actress, not a soldier.

COMMUNIST: All the better. We need people like you. Propaganda is the most important part of waging war. You realize how many millions there are in China? Why, if we reeducate half—just half—why, we could win, little sister.

(Shadows move behind the scrim. The COMMUNIST *looks around and lowers his voice.)*

COMMUNIST *(continuing):* Actors are important. Don't sell yourself short. *You* are important. Remember that. *(his voice fades)* Remember . . .

(The GUARD *returns with a magazine. He settles in his chair. The* COMMUNIST *has disappeared, but* CHIANG CHING *looks toward him.)*

CHIANG CHING: I will. I'll remember.

GUARD: Still at it?

CHIANG CHING: He said "Important." Important.

(The GUARD *grins.)*

CHIANG CHING *(continuing):* Don't sit there grinning at me. You think it's easy? Theater is cruel. Cold . . . like the wind from the Gobi . . . stinging stand. You have to be strong.

GUARD: And you are strong.

CHIANG CHING: You *know* that.

GUARD: And you will prevail.

CHIANG CHING: I always prevail. Even this . . . this isn't the end for me. They're waiting for me right now.

GUARD: Who's waiting? Who?

CHIANG CHING: People.

GUARD: Yeah?

CHIANG CHING: Oh, yes.

GUARD: You mean outside?

CHIANG CHING: Of course.

GUARD: Wonders never cease, do they?

CHIANG CHING: Say what you will. There are those who remember and love me.

GUARD: Still, nnh?

CHIANG CHING: They haven't forgotten. Why should they? I gave my heart. Everything. Rehearsed like no other actor. Ask anyone. Every time I was tired, disillusioned, I'd remember Chucheng, and nothing was too hard. Everything was possible. Didn't I prove that?

(Lights are rose colored. From the shadows, YU CHI-WEI *in handsome whiteface, in thirties' clothes, appears. He is clearly smitten. He enters* CHIANG CHING'S *dream dressing room.)*

YU CHI-WEI: Excuse me . . .

CHIANG CHING: Oh!

YU CHI-WEI: I had to come back stage, Miss Li. I enjoyed the play very much. Very much.

CHIANG CHING: Why, thank you.

YU CHI-WEI: Ah! How can I tell you? I'm not in the habit of visiting backstage, but . . . Ah! You were magnificent! Unforgettable!

CHIANG CHING: Thank you.

YU CHI-WEI: My name is Yu Chi-wei. I teach at the Tsingtao University. Would you . . . I mean, do you . . . do you have some time? I want so much to talk to you, Miss Li.

CHIANG CHING: Yunhe.

YU CHI-WEI: If you could spare a minute or two . . .

CHIANG CHING: Of course, ah . . .

YU CHI-WEI: Yu Chi-wei. Well . . . ah . . . shall we walk?

CHIANG CHING: All right.

YU CHI-WEI: Oh, but you must be tired.

CHIANG CHING: Well yes, a little, but a short walk would be nice. It'll help me relax.

YU CHI-WEI: Where would you like to go? *(pause)* To the park?

CHIANG CHING: Fine.

YU CHI-WEI: Or would you prefer the pier? It's a beautiful night.

CHIANG CHING: The pier. I love the water. I love watching the boats come in and the sea moving like . . . like quicksilver in the moonlight and . . .

YU CHI-WEI: Ah . . . Miss Li.

CHIANG CHING: And the smell of salt wind from the harbor.

YU CHI-WEI: You mustn't distract me like this, Yunhe. I could . . . I could fall in love.

(CHIANG CHING *almost puts her arms around him. He draws away imperceptibly.)*

CHIANG CHING: So why not?

YU CHI-WEI: I know you have lots of suitors.

CHIANG CHING: None as handsome as you.

YU CHI-WEI: Ah! I must remember you're an actress . . . a consummate actress . . .

CHIANG CHING: Let's forget for a moment that you're you and I'm me and let's explore the possibilities . . .

YU CHI-WEI: I'm sorry, I'm sorry. I'm afraid I gave you the wrong impression. I can't . . .

CHIANG CHING: It's too late. I've already crossed the bridge.

(YU CHI-WEI *turns away.)*

CHIANG CHING *(continuing):* You're saying you're married, aren't you?

YU CHI-WEI: My commitment is stronger than marriage. Deeper.

CHIANG CHING: What can be deeper than love?

YU CHI-WEI *(earnestly):* China, Yunhe. China. You feel it too, don't you?

CHIANG CHING: Of course.

YU CHI-WEI: Then you must feel the pain, too.

CHIANG CHING: I do. But let's forget that for now. Let's talk about us.

YU CHI-WEI: China IS us. You and me and the millions. When *one* is hungry, *all* of us suffer. We can't escape it. *(pause)* We must save China, Yunhe.

CHIANG CHING: Ah . . . You're one of them.

YU CHI-WEI: I'm one of them.

CHIANG CHING: It's not fair. Why did you come to me? If you're so committed, why did you come to me?

YU CHI-WEI: I don't know. I guess I'm human too.

CHIANG CHING: And you plan to change history? You and the "Maverick Warrior"?

YU CHI-WEI: History is already changed. There's no turning back now. Already we have an army to be reckoned with. Listen to me, Yunhe: the plan is to march to Yenan and—

CHIANG CHING: Yenan? On foot? Impossible.

YU CHI-WEI: We can do it. In Yenan we'll build farms, start universities and—

CHIANG CHING: Or die on the long march.

YU CHI-WEI: Some of us, yes.

CHIANG CHING: But . . .

YU CHI-WEI: Is it better to starve to death or to die fighting? The dynasties are gone, but the generalissimo is just as bad. Just another corrupt dictator.

CHIANG CHING: I know that, but—

YU CHI-WEI: It's a strange time, Yunhe. A wonderful time. Don't you want to be a part of it? Come with me. Work with me.

CHIANG CHING: I'm not a soldier, you know.

YU CHI-WEI: All soldiers don't carry guns. There are other ways to

116

fight. Join a troupe of actors. They go from village to village doing plays, songs . . .

CHIANG CHING: I know. We had them in Chucheng too.

YU CHI-WEI: You'll visit factories . . . inform the people of their rights. There's a lot of work you can do.

CHIANG CHING: I can do it.

YU CHI-WEI: But I must tell you: it's dangerous. As dangerous as marching to Yenan. You may be arrested . . . tortured.

CHIANG CHING: Oh, I'm not afraid.

YU CHI-WEI: And there's little or no pay. But you'll be with the people. The REAL people, Yunhe. You'll perform . . . share their millet. You'll travel. Oh, you'll see how big China is. It's exciting—gratifying. The people will love you.

CHIANG CHING: All of China will know me!

(Behind the scrim in a gray light a NATIONALIST SOLDIER *saunters about as though waiting for someone. The* WOMAN SPY *passes him silently and nods.)*

YU CHI-WEI: You'll be constantly on the move. Some days you'll be so tired and discouraged—

CHIANG CHING: Yu Chi-wei?

YU CHI-WEI: Nnn?

CHIANG CHING: Will we be together?

YU CHI-WEI: When we can. As much as possible.

(The WOMAN SPY *enters downstage, watches the two embrace and calls as though in trouble.)*

WOMAN SPY: Yu Chi-wei . . . Come quickly. Yu Chi-wei . . .

(The WOMAN SPY *exits silently and reappears behind the scrim. She whispers to the* NATIONALIST SOLDIER *and calls once more from behind the scrim—faintly.* YU CHI-WEI *stops, listens, and prepares to leave.)*

CHIANG CHING: Where are you going?

YU CHI-WEI: Someone's in trouble. Don't you hear her?

CHIANG CHING: Don't go. Please . . . please . . .

YU CHI-WEI: I must, Yunhe.

(YU CHI-WEI *exits and immediately reappears behind the scrim. He looks around for the* WOMAN SPY. *The* NATIONALIST *hand-cuffs* YU CHI-WEI *and leads him away. The scrim turns blank.* CHIANG CHING *sits dejected.*)

CHIANG CHING: I loved him, but I couldn't wait. The loneliness was . . . I missed him so much—Yu Chi-wei.

GUARD (*rather sympathetically*): Un-un-un.

CHIANG CHING: I worked hard and sacrificed my . . . my career to work in remote . . . remote villages to . . . Some of those places . . . life hadn't changed for them for hundreds . . . maybe thousands of years. We traveled in groups of five or six, you know? Do they still do that?

GUARD: We have television now.

(CHIANG CHING *reverts to her dream. A crowd cheers.*)

CHIANG CHING: Ah! Listen.

GUARD (*not hearing the sounds*): Uh-huh.

(CHIANG CHING *climbs on the platform of her bed.*)

CHIANG CHING: Comrades! I bring a gift to you! I bring hope!

(*The crowd roars.*)

CHIANG CHING (*continuing*): Are they cold? (*pause*) The rich eat well, but our children are hungry. (*to the* GUARD) You see them? (*back to her speech*) There are people who eat, but not us. There are people who wear warm and beautiful clothes, but not us. We shiver in our thin quilts, pull them over our thin bones. Brothers, sisters, let's end this tradition of inequity. Let's pool our energy. Let's work together to build a better China for all of us. We can do it. The rich are few. We are millions. Together we can do it.

(*Two* NATIONALIST SOLDIERS *in ghostly whiteface appear behind the scrim.*)

SOLDIER ONE: Well, well, well, what have we here, anh?

SOLDIER TWO (*overlapping*): Come along, come along.

CHIANG CHING: What d'you want from me? What did I do?

SOLDIER ONE: The generalissimo wants to hear you sing, Little Canary.

(They laugh raucously.)

CHIANG CHING: Nationalist pigs! Get out of my way. I have a performance to make.

SOLDIER ONE: What's your hurry, Canary?

SOLDIER TWO: Yeah, you ain't going no place.

(They threaten behind the scrim.)

CHIANG CHING: Pig!

SOLDIER TWO: You're coming with us pigs. *(he grunts like a pig)*

(Downstage, CHIANG CHING *mimes being handcuffed.)*

CHIANG CHING: You can't arrest me. What did I do?

SOLDIER ONE: Quiet, quiet. You'll wake the whole village.

SOLDIER TWO *(overlapping):* Noisy little bird, ain't ya?

CHIANG CHING: You can't do this. There're still laws around here. Or did your general take care of that too?

SOLDIER TWO: You catch on quick. Come along.

CHIANG CHING: Leave me alone!

SOLDIER ONE and the GUARD *(simultaneously):* Shhh! Quiet!

(The SOLDIERS *disappear as* CHIANG CHING *turns to the* GUARD.)

GUARD *(continuing):* Keep it down. Keep it down. Sick people are trying to sleep. Gya-gya-gya-gya. Telling the same old stories. Gya-gya . . .

CHIANG CHING: Same old stories . . .? How would YOU like to be thrown in jail . . . plucked off the street and thrown in a stinking jail. Eight months in—

GUARD: Three.

CHIANG CHING: Eight months in a stinking jail, starved . . . tortured.

GUARD: That's when they got the confession out of you.

CHIANG CHING: Anh?

GUARD: Confession. That's when you betrayed the party.

CHIANG CHING: Ridiculous. Where's the evidence, anh?

GUARD: Well, you went back and destroyed it. You and your gang.

CHIANG CHING: Not true.

GUARD: Plenty of people say that.

CHIANG CHING: You believe everything you hear?

(The cell is slowly drenched in a yellow light. The GUARD shrugs and goes to the window. He lights a cigarette.)

GUARD *(softly to himself):* Day's almost over.

(CHIANG CHING looks past the prison walls to a sunset not visible to her.)

GUARD *(continuing):* Another day gone.

CHIANG CHING: Another day. About now mists hang over the mountains of Lu Shan. Everywhere in China, workers return home to supper . . . the supper we won for them. *(pause)* What a sunset it must be!

GUARD *(also looking at the sunset):* Nnn.

CHIANG CHING: Children play outside, nah?

GUARD: I suppose.

CHIANG CHING: I miss that . . . their laughter in the late afternoon. *(pause)* I have a daughter, did you know?

GUARD: So I heard.

(LI NA appears behind the scrim, fainter than the first time.)

CHIANG CHING: Had to send her away. It was dangerous. You understand that, don't you? Dangerous. All that bombing. You understand—

GUARD: Haunts you, anh?

CHIANG CHING: I had no choice. They bombed us day and night— the Nationalists. The generalissimo.

GUARD: I hear she's schizo.

CHIANG CHING: No-no. Just mixed up. Mixed up.

GUARD: Well, you mixed her up with all that pushing and pulling. You messed up a lot of us. Lot of us. Never be the same.

CHIANG CHING: Eh. You know nothing.

GUARD: I know plenty.

CHIANG CHING: Maybe too much for your own good. What's your name? What's your name, anh?

GUARD: Going to call your Red Guards? Yeah, call your gang. See if they can catch me. *(he laughs)*

CHIANG CHING: Little shit. You don't know what it is to be a real soldier. I've seen boys of fourteen, fifteen . . . some younger— braver than men. I've seen them march seven thousand . . .

GUARD: You didn't go on that march.

CHIANG CHING: Well, I was in Shanghai doing other work: teaching factory workers about unions, about their rights, sharing my food with them. It was hard for me too. Eight months in jail . . .

GUARD: Three.

CHIANG CHING: Beaten like a dog. They let me go, but they hounded me. Had to change my name.

GUARD: You changed your name because you betrayed the party.

CHIANG CHING: Lan Ping. Ever hear of Lan Ping?

GUARD and CHIANG CHING *(together)*: The Blue Apple of Shanghai.

CHIANG CHING *(continuing)*: You remember, anh?

(Lights change. Crowds call, "Lan Ping, Lan Ping!" CHIANG CHING *runs to make up her face.)*

CHIANG CHING: Fans, fans, everywhere. I was late. It was hard to keep the schedule.

(The STAGE MANAGER *calls from behind the scrim.)*

STAGE MANAGER: Ten minutes, Miss Lan Ping.

CHIANG CHING: All right, all right, I'll be ready. Just need a couple of . . . couple of minutes. They followed me, you know, all the way from the studio . . . right up to the stage door. Autographs, autographs. Guess I'll just have to start out a little earlier. They never saw Ibsen before. They think I'm the real Nora. *Doll's House* changed my luck. Nora turned my life around.

STAGE MANAGER *(offstage)*: Places!

(Lights grow bright. An approving crowd applauds. CHIANG CHING *takes a deep breath and is on stage—on the bed.)*

CHIANG CHING: "I'm a human being—just as you are . . . but I can't be satisfied with what's in the books. I must think things out for myself. I must find out which is right . . . the world or I. The world or I!"

(A tremendous applause follows.)

CHIANG CHING *(continuing):* Hear that? "Breathtaking!" "1935 is the year of Nora!" Oh, yes. They surround me like flies to honey. Wine and dine me. Plenty to eat and plenty to drink and plenty of handsome young men.

(Night lights appear behind the scrim and we hear muted street sounds: rickshaws, bicycle bells, street vendors. CHIANG CHING *walks off the stage, head high.* TANG NA, *the Shanghai critic, appears in a flowing cape. He sweeps downstage. As with all remembrance characters, he is in whiteface.)*

TANG NA: Ah! Miss Lan Ping, the famous Shanghai actress. At last we meet—in the famous French Concession. Is this fate?

CHIANG CHING: Tang Na, the famous Shanghai critic. Thank you for the nice review.

TANG NA: Nice? That was a *rave* review!

CHIANG CHING: Yes, it was very kind of you.

TANG NA *(in her ear):* You wretch!

CHIANG CHING: Excuse me?

TANG NA: You're insatiable. Just as they said.

CHIANG CHING *(laughing):* Anh?

TANG NA: Your reputation precedes you, my dear—a woman of great appetites. What will you have of me tonight? My soul? Or would you be satisfied with simple *earthly* delights?

CHIANG CHING *(laughing):* Isn't it a lovely night?

TANG NA: Too warm for my taste. Too close.

(He takes a deep breath.)

TANG NA: Smell. Greasy food from the stalls . . . *(he sniffs)* perfume of whores . . . lovers' steamy emissions. The wind from the sea humid with the breath of slimy creatures. Much too warm.

CHIANG CHING: Well then, take off your *(indicates the cape)*

TANG NA: My cape is not removable. It is to me what a shell is to a tortoise. Without it I'm naked. Here, I'll show you. This is where I do my best work.

(He opens up his cape and envelopes CHIANG CHING in it. She giggles and permits him intimacies. He whirls her around and they fall on the bed laughing. Lights black out. TANG NA disappears. The stage is dark for a moment. The GUARD lights a cigarette, bringing back the cell lights.)

GUARD *(muttering):* Lan Ping, Lan Ping. I know what's coming next. "Toast of Shanghai!" "I was Nora for the women of China." "I showed them they could be Nora, too . . ."

(The GUARD sees CHIANG CHING covered in her blanket, still in her dream, making love to herself. He tactfully exits. Lights change. CHIANG CHING sleeps in her room. Ornate shadows of her windows make patterns on the floor. Behind the scrim is a poster with graffiti in Chinese characters. TANG NA returns without his cape. He is furious. He carries a crumpled paper.)

TANG NA: Wake up. Wake up!

(CHIANG CHING yawns sleepily.)

TANG NA *(continuing):* These are in every public toilet in Shanghai. *(he sees the scrim)* Look! Here too. Who is this Ci and Shu and Muzhi?

CHIANG CHING: Enh? Ci and Muzhi? They're friends.

TANG NA: Friends! That's not what it says here!

CHIANG CHING: Well, we work together. Muzhi is a director.

TANG NA: Director, eh? Just what does he direct?

CHIANG CHING: Gossip, Tang Na. You know how rumors spread. Aw . . . come here, sweetheart. Don't be angry. It's jealous people making trouble. Jealous people. They're not content to interfere with my work; they want to ruin my personal life too.

TANG NA: You're going to leave me, aren't you?

CHIANG CHING: Where did you get *that* idea?

TANG NA: You didn't answer my question.

CHIANG CHING: Tang Na, don't torture yourself. And don't listen to other people.

TANG NA: You see how she avoids my question? You see? It's true. These are true!

(TANG NA *throws the crumpled papers at* CHIANG CHING. *She can hardly contain her anger.*)

TANG NA: *(continuing):* Everyone's laughing at us!

CHIANG CHING: Not at us, Tang Na. At *you.*

TANG NA: Yeah? Well, I'm a respected Shanghai journalist. You? Everyone knows you're an ambitious, greedy . . . slut.

CHIANG CHING: Tang Na, why don't you just jump off a bridge or something? End your miserable life. Leave me alone.

TANG NA: Oh, you'd like that, hanh? You'd love it. Then you can fuck Ci and Muzhi and—

CHIANG CHING *(tiredly):* Oh, please. Take a dozen pills or something.

TANG NA: I'll do that. To make you happy. To free you.

CHIANG CHING: I'm free already. I'm free to do whatever I please. That's why people are so jealous.

TANG NA: Jealous! That's what you always say!

CHIANG CHING: Well, don't do it for me. I'm all right. Do it for yourself.

TANG NA: For myself. You're right. For myself. All right. Would you like it here, or shall I go outside?

(*A vial of pills materializes in* TANG NA'S *hand.*)

CHIANG CHING: Put those back, Tang Na! They're for my stomach. What would I do for my pain if you take them all?

(*They tussle for the pills.* CHIANG CHING *changes her tactics and becomes loving.*)

CHIANG CHING *(continuing):* Please . . . Tang Na . . . please.

TANG NA: Oh, Lan Ping, why do you torment me so? Don't you know how much I love you? Don't you love me too?

CHIANG CHING: Of course, I do. Come here to me.

(CHIANG CHING *pulls* TANG NA *to the bed.*)

CHIANG CHING *(continuing):* I love you. That's why I must let you go.

TANG NA: Oh, no. No. If you love me, that's all that matters. We can work the rest of it out, Lan Ping. We can. We can.

CHIANG CHING: I'm no good for you. I make you miserable. Why do you still want me?

TANG NA: It's your infidelity. Only that. Just stop the fooling around. Just that.

CHIANG CHING: It's more. It's always more.

TANG NA: That's all. Just put an end to the gossip. Be true to me. Be my wife. Marry me. Please marry me. We can have a family.

CHIANG CHING: The reality, Tang Na . . . the reality is, we've outgrown each other.

TANG NA: No-no-no. That's not so—

CHIANG CHING: It won't work. We have to break up.

TANG NA *(stiffening):* They were right. They said it'd be this way.

CHIANG CHING: "They were right"?

TANG NA: Everyone said you'd leave me. Just like Nora left Torvald. They said I was a fool—

CHIANG CHING: Nora? Why, Tang Na, she's just a character in a play. *(pause)* So that's it. It's Nora you want. Nora the doll, anh? Well, I'm nobody's doll!

TANG NA: No! It's you. I want YOU.

(*He gets on his knees and tries to kiss* CHIANG CHING'S *hand.*)

CHIANG CHING: Get up. Get up! Stand like a man!

TANG NA: Please . . . Lan Ping. Please . . . please . . .

CHIANG CHING: Don't beg! I hate a beggar. Get out. Get out!

(*Lights change. The cell bars are back.* TANG NA *is gone.*)

CHIANG CHING (*continuing; slightly disoriented*): He tried to ruin me.

(*The* GUARD *returns.*)

GUARD: Hunh? Who's that?

CHIANG CHING: Tang Na. He said I confessed, you know, while they had me in jail. Said I betrayed the party. Said my films were Nationalist propaganda.

GUARD: Well, everyone knows that. That's why you went back—to destroy the evidence. Killed to get back those films . . .

CHIANG CHING: I went back to get evidence of traitors. Theater was infested with traitors. I made Communist films.

GUARD (*sarcastically*): That's right. Communist films.

CHIANG CHING: What about *Blood on Wolf Mountain?* Was *that* Nationalist propaganda? What about *Old Bachelor Wang?* Was that Nationalistic—

GUARD: All right, all right. Go back to sleep.

CHIANG CHING: Sleep? There's still daylight left.

GUARD: That's all right. You can make your own rules today. Sleep.

CHIANG CHING: How can I sleep? I have all this work to do. Got to pass out these leaflets at five . . . before the spies come out. Talk to women at the cigarette factory. On top of all this, I must rehearse. (*pause*) Everyone sleeps, but Lan Ping must rehearse.

GUARD: All right. Rehearse then.

(*Lights change. Night sounds—a sewing machine on the floor above, a door slamming somewhere, soft whispers—support* CHIANG CHING'S *delusion.*)

CHIANG CHING (*continuing*): Only the tailor is up sewing. The night worker returns, but Lan Ping must rehearse.

(*The crowd applauds.* CHIANG CHING *stops, listens, and rushes to the platform. She bows deeply.*)

CHIANG CHING (*continuing*): Thank you . . . thank you . . . thank you.

(*Interspersed with the applause are the voices whispering: Tia-*

nanmen . . . Tiananmen . . . The STAGE MANAGER *pokes out his/her head from stage left.)*

STAGE MANAGER *(whispering loudly):* Lan Ping, the Long March is over.

CHIANG CHING: Nnh?

STAGE MANAGER: The Long March is over! Mao Tsetung is in Yenan!

CHIANG CHING: People! People of China! *(she quiets the crowd)* The Long March is over! Our warriors have reached Yenan! Comrade Mao is safely in Yenan!

(The crowd roars. CHIANG CHING *bows. Lights turn red as the voices continue faintly: Tiananmen . . . Tiananmen . . .* CHIANG CHING *raises her fist. Lights fade.)*

End of Act One

ACT TWO

(Time: A short time later. On rise: lights are dim. CHIANG CHING *dozes in her chair. She hears the bombing and strafing of a recurring dream. She ducks under the bed. The* GUARD *sits reading in the shadows outside the bars.)*

GUARD: Wei-wei! *("Hey-hey")* What are you doing there? Get up. Get up!

CHIANG CHING: Ha ha. Had that dream again. Bombs falling on Shanghai. The Japanese, you know, leveled the city. I was there.

GUARD: You know you're not supposed to do that. Do I have to keep an eye on you every second?

CHIANG CHING: Or was it Yenan? Anh! Yenan.

GUARD: Japanese didn't bomb Yenan.

CHIANG CHING: Not Japanese. I didn't say that. The generalissimo. General Chiang Kai-shek. After the war. After World War II. After the Japanese surrender. Chiang Kai-shek bombed Yenan *after*, don't you know? Civil War! Bombs dropping day and night. Worse than Shanghai. Got so bad, I had to send Li Na away. Li Na grew up without me. Without her father.

GUARD: Un-un-un.

CHIANG CHING: You know Yenan, anh? Yenan? The Long March?

GUARD: I know Yenan. Think I'm stupid?

CHIANG CHING: Go there sometime and see your history. What your ancestors did with their bare hands. Centuries of peasants patiently carving . . . scooping out a city of caves in the hard cliffs . . . building massive walls. Three thousand years ago, mind you. Yenan was the strong-hold of bandits. Our warriors marched there to start a huge commune of farms, universities, theatre—

GUARD: I know, I know.

CHIANG CHING: Nnh! What a history! Li Na was born there.

GUARD: I know.

CHIANG CHING (*taking a deep breath*): The air is clear, the sun brilliant on the hills. The caves are warm in winter, cool in summer. Oh, did we have a lot of conferences in those big rooms. Wooh! Lots of important people sitting around all night . . . you heard of them: Chou En-lai, Liu Shaochi . . .

(The GUARD *looks up.)*

CHIANG CHING (*continuing*): Deng Xiaoping—the varmint. He was there too.

(Voices, very faint: Deng, Deng Xiaoping . . .)

GUARD (*overlapping*): Everyone knows you went to Yenan to seduce Comrade Mao. You were after his sweet ass.

CHIANG CHING: Not true. I went to work for the revolution. I gave up stage and screen to work for the people of China.

GUARD: Everyone knows you stood up at his lectures and clapped 'til he finally noticed you. You chased him to every hall and drooled and fawned 'til he finally noticed—

CHIANG CHING: Me drool? I was already a star!

GUARD: You made second-grade movies.

CHIANG CHING: Star! I'm Nora, Ibsen's Nora—

GUARD *(overlapping)*: And you're a collaborator.

CHIANG CHING: Not true! I went to Yenan because I couldn't watch what was going on in Shanghai. Traitors everywhere. I had to leave.

GUARD: The Central Committee believed it.

CHIANG CHING: Oh, that Committee. They spread all kinds of awful gossip. They didn't want me to marry Comrade Mao. They hated me. All of them. Chou En-lai, Liu Shaochi, the same old bunch. Liu's wife, Wang Guangmei. The same old . . . she was the worst.

(WANG GUANGMEI *appears with the sound of wind. Young, beautiful, she wears a fluttering rayon dress [1935], and a cloche hat.*)

CHIANG CHING *(continuing)*: There she is. Look at her clothes. Bourgeois!

WANG GUANGMEI: I went on the Long March with Liu Shaochi. Is THAT bourgeois? He's one of the founders of the revolution. We were there from the beginning. Were you? No. You're the upstart. Chou En-lai, Deng Xiaoping . . . we all knew what you were up to. Riding to Yenan on a horse! Expecting star treatment. What a laugh. Ha ha. We knew what was going on. Only Comrade Mao . . .

CHIANG CHING: All of you. You tried to set him against me, but it was ME he loved.

WANG GUANGMEI: You knew his weakness for women.

CHIANG CHING: I wasn't just another woman to him.

WANG GUANGMEI: Well, there were plenty before and plenty after you.

CHIANG CHING: He named me Chiang Ching. Chiang Ching after the green river that runs through his village. He wrote poems to me. Isn't that love? Admit it. You all gave in to the face of true love.

WANG GUANGMEI: Admit it. You stormed in the committee meeting with your belly swollen (with) . . .

CHIANG CHING: With Li Na. I walked into that meeting . . . all of them there and Mao said, "I can't continue the revolution without Chiang Ching." "Can't continue." You heard him.

WANG GUANGMEI: The marriage was sanctioned only with the condition that you stay out of politics . . .

GUARD: What happened to that? You promised to stay out of politics for thirty years.

WANG GUANGMEI: What happened to that?

(CHIANG CHING *looks from one to the other, confused.* WANG GUANGMEI *disappears with the sound of the wind.*)

CHIANG CHING: You didn't expect me to honor that, did you? It wasn't my fault anyway. Everyone . . . everyone tried to get me involved: "Chiang Ching, Chiang Ching . . ." All day. "Chiang Ching, get me an appointment." "Chiang Ching, inform him of my project." All day long. Gifts and flattery and everything. Never let up. All the favors I did for them. You'd think they'd be grateful, but no. Back-biting, gossiping. Oh, I kept out for a long time. Took care of him, cooked his millet, darned his socks, was his secretary . . . transcribed all his notes. Oh, yes, served his guests—they came from Europe—all over. Even America. I was busy seeing their cups were full, keeping my mouth shut and serving—

GUARD: That was the hardest, heh? Keeping your mouth shut?

CHIANG CHING: . . . serving his hot peppers—he's from Hunan, you know—putting peanuts—he loved peanuts—used to hold out his hand (*she holds out her hand*) and I'd put peanut . . . (*she demonstrates*) Ha ha. I did that. I tell you, it wasn't my fault. They started it—sucked me into it. Followed me all over Yenan . . . to the farms, the kitchen . . . to the dances . . . the Saturday night dances at Pear Orchard.

(*Behind the scrim, lanterns hung on trees sway in the wind. Dancers move to the strains of "The Blue Danube."*)

GUARD: And you danced with them all.

CHIANG CHING: With them all. Generals, lieutenants, foot soldiers . . .

(CHIANG CHING *waltzes.* CHOU EN-LAI *in whiteface appears.*)

CHOU EN-LAI: May I have this dance, Madam?

CHIANG CHING: Why, Deputy Chou En-lai. Where is your wife this evening?

CHOU EN-LAI *(laughing):* Oh, she's given me permission to dance with you.

CHIANG CHING: I didn't mean that. You're such a wonderful dancer, I just thought she might be unwilling to let you go.

CHOU EN-LAI: On the contrary. I'm letting *her* go. There are so few women—as you know—those of us with wives must be generous. Sometimes more than we want.

CHIANG CHING: Are you saying that Comrade Mao should—

CHOU EN-LAI: No-no. Nothing like that. I just want to talk to you this evening.

CHIANG CHING: Yes?

(CHOU EN-LAI holds out his arms and they begin dancing.)

CHOU EN-LAI: I know the farm group has been pressuring you to talk to Mao about their water project.

CHIANG CHING: Not just the Agricultural Committee, all of them. The Department of Transportation . . .

CHOU EN-LAI: That's what I want to talk to you about.

CHIANG CHING: Transportation?

CHOU EN-LAI: This is just a little advice from an old trouper. *(pause)* Chiang Ching, you must try not to get involved. Taking a position—any position—may get you in way over your head.

CHIANG CHING: You're saying I may not have the intelligence to . . .

CHOU EN-LAI: Absolutely not! I have the utmost respect for your intelligence.

CHIANG CHING: Always the diplomat, anh? Do you remember, Chou En-lai, when you stumbled over Mao and me in the fields on that night?

CHOU EN-LAI: In the fields . . . I've tripped over so many lovers in the fields. Looks like that's where most of the activity takes place. Whatever happened to beds?

CHIANG CHING: Husbands and wives do it in beds.

CHOU EN-LAI: Well, it's a lot more comfortable.

CHIANG CHING: You were looking for Mao. You had a very important message from the . . .

CHOU EN-LAI: Oh, yes, from the generalissimo.

CHIANG CHING: And you were calling, "Mao . . . Mao . . . A message from the general . . ." And you carried this lantern, swinging it back and forth. We were lying in the bushes, trying to be very quiet and suddenly you stumbled . . . fell right on top of us. You held the lantern *(she demonstrates, laughing)* . . . I'll never forget: you, nose to nose, eyeball to eyeball with Mao. Then you stood up and walked away.

CHOU EN-LAI: Ah, I seem to recall some such incident.

CHIANG CHING: And Mao said, "That's Chou En-lai. Diplomat to the bone."

CHOU EN-LAI: Bad timing, wasn't it?

CHIANG CHING: What did you really want to tell me?

CHOU EN-LAI *(slowly):* Just what I said: the best service you can do for the party is to take care of Comrade Mao.

CHIANG CHING: I *do* take care of him.

CHOU EN-LAI: Of course, you do. But I mean, stay neutral. Don't take sides. Let Mao make his own decisions. Stay away from Yenan politics. All politics. Power is addictive, Chiang Ching. Be careful. Addictive.

CHIANG CHING: Are you speaking from experience? Ha ha.

(CHOU EN-LAI *laughs.*)

CHIANG CHING *(continuing):* Well, Mao relies on me. Well, I've been his secretary for a long time and I transcribe all his notes and I know everything that goes on in Yenan. You want me to stop helping him?

CHOU EN-LAI: It's probably gossip, but there's talk that you're interfering in cultural affairs.

CHIANG CHING: I've been in the theater all my life and Mao consults me about these things. But interfere? No. There are people here who are extremely hostile toward me.

CHOU EN-LAI: You understand, my dear, I'm not telling you what to do. I just want you to be aware.

CHIANG CHING: You're right. You're not telling me what to do.

(The music stops. CHIANG CHING *pulls away abruptly.)*

CHOU EN-LAI: No need to get all worked up over it. Just keep it in mind. That's all I say.

CHIANG CHING: No one . . . no one tells me what to do. I want you to keep that in mind, too.

CHOU EN-LAI *(still smiling):* As good as done, Madam.

("The Merry Widow" waltz begins. CHOU EN-LAI *holds out his hand.)*

CHIANG CHING: I've been on my feet all evening. I'd like to sit this one out.

CHOU EN-LAI: Of course.

*(*CHOU EN-LAI *exits.* CHIANG CHING *sits massaging her feet.)*

CHOU EN-LAI *(continuing; offstage):* Ni ha . . . May I have this dance?

WANG GUANGMEI *(offstage, laughing):* Of course, of course.

*(*CHOU EN-LAI *and* WANG GUANGMEI *fade in behind the scrim. She wears her cloche hat and fluttering rayon dress. They laugh softly as they whirl gracefully to the music.)*

CHIANG CHING: Look at them. Just look at her. Always showing off. Probably talking about me. Well, I don't care. I don't care. *(muttering)* Always trying to make me look bad. Trying to make me feel like a kid in rags.

GUARD: Rags, Yunhe.

CHIANG CHING: Shut up.

GUARD: Duck eggs, duck eggs.

CHIANG CHING *(overlapping):* Don't you worry. Your time will come. They still wait for me you know.

GUARD: Well, I'm just terrified. You see how scared I am?

CHIANG CHING: You're lucky, young man. We fought your battles so you could sit on your fat ass and be impertinent. Be careful and don't turn your back.

GUARD: Sit on my ass? I pulled a lot of strings to get this job.

CHIANG CHING: You pulled strings to get *this* job?

GUARD: Especially when no one's supposed to know where you are. It wasn't easy.

CHIANG CHING: So you could sit here day after day and torment me, anh?

GUARD: Precisely.

CHIANG CHING: Well?

GUARD: Well, what?

CHIANG CHING: Well, did you get your revenge? Are you happy? Do you thank God every day that Chiang Ching's in jail?

GUARD: Oh, yes, that's my passion.

CHIANG CHING: Passion is for patriots. Not people like you.

(The GUARD shrugs.)

CHIANG CHING *(continuing):* Yenan was built with passion and bare knuckles. It's passion that won the war. They had an army seven times larger . . . the generalissimo. The world was against us. Truman wouldn't help. Stalin wouldn't help. "Make peace with the general," he said. But we beat them. Took twenty-eight hard years and all our passion. That's Chinese, you know— never to give up. You think I've given up?

GUARD: Aw, shut up.

CHIANG CHING: Well, sometimes it gets difficult. Sometime victory is harder . . . Success changes things. *(pause)* It was sickening: "Oh, Chairman, Chairman . . . our glorious leader. We must have a portrait . . . Swimming the Yangtze, of course. Our Great River, our Great Leader. Oh, you look wonderful, Chairman; doesn't he look well?" What lies! Shit. Pure shit. Already he was bloated from the rich food and . . . and his excesses.

GUARD: Don't piss on him, woman.

CHIANG CHING: That's the truth.

GUARD: Your truth. One man's truth is another man's lie. You ought to know that.

CHIANG CHING: Oh, profound. Sounds suspiciously like a Western adage. A little something from the corrupt West, eh?

GUARD: It's a different China from the one you knew. You could never get away with it now.

CHIANG CHING: With what?

GUARD: Another massacre.

(The voices start very softly: Tiananmen . . . Tiananmen . . .— overlapping very softly—beat-her-up . . . beat-her-up . . .)

CHIANG CHING: Why, the whole idea of a revolution is to get rid of oppressors and old oppressions. That means traditions, too.

GUARD: And patriots too, anh? You sent Deng Xiaoping into hiding —nearly killed his son, tortured thousands—

CHIANG CHING: They were traitors.

GUARD: Patriots! Deng Xiaoping, Liu Shaochi, Wang Guangmei . . .

CHIANG CHING: They thought they could take over the party.

GUARD: My brother stood up for Liu. Only said a few good words in his behalf and you . . . killed him.

CHIANG CHING: I didn't even know your brother.

GUARD: You buried him alive!

CHIANG CHING: I said I didn't know—

GUARD: It's why I'm here, old woman. You want to know why I'm here . . . I dedicated my life to guarding you. For my brother. I want to be here when you die. For my brother.

CHIANG CHING: That's all right. Spend your life guarding me. You're as much a prisoner as I am.

GUARD: That's my sacrifice!

CHIANG CHING: That's all right. Blame me. They blame me for everything anyway. Once they loved me. Bunch of hypocrites. I knew what was going on. They sent me away to Moscow to recuperate. I was sick, yes, but to Moscow? Ha ha. I went.

GUARD *(muttering):* What's the use. What's the use?

(He looks at his watch and leaves.)

CHIANG CHING: In Moscow they gave me a grand reception—vodka, caviar—gallons of caviar. They loved that. And people! So many people in that great hall: diplomats, consuls, party officials . . . everybody! They all ask, "Where's the chairman? Where's the chairman?" And everything stops. *(pause)* Stalin doesn't show. No Stalin. Four times. I went to Moscow four times for the treatment. Four times, the same. No Stalin. Ha ha. No chairman, no Stalin.

(MAMA, *dim and faded, appears behind the scrim.)*

MAMA: Didn't I tell you that? Didn't I tell you, Yunhe? Things don't change. It was like that for my mother and it will be like that for you.

CHIANG CHING: No! I lived in the Imperial Palace. Did you ever think I'd be there? The Imperial Palace, Mama. Oh, yes, the Central Committee settled in the Imperial Palace. Silk scrolls, marble floors . . . far from the hut of Chucheng . . . far from the dirt floors. Un-un-un. The seduction of opulence.

MAMA: He had another woman, Yunhe.

CHIANG CHING: I know that. I know. A new secretary. High heels, paint . . . plenty of paint. I'm not against makeup, but that much? This one had skinny legs.

(MAMA *fades. The* GUARD *returns with* SHANSI, *a young guard. They enter talking.)*

GUARD: You shoulda brought something to read. Paper. Write your letters here. Gets boring otherwise.

CHIANG CHING: She was the sister of Yu Chi-wei.

SHANSI: Talks to herself?

GUARD: To herself, to the chair, bed, to dolls . . .

SHANSI: Dolls?

GUARD: She sews dolls.

SHANSI: Is she . . .? *(he taps his head)*

GUARD: Nah. She'd like you to think that. See, when you turn off the lights, you put on this one here *(small night light)* and always keep your . . . She'll drive you crazy. Always keep your flashlight handy because—

SHANSI: What's the matter with her?

GUARD: Lonely. Been in jail eleven years, you know. Just lonely. Nothing's likely to happpen, but keep an eye on her all the—

CHIANG CHING: Hanh?

SHANSI: He said "lonely."

CHIANG CHING: I'm never lonely. Listen: I've been shunned by the whole world—presidents, kings. You're nobodies. Bad peanuts. I spit you out.

GUARD *(to* SHANSI*)*: Where you from?

SHANSI: Shansi province.

CHIANG CHING: Shansi? I've been there. I know Shansi. Stayed there three days . . . a week? I remember Shansi. The women there: "Give us guns! We're strong as men!" What do you think of that?

GUARD *(to* SHANSI*)*: How's it going out there?

SHANSI: Tiananmen Square?

GUARD: Yeah.

SHANSI: They're still there. Got to hand it to them. They're still out there. More and more people behind them now. Thousands. Not just students anymore.

GUARD: They got lots of guts—young people. They don't know how dangerous it is. Just takes a second for things to change.

SHANSI: You should see it. Square's full of people and tents and banners. Orderly, though. Very orderly.

GUARD: My son's out there.

SHANSI: Your son?

GUARD: I told him, "Don't do anything you'll regret."

CHIANG CHING: China is in chaos . . . famine, discontent . . .

GUARD: You get caught up in something like this, you can regret it the rest of your life. Well, maybe it'll blow over.

SHANSI: Been going on almost a month.

GUARD: I know. I know. *(pause)* Night watch is bad. The worst. Light out at 9. Wooh! When she can't sleep, she rattles on and on—like a dry branch scratching on a window.

CHIANG CHING: All the chairman's great plans . . .

GUARD: On and on. Over and over. The Rectification Movement, the Hundred Flowers Movement—

CHIANG CHING: "Let a hundred flowers bloom and a hundred thoughts contend." Liu Shaochi laughed. He thought he knew so much. Already he was pushing his way up.

GUARD: On and on. You want to cut off your ears. *(pause)* Young people have all the energy . . . they got to find some place to put it. They got to find a cause.

CHIANG CHING: The great leap forward failed too. All failed.

SHANSI *(to GUARD)*: Something's going to happen. I know it.

GUARD: Eh! It'll all blow away. Yeah, it'll blow away.

CHIANG CHING: And him, the Warrior, sitting in Shanghai all huddled in despair . . .

SHANSI: I doubt it.

CHIANG CHING: Three failed projects. People: "Where's the Great Leader? Waged war but can't wage peace. Can't wage prosperity."

GUARD: What you trying to tell me?

SHANSI: Nothing! I don't know—

CHIANG CHING: Food. Food.

SHANSI: Lady, we're trying to talk.

CHIANG CHING: Lady?

GUARD: Now you did it.

CHIANG CHING: My name is Chiang Ching.

SHANSI: Madam Mao?

CHIANG CHING: Chiang Ching.

SHANSI: Why, she looks like my grandmother.

CHIANG CHING: Well, I'm not your grandmother.

SHANSI: You killed a lot of people, lady.

GUARD: Not many grandmothers can say that, anh?

CHIANG CHING: Not me, I didn't kill them.

GUARD: "Not me, not me!" Who the hell did it then? It's not you and it's not me. Who the hell's responsible then? *(sounds of gunfire and the voices, distorted, moan: Massacre . . . Massacre . . .* SHANSI *seems to hear.)*

SHANSI: What's that?

(He exits in haste.)

CHIANG CHING: Old ideas, useless traditions must be destroyed before new seeds can sprout.

GUARD: You serve the people by killing them? You killed my brother . . . you killed Liu Shaochi.

CHIANG CHING: He died of pneumonia. Check the coroner's report.

GUARD: In a cold cell, no medicine, no doctor, brutally beaten. Tell us what you did to his wife.

CHIANG CHING: That idiot?

(Light changes. We hear the sound of leaves blowing over a pavement. CHIANG CHING *picks up a paper and glances through it. Her face turns sour and the light turns red with her jealously.* WANG GUANGMEI, *whitefaced, in her cloche hat and fluttering dress, a showy necklace at her throat, enters smiling.)*

WANG GUANGMEI: Over here, Chiang Ching.

CHIANG CHING: Oh, you. You enjoyed your trip, I see.

(She taps the paper.)

WANG GUANGMEI: Oh, yes. President and Mrs. Sukarno send their best. I brought a small gift for . . .

(She reaches into her purse and mimes . . .)

CHIANG CHING *(rudely):* Set it on the table. Is that what you wore for the reception, Wang Guangmei?

WANG GUANGMEI: Yes. Oh . . . black was . . . the black you recommended was too warm for Jakarta. In fact, Mrs. Sukarno advised me not to wear black . . .

CHIANG CHING: Well, my suggestion was to dress conservatively. This is the People's Republic, Wang Guangmei. I'm sure you understand that. In fact, I'm right now designing a dress that every woman in China can wear.

WANG GUANGMEI: Every woman?

CHIANG CHING: This is Communist China, Wang Guangmei. Have you forgotten? There is no rich, no poor . . .

WANG GUANGMEI: But we mustn't lose our individuality, Chiang Ching. We must keep that. You're different, I'm different . . .

CHIANG CHING: Nor must we become slaves to fashion and . . . and to capitalist bauble.

(She points the rolled up paper at WANG GUANGMEI'*s necklace.* WANG GUANGMEI'*s hands instinctively protect her throat.)*

WANG GUANGMEI: This is a gift from President and Mrs. Sukarno. I'm expected to wear it.

CHIANG CHING: Perhaps in Jakarta, but not here.

WANG GUANGMEI: And if I choose to wear it?

CHIANG CHING: Of course, it's your choice. *(pause)* I see that Liu Shaochi gave a talk at the university.

WANG GUANGMEI: Oh, yes. It was a request from the chancelor. In fact, he spoke at other assemblies—

CHIANG CHING: I think your husband should keep his talks strictly to the party line at prearranged places.

WANG GUANGMEI: My husband believes we must have allies in Southeast Asia. We cannot survive without friendly neighbors. My husband is loyal, Chiang Ching. I think you know that.

CHIANG CHING: Some say he's trying to form his own power base.

WANG GUANGMEI: That's not true! Read the text of his speech. You won't find anything in it that criticizes the party. Read the text!

CHIANG CHING: There are those in the party who've already read it. They find problems with it.

WANG GUANGMEI: Liu Shaochi is loyal! How dare you question his loyalty?

CHIANG CHING: Some say the chairman is not long for this world and Liu Shaochi is getting ready for the transfer of power.

WANG GUANGMEI: It's *you* who's getting ready! You're taking over. No one can get to the chairman anymore. You and your gang have closed off all avenues to him. He doesn't know what's going on anymore.

CHIANG CHING: You're excused, Wang Guangmei.

WANG GUANGMEI: So I'm excused, am I? Who are you anyway? Empress Wu?

CHIANG CHING: Shall I get an escort for you?

WANG GUANGMEI: Be careful, Chiang Ching. It will come back to you one day. It will all come back tenfold.

CHIANG CHING: Perhaps you didn't hear. You're excused, Wang Guangmei.

(WANG GUANGMEI *exits with the rustle of wind.*)

GUARD: Anh? Annngh? Wang Guangmei. What happened to her?

CHIANG CHING: I don't know.

GUARD: Oh, you know all right.

(*A spotlight falls on a table behind the scrim where* WANG GUANGMEI *stands, a sack over her head, a string of table tennis balls painted with skulls around her neck. Her rayon dress flutters; she stands in the jet position, her arms behind her, her knees bent. We hear jeering and hooting.*)

CHIANG CHING: That was her punishment. Her sentence. That's the sentence of all counterrevolutionaries. They do the "Struggle and Criticism."

(*Slowly in the dim light, whitefaces in agony appear one by one at various heights.*)

GUARD: "They do the Struggle and Criticism." Struggle and criticism. Like it was a dance or something.

CHIANG CHING: It wasn't *my* decision, you know. I didn't actually sentence her. I only recommended—

GUARD: There it is again: "I didn't do it. It wasn't me."

CHIANG CHING: You must realize the Red Guards were responsible for a lot of the destruction and the arrests, too—

GUARD: You organized them! You and your gang.

CHIANG CHING: Amazing! Once they got started, it was like a forest fire. They combed the country—zoom-zoom—unearthing traitors, conspirators, plotters . . . in universities, colleges . . . in high offices . . . hiding under rocks.

GUARD: Arresting and . . . and . . .

CHIANG CHING: Of course, arresting.

GUARD: . . . torturing, maiming, killing. Setting son against father; brother against brother—

(He stops abruptly. CHIANG CHING *looks up.)*

CHIANG CHING: So that's it. Brother against brother, anh? Well, if he was innocent, why did you testify against him? That's your first mistake.

GUARD *(shaken)*: A kid of fifteen ratting against his brother? Doesn't the state take some responsibility for that? It's the state that sets the pattern for suspicion and betrayal.

CHIANG CHING: You don't understand these things. In politics you must keep one step ahead. One step ahead. And sometimes things move so quickly, they get out of control. The chairman was sick. Old. I had to find . . . find people—loyal people who would implement his goals or lose everything we gained. I had to lead or lose everything. Sometimes harsh measures . . .

CHIANG CHING *(continuing)*: All the world came to our door then: Senora Marcos, Prince Sihanouk . . . they all came. President Nixon was here too. I ask, "Mr. Nixon, why didn't you come to China before?" Ha ha. He pretends not to hear. And Mrs. Nixon smiles. And drinks. That's what happens to most political wives, you know. They learn to smile and drink.

GUARD: The Chinese . . . Chinese blood flowed like the Yangtze. You can't wash that away, woman.

CHIANG CHING: Once upon a time you admired me. My word was

law. You would betray your brother to obey. I am the same Chiang Ching. What has changed? I am the same.

GUARD: I am not.

CHIANG CHING: Eh! You're nobody.

GUARD: I'm everybody. I'm all the people whose lives you wrecked . . . who stood helplessly by while you killed—

CHIANG CHING: One Nixon smiling; one not hearing. And Chou En-lai—the premier himself—hovering nearby . . . fluttering his hands, afraid I'd say something . . . something "gauche," he called it. Always trying to patch things up. Who cares?

GUARD: So you walk on his grave.

CHIANG CHING: I did no such thing.

GUARD: What do you call it when the world comes to pay respect and you won't even take off your cap—at his funeral. At his funeral!

CHIANG CHING: Much ado about nothing.

GUARD: Yeah, nothing. The world comes mourning and you refuse to take off your cap.

CHIANG CHING: Chou En-lai was not a nice man. Sure, he smiled and all that but he always tried to hold me back . . . hold me down. Never once said, "Good job, Chiang Ching." Never.

GUARD: You couldn't fool him. Not Chou En-lai. Everyone else was kissing your ass, but he knew. He knew. Reached from his grave to warn us.

CHIANG CHING: Reached from his grave, anh?

GUARD: Qing Ming. Festival of the Martyrs. Remember Qing Ming?

(Overlapping the sound of an angry crowd, voices begin: Tiananmen . . . Tiananmen . . .)

GUARD *(continuing)*: Sure, you remember. April of '76. Tiananmen Square, enh? The day thousands, maybe millions, came to honor Chou En-lai . . . the square filled with flowers and poems. And you swept them out. Swept them all out. And we nearly killed you. Remember?

CHIANG CHING: The square is no place for dead flowers.

GUARD: Tiananmen Square is where we come to honor our heroes and support our common goals. Why, even today, students assemble to . . . to . . .

CHIANG CHING: To what?

GUARD: I don't know. They want more freedom . . . within party lines, of course.

CHIANG CHING: Oh-oh! So Deng is out of favor, anh? Deng the great, the people's chiose. Deng Xiaoping, the indestructable. Deng, your man.

(CHIANG CHING *laughs heartily.*)

GUARD: I didn't say that. I just said the students are rallying—Hey. You remember that day, don't you? The memorial for Chou En-lai? The day he reached from his grave to warn us—

CHIANG CHING: Chou En-lai, Chou En-lai. What about me? All the work I did? Everyone moaning and wailing at the square. They forget so soon. The cap . . . the flowers . . . so what? It's no reason to get so ugly. A public humiliation—right in the square. All I can say is, good thing the Red Guards were there.

(*Gunfire and the roar of panic and anger are heard. Then more gunfire. Out of the din, a rhythm grows: beat-her-up, beat-her-up, beat-her-up.* CHIANG CHING *covers her ears and echoes the crowd.*)

CHIANG CHING (*continuing*): Beat-her-up, beat-her-up . . . What did I do? Beat-her-up . . . Deng Xiaoping's at the botton of this.

(SHANSI *enters, extremely overwrought. The* GUARD *is puzzled.*)

GUARD: Shh! (*to* SHANSI) What's the matter? What's the matter?

SHANSI: Disaster! Massacre! Murder!

(Voices simultaneously: massacre . . . massacre . . .)

GUARD (*overlapping*): Tiananmen? What happened?

SHANSI: They sent in the troops. Guns! Tanks!

CHIANG CHING: Got tea for me, Shansi?

GUARD (*overlapping*): Oh, God! My son!

SHANSI: Tanks rolled into the square shooting at the crowd. Hundreds dead and wounded. Bicycles flattened like pancakes. They rallied to the front and were shot down . . . line by line . . . line by line.

CHIANG CHING: Got tea for me, Shansi? *(she sees him crying)* Ah, Shansi, you're too gentle. Too soft. You'll never survive in this world. You got to he hard. Like me. Like me. I shall always prevail.

GUARD *(overlapping):* Wounded? What? What?

SHANSI: Wounded. Killed.

GUARD: Killed? Who? How many? How many?

SHANSI: Hundreds!

GUARD: Names. Do they have names?

SHANSI: No! I don't think so. Too many.

GUARD *(in anguish):* Anngh! When will it stop! It goes on and on. When will it stop?

SHANSI: They won't give up. I tell you, they're not giving up.

GUARD: The fools! They'll be slaughtered. They're unarmed. Someone has to stop them.

CHIANG CHING *(downstage):*
They wouldn't let me touch him, Shansi—my own husband. Said I was laughing and playing playing cards and eating like a pig while he lay dying. Not true. I made a wreathe for him . . . with my own hands. I have pictures. This doesn't show the true colors, but isn't it beautiful? Thorns tore my fingers. Here. All around. See them crying? Wah-wah-wah. What a farce, eh, Shansi? It was hard for me, too. I loved him once. But he was a different person. Funny . . . while he lay dying, the sickness left his face and he was handsome again and time reeled back and we were young again— in love again—and just for an instant, the old fire was in his eyes again. Then he was gone. "Help Chiang Ching carry the flag," his last words.

SHANSI: Stop who? The students? The army? Stop who? Your son?

CHIANG CHING: Ah, Shansi, be strong. Never show your underbelly. Never, Shansi.

SHANSI: Don't call me that! My name is not Shansi!

(The GUARD suddenly rushes out. SHANSI follows him, calling.)

SHANSI *(continuing):* Where you going? Wait! Wait!

CHIANG CHING: No matter what. Even when they come at you with guns.

(The scrim is dark. A spotlight focuses on a SOLDIER aiming a gun at CHIANG CHING. He is in whiteface. Another SOLDIER stands behind. Downstage, a spotlight is on CHIANG CHING.)

CHIANG CHING *(continuing):* Ai! Now that the chairman is dead, you come to get me, nah? Body's not even cold. What brave men you are!

(CHIANG CHING fights them as though being arrested.)

CHIANG CHING *(continuing):* "Help Chiang Ching carry the flag!" Do you defy the chairman's last request?

(She faces TWO JUDGES in whiteface. Their dark robes make them appear to be floating. They rap gavels.)

CHIANG CHING *(continuing):* Anngh? What's the charge?

(Noisy confusion prevails with the gavels pounding louder and louder.)

CHIANG CHING *(continuing):* You keep me in solitary four years without a charge and you tell me to shut up? I am a revolutionary—a soldier. I am not afraid to die. I will not crumble like the others. On the crest of a wave or under, I am Chiang Ching. *(to the JUDGES)* You sit up there so high and mighty. There was a time when . . . Remember me? Remember begging for an appointment—? Liu Shaochi and Wang Guangmei were arrested according to the authority of the time. Chou Enlai was in charge. Not me. You did the same. You criticized him too! What proof . . . You have no record. You know more about that than I do. You know exactly how many and where the bodies are buried. I wouldn't be surprised if some of you were in the plot to kill the chairman—

(ZHANG YUFENG *in whiteface, Mao's last secretary and lover, appears.*)

CHIANG CHING *(continuing):* What's *she* doing here? Poxieh! I know about you . . . all about you . . . you pig's all. Jumped in the chairman's bed while I was away . . . away . . . doing . . .

ZHANG YUFENG *(overlapping):* Zhang Yufeng, secretary to the chairman.

CHIANG CHING: Secretary, anh? Took his notes, I bet. I know that old story.

ZHANG YUFENG: There were lots of rumors about her in Shanghai.

CHIANG CHING: I worked hard in Shanghai—clawed my way over the nepotism of directors and bodies of jealous lovers.

ZHANG YUFENG: Well, not good. They say she was . . . everyone knows what she did—even the chairman.

CHIANG CHING: What. What.

ZHANG YUFENG: There's the old story about . . .

CHIANG CHING: Lies!

ZHANG YUFENG: . . . story about the night she got so drunk and in the morning found herself in someone's bed and on—

(Muted sounds of courtroom laughter.)

CHIANG CHING: Tang Na! He spread that—

ZHANG YUFENG *(overlapping):* She wasn't around much while I was there. Touring the country, they say. Well, a Ping-Pong player . . . I forget his name and a couple of . . . well, of course, those three men—the gang. They were always together. Maybe others. I don't know.

CHIANG CHING: I worked! Not like the work *you* do. On your back.

ZHANG YUFENG *(overlapping):* Chairman Mao did not want to dismiss Deng Xiaoping. It was *her* idea. She insisted—

CHIANG CHING: Not true!

ZHANG YUFENG: . . . insisted on it. She made it very hard for him. You know he was very ill.

CHIANG CHING: That's what I said. Exactly what I said.

ZHANG YUFENG: Hardly able to defend himself. But he always said—not only to me but to others as well—"Beware of the Gang of Four."

CHIANG CHING: How can you believe this . . . this . . .

ZHANG YUFENG: That's what he called them—"Gang of Four." Oh, no, I can't repeat what he called her.

CHIANG CHING: Lies, lies. He called me to him. I was doing other work and he called . . . All his other projects failed and he called . . . What does *she* know? I'm the chairman's wife. Where was she when . . . *(to* ZHANG YUFENG*)* What do you know about struggle and sacrifice? You know hunger? You eat millet day after day 'til your stomach turns against you and . . . Ever smell guts spilling from a soldier's wounds while his feet still march?

*(*SHANSI *enters with his arm over the* GUARD'S *shoulder, talking softly.)*

SHANSI: We'll find him. I'll talk to my friend—he knows everybody—and we'll find him.

CHIANG CHING *(to* ZHANG YUFENG*)*: You spend one day . . . just one day in a filthy jail, covered with fleas and lice? Ever been to a cigarette factory? Ever send your only child . . . Li Na . . . not to see her again 'til . . .'til love is . . . is . . .

SHANSI *(continuing)*: Nothing we can do right now.

SHANSI *(continuing; to* CHIANG CHING*)*: Shhh . . . Shhh . . .

CHIANG CHING *(to* ZHANG YUFENG*)*: That's what struggle and sacrifice is all about . . . What do *you* know? Revolution! Revolution! Revolution—

GUARD: Shut up!

*(*CHIANG CHING *sees* WANG GUANGMEI *in a dim light behind*

the scrim. She wears a muted green dress and a yellow scarf and her old cloche hat.)

SHANSI *(to the* GUARD): Listen: I have lots of friends at the rally. I'll help you look for him. When I get off, nah? Later, nah?

CHIANG CHING: She's out now, is she? Rehabilitated, anh? Well, don't you worry. One day I'll be out and you'll put up a statue of me . . . in Tiananmen Square where all that ruckus . . .

(The GUARD *shakes* SHANSI *off and enters the cell, his jaw set and fists rolled.* CHIANG CHING *sees him.)*

CHIANG CHING: You don't think so? Politics is like fashion. Styles change. Yesterday I was in fashion. Today you. Tomorrow me, again.

(The GUARD *lunges for* CHIANG CHING'S *throat.* SHANSI *rushes to stop him.)*

GUARD: Don't say that! Don't say that!

SHANSI *(overlapping)*: Wei-wei-wei! Stop! Stop!

*(*CHIANG CHING *slips away.* SHANSI *holds the* GUARD.)*

CHIANG CHING: Ah, Shansi, did you bring my dolls?

GUARD: I'll kill . . . I'll kill her.

SHANSI: Come on, she's an old woman. An old woman. Come on . . .

CHIANG CHING: Not an old woman. Chiang Ching.

GUARD *(overlapping):* Tiananmen all over again. Over and over and over. It's *her* fault. She started it all!

CHIANG CHING: Lots of fleas in Shansi, nah? Women strong as men. "Give us guns . . ."

GUARD *(overlapping):* Shut up! It's your fault!

SHANSI: It's everyone's fault! We follow our leaders like sheep. It's wrong! We're all to blame.

CHIANG CHING: Be strong, Shansi, be strong. Politics is like fashion. Yesterday me; today you; tomorrow . . . tomorrow . . .

(Lights fade as SHANSI *holds the* GUARD *and* CHIANG CHING *sits on her chair.)*

End of Play

Genny Lim

GENNY LIM WAS BORN IN 1946 in San Francisco, where she grew up as the youngest of seven children. Her parents, Edward and Lin Sun Lim, are both natives of Kwantung, China. Her father resided in the Bay Area as a young boy and met Lim's mother on a return trip to China. Lim studied theater and liberal arts at San Francisco State University as an undergraduate and went on to earn a master of arts in English with a creative writing emphasis. In addition, she was a graduate fellow in the Columbia University Broadcast Journalism Program for Minorities in 1973. An artist whose work has been widely produced and acclaimed, she lives in San Francisco with her two daughters. Lim teaches at the New College of California where she coordinates the Performance Program under the Department of Arts and Social Change. She also teaches poetry to elementary through high school students and curates the Poets-in-the-Galleries exhibition at the De Young Museum in San Francisco.

Frustrated at the lack of authentic representation of Asian Americans in theater and other areas of the entertainment industry, Lim began to write plays in 1978. "As an Asian American woman writer, I feel it is my responsibility to tell the truth about my culture and gender," Lim says. "The two are inextricably bound and unavoidable." But Lim is quick to point out that some people do not wish to hear such truths: "I suppose it initiates some contact with their own consciousness and, therefore, with a sense of responsibility, which they interpret as guilt." Lim prefers, she says, to arouse people with her writing, to force them to think. She makes no apologies for this preference because she believes that, often, artists have to make people feel uncomfortable or "even provoke them" in order to be heard. "Art should engage the mind and the spirit," Lim says. "It should mobilize people into social action whenever social change is necessary."[1]

From Lim's point of view, one shared by the other playwrights in this volume, social change remains a key concern for women of color. "We are living in such adverse times—ecologically, economically, morally and spiritually—that any effort made to mobilize peoples' consciousness into self-determination, self-validation,

[1] This and following quotes from Lim are from personal conversations with the editor, 11 February 1992.

153

compassion, and racial, class, and sexual understanding is a step further along in the difficult journey of human survival on this planet."

Lim notes that she believes that gender and race are two of the biggest issues of our time, at the core of our problems as a "dominant Western male imperialistic society." She contends that the "traditional social stigmas" of race and gender cannot be separated from the realities and political issues of ecology, AIDS, nuclear arms, technology, homelessness, drugs, guns, and violence. "Women are abused, raped, battered, and deserted with their children on a daily basis," Lim says. "Women of color must stand and watch their sons become involved in wars or imprisoned or killed in their own city streets. If we don't confront these realities squarely and honestly, we, as a culture, will be undermined by them, as we already are witnessing."

Lim acknowledges that American theater, much like other elements of American society, has been patterned after a patriarchal European tradition, a tradition she points out has been called into question only recently. Because of this tradition, Lim feels that Asian American women have been allowed only a marginal role in the American theater; they have been denied the opportunity to participate in production and in the publishing of plays because of gender and race oppression. "Social change has been slow in coming for people of color in general and even slower for women of color, who historically represent the last people to become liberated in repressive Western colonial societies," Lim says. She believes that it is not "merely chance" that Asian American women find it difficult to climb the male, European American–dominated theater hierarchies with success.

For women, Lim feels that the difficulty of being successful in the theater is exacerbated by the fact that the life of a theater artist is one of "economic vicissitudes, migrancy, late hours, and personal sacrifice." "Many of us are working-class mothers who have to juggle family, career, and art," she notes. "I am a single mother and cannot travel from theater to theater to follow my productions or serve in out-of-town residencies." Because theater hierarchies usually expect such flexibility in artists' life-styles, there are inherent conflicts and obstacles in the situation for the single-parent artist. If opportunities are limited for an aspiring playwright in the U.S. today, they are even more limited for female playwrights of color, and women of color virtually are unrepresented in the artistic staffs of a majority of regional theaters in the U.S. All in all, the prospects for Asian American women playwrights seeing their work produced appear remote.

Despite these challenges, the artistic contributions of these playwrights are at an all-time high. Lim is working on collaborative projects that combine poetry and music in interdisciplinary settings. Recently, she participated in a collaboration of musicians and poets entitled *SenseUs: The Rainbow Anthems* with artists Max Roach, Sonia Sanchez, John Santos, Victor Hernandez Cruz, and Jon Jang. Lim explains that the group composed new American anthems from their own culturally specific voices so that "we might redefine the anachronistic white Yankee stereotype, which the national anthem, a British drinking song, conjured up."

In addition, Lim is working on a new collaboration with composers/musicians Jon Jang and Francis Wong. They are exploring a contemporary Asian American musical expression, theater as ritual and event, and theater as a communal and personal experience. Lim also plans to collaborate with the visual and performance artist Guadelupe Garcia on "La China Poblana," the story of a Chinese woman who landed in Mexico during the 1600s and influenced the native dress and culture. Their intention is to focus on the cultural exchange that took place between Asia and the Americas in the sixteenth and seventeenth centuries.

Family is important to Lim. She is the single parent of two daughters, high-school student Colette and elementary-school student Danielle. Lim describes Colette as a "bright, gifted writer" who is at that "age of transition when all the hormones are swarming." She said that Danielle also is bright and, like her sister, has participated in the program for gifted children in the San Francisco public school system. "Danielle still identifies with me a lot," Lim said, "but soon she will reach the age of twelve, when she will start the transition that Colette is experiencing now." Colette has developed a taste for rap culture because she perceives it as being a radical departure from the artistic culture of her mother. But Lim points out that rap is a type of "contemporary poetry" and does not challenge her daughter's interest. "Colette is looking to carve her own identity," Lim said. Lim said she feels that her daughers are much more self-confident than she was at their ages because she had no role models who encouraged her to be self-sufficient and independent. Reflecting on her native Chinese parents with respect and clarity, Lim said that they did not feel there was a need for their children to go to college.

"My daughters and I are three females who are so bonded and have so much in common," Lim said. "There's no extended family, so I have to be all things to them at all times. There's not much support in society for the family and especially the single-parent family." Lim said her mother, who is now eighty-six, cooks dinner for them once a week, packaging food for them to take home. "My mother gets tired and she doesn't speak English, so it's hard for the girls to understand her as a role model," Lim noted. Lim's siblings are scattered around the country and she does not see them very often.

Lim gave her daughters French names because she also was given a French name at birth: Genevieve. "I thought I'd keep it consistent," Lim said with a smile. "I asked my father the source of my name. He said he wanted my name to be Jennifer but that the people at the hospital must not have understood him because he had a thick Chinese accent. I'm not sure if that's a true story. I was never able to verify it one way or another before my father passed away."

A political, poetic playwright who has managed to create rich theatrical portraits while raising a family on her own and teaching, Lim clearly writes with hope for social change, but she also writes for "self-recovery." She says that she writes for the theater of the future, because the traditional American theater is too entrenched in the past, but she looks to history—with all its unanswered questions—for answers. Lim's plays *Paper Angels, Bitter Cane,* and *XX* all deal with important aspects of history. Journalist Margo Skinner, writing in *Asian Week* about Lim's *Bitter Cane,* noted, "It is a powerful and moving work in which she has wedded traditional fairy-tale elements to social concern."[2] Of *XX,* Robert Hurwitt of the *San Francisco Examiner* said that it "plays like variations on Federico Garcia Lorca's 'To be born a woman is the worst punishment.'"[3] Noting a foot-binding scene, he said that Lim manages to make this

---

[2]Margo Skinner, "Lim's *Bitter Cane* Weds Fantasy with Reality," *Asian Week,* 29 September 1989.

[3]Robert Hurwitt, "Erratic New Play Rewards Patience," *San Francisco Examiner,* 27 July 1987.

"violation of the individual imposed by society at large" so "vivid and fresh that its horror takes hold anew."[4]

Paper Angels focuses on the story of poor immigrants from rural China who are held at Angel Island in the San Francisco Bay as they await permission to enter the United States. It is set in the first decade of this century and the immigrants fall victim to the Chinese Exclusion Act of 1882 that allowed U.S. immigration officials to make it difficult for lower-class Chinese to gain entry. Identity papers had to be falsified to make immigrants appear as if they came from families of wealth and higher status. Acquiring such papers, however, was not easy and often led to years of limbo on Angel Island under less than adequate living conditions. Lim is a descendent of two generations of Angel Island immigrants.

Lim's *XX*, a multimedia play chronicling the experiences of myriad Chinese women, was called "a remarkable statement, made through music, poetry, symbolism, [and] the techniques of Asian theater combined with the West" and was termed "a drama of exploitation and betrayal" by *Asian Week* when it was produced at The Lab in San Francisco in 1987.[5] Lim acted in and directed this production.

Her contribution to this volume, *Bitter Cane*, is about Chinese laborers, recruited to Hawai'i in the 1880s to work in the sugarcane fields, and the way they were exploited by white plantation owners and the Chinese foremen who were under the owners' thumbs. Sixteen-year-old Wing Chun Kuo hears the sounds of his dying mother as he packs to leave for America. She reminds him of his history and how to preserve its wisdom to lead him into the future with integrity: "You are my blood, my color, the offshoot and stem of my bones. There is no place you can walk without shadow. . . . You must remember, my only son, never to dishonor yourself. . . . Do not spill black ink on the ancestral graves. . . . Will you break the cycle of pain or will you pursue another grievous lifetime? . . . The sun and wind carry the seeds of memory. Do not forget my words." Wing comes to Hawai'i to lift the dishonor that his father brought to the family. His father, Lau Hing, worked on the same cane plantation years prior and reportedly drowned due to opium intoxication.

[4]Ibid.

[5]Margo Skinner, *Asian Week*, 3 July 1987.

Not understanding the exploitation of the Chinese laborers—which included plantation owners supplying the laborers with opium on a nightly basis, according to Lim—Wing and his mother assumed the father to be a liar who broke his promises to the family and brought them disgrace. Wing's loneliness compels him to become acquainted with the beautiful prostitute Li-Tai, and he falls in love with her as his father had. Wing realizes with anger and despair that his father's obsession and dream are his obsession and dream.

Li-Tai gives Wing further cause for escape when she reveals to him that he is multiracial—his grandfather returned to China with a Polynesian woman who died after giving birth to Lau Hing. Li-Tai also tells Wing that Lau Hing's marriage had to be arranged by a relative and that Lau Hing was cheated out of his share of the family land because he was multiracial. Wing is shocked at this discovery of his racial identity. He says to Li-Tai, "If we can't change our past lives, then let us at least have our future!" He is speaking about them running away to Honolulu together, but his words resonate to a universal history and future, especially for people of color. Li-Tai tells Wing, "Life is going after what you want, no matter what." She learned this lesson the hard way; she had refused to run away to the U.S. mainland with Lau Hing because she was terrified. She says with remorse, "The idea of freedom was as frightening as death."

Bitter Cane deals not only with the history of oppression of Chinese laborers on sugarcane plantations in Hawai'i but also with the history of racism against persons of mixed race in China, the authoritarian presence of Christianity in Hawai'i, the slow genocide of indigenous Hawaiian people and their culture as evidenced in the legacy of Wing's Polynesian grandmother, the history of family, and the power of destiny as the heartbreak and despair of a dead man's spirit is recycled into the dreams and adventures of his son. This leads full circle—through the woman they loved—back to their beginnings in China, back to history. The answers that Wing finds in history alter his life considerably. His race is clarified. His perception of his father and origins of his manhood are given new meaning, meaning that creates anger over the destruction of his mother's life and creates a sense of determination about his future and how he must make it happen.

In *Bitter Cane*, Lim examines the truth of gender exploitation in the deftly drawn character and unfolding heart of Li-Tai. She had come to Hawai'i seeking paradise and, instead, found enslavement of her body in marriage and, finally, enslavement of her soul when her husband died and she was forced to work as a prostitute for Fook, the plantation foreman. Li-Tai seeks escape and redemption, just as the spirit of Lau Hing does. Her soul is delivered to heaven and to her true love, Lau Hing, who has been waiting patiently for her to summon the courage finally to escape.

The play asks us to consider the history of oppression of Chinese in the United States—cane cutters lured to Hawai'i and railroad builders lured to the American mainland with false promises; Lim reveals the burdens of men living apart from their wives and children or unable to begin a family in the first place, lacking adequate food and living conditions, and being seduced by the opium provided by plantation owners. In considering this history, which American history books have chosen to forget, we are challenged to contemplate a future in which we can avoid repeating past mistakes.

Lim calls history "the repository of the memory, the memory of where we've been as a people." "I feel that if we can examine history closely, we can learn from our mistakes and move on to firmer ground," she says. "Otherwise, like the cat chasing its own tail, we'll be doomed to doing the same."

Plays and Performance Pieces	**Production History**
Paper Angels	Asian American Theater Company (1980, world premiere), New Federal Theater (1982), San Francisco Chinese Culture Center (1982), Asian Theater Group at the Ethnic Cultural Center in Seattle (1983)
Daughter of Han (performance piece)	Bay Area Playwrights Festival VI (1983, world premiere)
I Remember Clifford (performance piece)	Bay Area Playwrights Festival VI (1983, world premiere)
Pigeons (one-act play)	San Francisco Chinese Culture

	Center (1983, world premiere), Hampden Theater, University of Massachusetts (1985)
XX	The Lab in San Francisco (1987, world premiere)
The Pumpkin Girl	Bay Area Playwrights Festival (1987, world premiere)
Winter Place ("epic jazz poem" in an interdisciplinary collaborative live performance piece combining sculpture, music, and theater)	San Francisco's Hatley-Martin Gallery (1988, world premiere)
Faceless (performance art collaboration piece with Paul Kwan and Arnold Iger of Personal Grata)	San Francisco's Magic Theater, Multicultural Playwrights Festival (1989, world premiere)
Bitter Cane	Bay Area Playwrights Festival XII (1989), Group Theater Company, Multicultural Playwrights Festival (1989, staged reading)
The Magic Brush	World of Tales, Bay Area children's theater company (1990, world premiere, tour)
SenseUs: The Rainbow Anthems	Life on the Water and Asian Improv Arts for Festival 2000 at Davies Symphony Hall, San Francisco (1990)

Films and Audio-Visual Works

Paper Angels	PBS American Playhouse (1985)
Fei Tien (film adaptation of Lim's play, *Pigeons)*	Producer: Christine Choy

*The Only Language She
Knows* (short subject feature)

PBS, Producers: Steven Okazaki
and Amy Hill on "Silk Screen"
series (1987)

Streetfare (nationwide
municipal bus poetry
poster program)

Sponsor: Winston Network
(1988)

Poetry and Prose

Winter Place (collection of poetry) (1989)

*Island: Poetry and History of Chinese Immigrants on Angel Island,
1910–1940*, coauthored with Him Mark Lai and Judy Yung
(1980)

Wings for Lai Ho (1982)

Through Our Voices: An Anthology, edited by Lim (1990)

*The Chinese American Experience: Papers from the 1980 National
Conference on Chinese American Studies*, edited by Lim (1984)

Lim's work is included in the following anthologies: *The Heath Anthology of American Literature*, "Carved on the Walls: Poetry by
Early Immigrants" (1990); *The Statement of Two Rivers: A Chinese Translation of Poetry by 16 Chinese Americans* (1990); *The
Forbidden Stitch*, coedited by Lim (1989); *California Childhood*,
"A Juk Sing Opera" (1988); *Calyx Asian American Women's Issue*,
"Children Are Colorblind" (1988); *Under the Bridge of Silence:
California Poets in the Schools*, "Children Are Colorblind" (1986);
This Bridge Called My Back, "Wonder Woman" (1981, 1983);
Homegrown, "An Excerpt from *Paper Angels*" (1984); *Breaking
Silence* (1983); and *American Born and Foreign* (1979). The playwright also has had her work published in the following magazines:
Zyzzyva, scenes from *XX*, (Winter 1987); *Contact/II*, "If Sartre
Was a Whore" (Winter/Spring, 1986); *Bamboo Ridge, Pigeons,
The Only Language She Knows*, "People's Prayer," and "Made in
America" (Spring 1986); *Bridge*, "Journey to Death Valley" (Summer/Fall 1982); *Bridge*, "Atsuko" (October 1976); and *Y'Bird* (formerly *Yardbird*), "Seven Minus Zero" (1976).

Awards and Honors

New Genre Individual Fellowship of the California Arts Council (1988), the Zellerbach Family Fund Community Arts Program Grant for a new performance collaboration (1988), the California Arts Council Multicultural Program Fellowship for XX (1986–89), The Lee and Lawrence First Prize Playwriting Award for XX from the San Francisco State University Department of Creative Writing (1987), the Zellerbach Family Fund Community Arts Program Grant for XX (1987), the James Wong Howe Award for PBS' American Playhouse production of *Paper Angels* from the Association of Asian Pacific American Actors (1986), Award of Appreciation for valuable contributions in developing community mental health for Asians from the Asian Community Mental Health Services (1986), Certificate of Honor in Appreciative Recognition of Distinction and Merit from the Office of the Mayor of San Francisco (1985), the Downtown Villager Award for best new play for *Paper Angels* (New Federal Theatre production, New York) (1982), the American Book Award for *Island: Poetry and History of Chinese Immigrants on Angel Island, 1910–1940* from the Before Columbus Foundation (1982), and the Robert Frost Award for first place in poetry at the San Mateo County Fair.

Bitter Cane

Genny Lim

CAST OF CHARACTERS

Lau Hing Juo, the ghost of a middle-aged cane cutter
Li-Tai, a prostitute in her mid-thirties
Kam Su, a cane cutter in his early thirties
Wing Chung Kuo, the sixteen-year-old son of Lau Hing
Fook Ming, a middle-aged Chinese luna (foreman)

Scene One

(China. A bare stage. WING *is packing to leave for America. There are several tightly wrapped cloth bundles on the floor, ready to go.)*

Voiceover of HIS OLD MOTHER: Listen well, young man, and understand. You are my blood, my color, the offshoot and stem of my bones. There is no place on this earth where you can walk without shadow. The rain will pelt your shoulders like stones. The burning sun shall torment your flesh. Life is difficult and short. But the gods have given us laughter and song to forget our troubles.

You must remember, my only son, never to dishonor yourself. Do not be idle, do not wander aimlessly, without destination. Do not throw dust upon the gods' faces. Do not spill black ink on the ancestral graves. You have been formed, shaped like a thorn from my womb. You grow like the wound in my soul. Now it is up to you, my son. Do not kill me with shame as did your father. Will you break the cycle of pain or will you pursue another grievous lifetime? Beware of tigers everywhere. Snakes lie among the leaves like snares. The sun and wind carry the seeds of memory. Do not forget my words. They are all I have to leave you.

(Enter a funeral procession in a Chinese village during the mid-1800s. The drone of tantric Buddhist chants mingled with the weeping and wailing of women fill the air. White-robed mourners march across the stage bearing a litter with the shrouded body, paper effigies, and palace, symbolizing wealth and status in the afterlife. The objects are lowered to the ground in a funeral pyre. WING *approaches and halts apart from the rest. He presses his hands in prayer and bows three times. The mourners turn together and watch him in silence.* WING *takes up his bundles and exits. Blackout.)*

Scene Two

(Storm over Oahu. Kahuku sugarcane plantation. A weary, middle-aged Chinese traveler, wearing white and a coolie hat,

enters carrying a wrapped bundle. His movements should be stylized and suggestive of another world. He stops, listens, and puts down his bundle.)

LAU HING *(attentively):* Listen to that. Sounds like it's never goin' to stop. Hear it hammering down the tin roofs? Drilling through cracks, dripping down walls, fillin' empty tins on the floor? Yu-chiang, the master of floods, remembers our sins. *(miming)* Sometimes he cups the ocean in his hands and hurls a tidal wave! *(howling of wind)* Hear him growling? *(pauses)* There's nothing more lonely than the sound of wind and rain. But, once it stops, you're back in the fields, knuckling under the sun. Just when you think you'll collapse, you look up and there she'll be, the cane witch. Smiling at you from behind high stalks; long, black hair shining, naked brown arms beckoning you. You blink your eyes twice to see if you're dreaming and she laughs. You don't know where she came from or who she is, but you want her. You want her so bad you can feel your heart trembling. You chase her through row after row of cane till you're breathless. When you finally catch up to her, she spins around and looks at you. Her two dark eyes are caverns. You reach to enter, but a stabbing pain pierces your heart and she disappears. There's no trace of her. All you see is a lizard darting through the leaves. And the faint smell of pikake.

(Woman's laughter and sound of rain. LAU crosses downstage left, where he remains for the rest of the play. Light goes up on a wooden shack room with a vanity, a bed and a few feminine, Victorian articles. The set should be evocative, not literal. On the bed, LI-TAI is giggling as KAM SU tickles her.)

KAM: Teach me!

LI-TAI: I'm not Hawaiian.

KAM *(lifting her camisole):* Then you need exposure. *(kisses her navel)*

LI-TAI *(laughing):* Piko.

KAM *(tickling):* Piko, piko, piko!

LI-TAI: Diu-mao-gwai!

KAM: Who you calling a drunk?

LI-TAI *(puts out her palm in a no-nonsense manner)*: My money?

(Realizing the rules have changed, KAM *irritably picks up a fifth of whiskey from her dresser and takes several snorts. She grabs it from him and puts it back.)*

KAM: Payday is Saturday. I'll pay you then.

LI-TAI *(irate)*: What do you think I am? You pay me now!

KAM: I got one year left on my contract. *(digs into his pocket and hands her several coins)* One more lousy year. *(meaningfully)* Then I'm free.

LI-TAI *(looks at the coins with disgust)*: Fifty cents! Is that all you got?

KAM: Have a heart, Li-Tai. I came all this way in the storm!

LI-TAI: And you can go back in it!

KAM: Please . . .

LI-TAI *(indignant)*: You wouldn't do this to a haole woman!

KAM *(cajoling)*: Just this once. I'm begging you!

LI-TAI *(contemptuously)*: Jawk-gee! Do you think you're catching a pig?

KAM *(desperately)*: As a countryman!

LI-TAI *(throws the coins on the floor in anger)*: Get out.

KAM *(explodes)*: You think you so high and mighty? You think you too good for me, huh? Well I'll tell you something. You and that Pake luna are nothing but a pair of blood-sucking leeches!

LI-TAI: You are dirt!

(She slaps him. He grabs her violently, forces her onto the bed, grabbing her bound feet. She struggles helplessly underneath him.)

KAM *(aroused)*: Crippled woman, where can you go? You have no feet—only petals for toes.

(She spits at him. He twists her ankles. She clenches her teeth in pain.)

KAM: You can only submit! *(He bites the tip of her foot as if it was a delicacy.)* Like fish out of water.

(She struggles free and in a frenzy, gathers his coins and flings them at him.)

LI-TAI: Take your crumbs and get out!

KAM: Why spit on your own kind? Do you think you're better than me?

LI-TAI *(contemptuously):* Shit is better than you. *(hysterically)* Get out! Get out!

KAM *(pointing his finger):* One day, you'll be sorry.

(He exits, slamming the door violently. She takes his shirt, opens the door, and hurls it out. We hear him yell from outside.)

KAM *(offstage):* Pake snake! Mercenary whore!

LI-TAI *(screaming):* Fook will kill you if you ever come back here!

(She slams the door shut, leaning against it with eyes shut. She takes big gulps from the whiskey bottle. She goes slowly to the bed, sits, then lights the opium lamp on the bedside table and prepares the pipe. She takes deep tokes. The drug has an almost immediate calming effect on her. She picks up a cricket cage from her bed table and studies it with intense fascination. The room fills with smoke and the crescendo of rain, then the sound of a cane worker singing:)

> Hawaii, Hawaii
> so far, far from home,
> Hawaii, Hawaii
> My bones ache and my heart breaks
> thinking about the ones I left behind.

(The light fades on LI-TAI and comes up on KAM in the field, holding a machete and singing:)

> Hawaii, Hawaii
> so far, far from home,
> For every cane I cut, there are a thousand more
> With so many days to pay.
> Hawaii, Hawaii
> Don't let me die of misery.
> Don't bury me under the cane fields.

(LAU HING *watches him silently from a distance.* KAM *wipes his brow with his sleeve, then hacks the stalks with vengence.*)

KAM: Goddam sonovabitches! *(throws his whole body into cutting motion)* Take that! *(again striking)* And that, son-a-va-bitch!

(*A* CHINESE LUNA *enters with a new worker.*)

LUNA *(to* KAM*)*: Less mouth, more action! *(indicating newcomer)* I want you to teach this boy to cut cane. Make sure he doesn't cut the tops high. I want the stubs nice and low. Show him the right way. Stack 'em straight. No sloppy piles. No cheating. I got eyes. We'll have to lop this field by Saturday—otherwise, overtime.

KAM: No overtime! Our contract says no overtime Sunday!

LUNA: I'm boss here! If I say you work, you work. If I say you work overtime, you work overtime. Understand?

KAM *(stubbornly):* I understand the contract.

LUNA: Well now, I wouldn't want to violate your contract. If you don't like working Sundays, you can work nights.

KAM: No dinner, no work!

LUNA: No work, no pay! You got that, Chinaboy? *(waiting for response)* Now get back to work. That's what we pay you for.

(LUNA *exits.* KAM *takes the machete and lands it with force.*)

KAM: You haole lap-dog! *(strikes)* Profit from the blood of your countrymen! *(strikes)* Traitor to the white devils! *(strikes)* Bastard! *(to* WING*)* Back up! Look out for flying splinters. You're liable to lose an eye or nose! You want to learn how to cut cane, boy? This is how we cut. Nice and deep. Down to the bone. They want the juice in that stalk. Don't let it run to the ground. The bottom's where the vein's at. Easy. Nice and sweet for the mill to grind. If you can cut one, you can cut eight! Just think of each cane stalk as Fook Ming's skinny neck . . . Aiii-ee-eee!!!

(*A final angry blow. Fade out.*)

Scene Three

(Dinnertime outside the plantation shack. KAM *is too wound up to eat.* WING, *by comparison, wolfs down his bowl as if starved. There are two small packets beside each of their bowls.)*

WING *(with disappointment):* Is this all we get for dinner?

KAM *(with a bitter laugh):* What did you expect? A king's nine-course banquet? Cod fillet and shark fin soup? Deep-fried quail and tender, boneless barley duck? Ha ha. You'd better get used to limp salt cabbage and cold rice, cause you're gonna be eating a lot of it. *(pushes his bowl toward* WING) Go ahead, eat, friend.

WING *(eagerly seizes* KAM's *bowl):* Thank you.

KAM: Welcome to Kahuku, the land of bitter cane. I am Kam Su. Better known as Kam-a Su-tra. And who are you?

WING: Wing. Wing Chun.

KAM: You look like someone I know. *(slapping mosquitoes)* I must have sweet blood. I'm being crucified! *(laughs)* Like Jesus.

WING: I got stung by a wasp in the field. *(rubbing his ear)* Who is Jesus?

KAM: Christ. Wrap your head. The nests are hidden in the leaves. *(points to his unopened packet;* WING *hands it to him)* Jesus Christ. Nailed on a cross by his own gentle kind. Friendship is a rare thing. Greater love hath no man than this, that a man lay down his life for his friends. *(preparing his pipe)* And there are those who profit from the misery of their own. Judas saith unto him, not Iscariot.

WING *(perplexed):* What the hell are you talking about?

KAM: Christian delirium. Don't mind me. When the sun hits, I start babbling that holy drivel. *(takes a puff)* The only book we could get was the Bible. We recited passages from Matthew, Mark, Luke, and John, like little schoolboys, trying to keep our minds off sex. It only made it worse. (KAM *points to* WING's *unused packet)* Aren't you going to open yours?

(WING shakes his head disinterestedly.)

KAM: Then why don't I trade my rice for your powder?

(WING *shrugs and shoves his packet toward* KAM. KAM *eagerly takes it.*)

KAM: I give you a month before you're as depraved as the rest of us. Disciples of the golden poppy.

WING *(offended):* Don't be so sure.

KAM *(surly):* Oh? You don't shit?

WING *(stubbornly):* Every man's different.

KAM *(cynically):* I don't agree. I say all men are the same. Deaf and dumb. You come out of a hole, you go into a hole. Eventually you disappear. Like the cane. *(takes out his pipe and opens the packet of powder)* You're no different. *(puts the powder in the bowl of the pipe)* You came to make money and return to the village rich. When your contract's up, you'll go home and pick a wife. That's what we all thought. You'll see. The seasons pass without fail. Each day follows the next. You plant, you cut, you harvest, you haul, and you don't ask questions. Like a dumb plow ox. The only thing you got to break the monotony is gambling, opium, or women. Euphoria or Christianity. Take your pick. Can you think of anything more depressing than praying to some limp haole hanging from a cross? *(laughs)* He probably never understood a word of Chinese anyway! *(taps his pipe, then lights it)*

WING: Why did you stop believing?

KAM: When I realized this White God wanted no graven images before him. Father DeCarlo snatched up Kwan Kung and hurled him on the ground. There was no way on earth, I'd let him burn Kwan Kung! I carried him all the way with me from China. Why that'd be like spittin' on my father's grave! Father DeCarlo couldn't believe the endless string of curses I shouted at him. If their God was going to be so greedy, I said, I'd just as soon stay pagan. It was stupid to think of myself as Christian anyway. You can't spin silk out of cotton, no more than you can teach a pigeon to swim. Soon as I pay my debt, I'm going back. I have no illusions about this place. *(cheerfully)* I'll just spend whatever time I have left, playing, not praying. *(shrugs)*

If opium is evil, the white man's the devil. He gave it to us and it's him who's keeping us here. *(puffing)* Most of the fellas take any woman they can get their hands on. You can't drain away your manhood. Why wait five or seven years for a village girl? Some of the fellas marry Hawaiian girls. Some even marry prostitutes!

WING: Not me. I'm going to make my village proud.

(WING *takes out a knife and a hunk of wood from his pocket and starts whittling.* LAU *simultaneously takes out an invisible knife and his cutting movements repeat* WING'S.)

KAM: Look at the bastard talking! *(mocking him)* I'm going to make my mother proud! What are you anyhow? Mexican? *(amused)* You still a virgin? *(patronizing)* Listen, you don't have to be ashamed. No one's perfect. I was once one too. But once you've tasted wine *(a quick tug at his crotch)*, you never lose your thirst. *(smirks)* Know what I mean? You want a woman?

WING: I'll wait till I marry.

KAM *(disgustedly)*: Did you leave your dick in China? Is that what you're carving? Wake up! I got just the woman for you, China-boy. She can wrap her gaze around you till you think you're seeing double. She's a snake beauty. With a deadly bite.

WING: She must be a bad woman.

KAM: There are two kinds of women. The kind that reminds you of your mother and the kind every mother fears for her son. The first kind you marry and the other kind you lust. As long as you don't confuse the two, you'll be fine—know what I mean?

WING *(laughs)*: Oh you're a real expert, aren't you, Kam?

KAM *(a casual wave of the hand)*: Ah, I don't trust any woman. I don't let 'em get the better of me. If you're smart, you won't either. You gotta keep your knuckle on 'em. Don't take any chances. When you see a woman cry that's a sign of surrender. She'll be like that piece of wood in your hand. You can carve her into any shape you desire. (WING *laughs with disdain.*) She'll worship you like Jesus.

WING *(laughing)*: You're full of dung!

KAM: Hey take it from me! I know what I'm talking about. Every woman wants you to suck her dainty earlobes. She wants you to caress her creamy thighs and pinch her nipples till she cries with pain. And when you bite those tiny dewdrop feet with your teeth, she'll ache with such pleasure, she'll think she was just born! She'll arch her back up in a half-moon and that's when you'll know, the gate of heaven is open. She's ready for you to plunge into the heart of the flower. *(with a big self-satisfied sigh)* The secret of seduction, according to the analects of Master Kama Sutra, is mystification. *(both are laughing conspiratorially)* Now how about it, country poke? *(lascivious grin)* Ready to dip your brush?

WING *(shaking his head nervously)*: No.

KAM: You turnip, I give you one month before you come sweating!

WING *(stubbornly)*: Not me, I'm no red lotus-chaser!

KAM *(with knowing certainty)*: We'll see about that, Chinaboy. Anyone who whittles the way you do has got to have an itch! *(laughs)*

(Fade out.)

Scene Four

(Night time. Cicadas. Outside LI-TAI's cabin. There is the sound of a couple's laughter from inside. The two men, outside, are hiding behind bushes, spying. LAU joins them unnoticed.)

WING *(anxiously)*: What if he doesn't leave?

KAM: Then you go and knock.

WING *(nervously)*: What do I say?

KAM *(impatiently)*: Why does a man go to a woman in the middle of the night? You don't have to say nothin,' stupid!

WING *(misgivings)*: Maybe we should go.

KAM *(irate)*: You think we walked three miles for nothin'? You crazy!

WING *(nervous)*: Maybe this isn't such a good idea.

KAM: Shoot! I do it all the time. The lunas, they know we sneak away. They turn the other way. It just makes their job easier, that's all. *(craning to see)* I wonder who's in there with her?

WING: It sounds like a man's voice!

KAM: Oh, you don't say?

(Lights off on two men and up on FOOK *and* LI-TAI *in bed, drinking. He is slightly intoxicated. The room is lit by a single kerosene lamp.)*

FOOK *(stroking her in pleased tones):* You have the body of a virgin. Tight and firm as a stalk of cane. No one would suspect you were over thirty-five.

LI-TAI: I'm not.

FOOK *(grinning possessively):* You can't keep secrets from me, Li-Tai.

LI-TAI: Did you bring me a treat today?

FOOK: I'm going to wind up in the poorhouse over you, Li-Tai!

LI-TAI: Come on, give Li-Li some candy!

FOOK *(reaches into the pocket of his garment at bedside and takes out an envelope, which he reluctantly hands her):* That's all you get.

(She grabs the envelope.)

LI-TAI: My delicious poppy!

FOOK *(shaking his head):* My poor little slave! *(he slowly gets dressed and out of bed)* What will become of you?

LI-TAI *(annoyed):* Why do you always talk to yourself?

FOOK *(defensively):* I take good care of you Li-Tai. If it wasn't for me, you'd be stuck in a brothel. You should be grateful.

LI-TAI: Shall I get on my hands and knees?

FOOK: Is that the position you like? *(matter-of-factly)* Do you have my money?

(She crosses to the drawer and takes out some money, which she hands to a suspicious FOOK.*)*

FOOK: Is that all?

LI-TAI *(nervously):* Business is slow.

FOOK: You're smoking up my profits.

LI-TAI *(turns her back):* Don't start!

FOOK: Then be straight with me!

LI-TAI: I want a cicada.

FOOK: What? Another damn cicada? What happened to the last one?

LI-TAI: It died.

FOOK: I despise those ugly insects!

LI-TAI *(sadly holds the empty cage up):* That's all I have.

FOOK *(amused):* You're such a child, Li-Tai. *(he tries to kiss her, but she turns her cheek)* You enjoy wearing me down, don't you? Don't you?

LI-TAI *(wearily):* Shouldn't you be going?

FOOK *(aroused):* I ought to turn you over my knees and spank you. Do you realize that in another year, I'll have enough to buy some land of my own? The rest of these coolies don't have the smarts to do anything but smoke and gamble. They have no ambition. They'll never make a cent because they're not willing to invest time to make money. Not me. Sugar is a good cash crop and prices are climbing. Soon I'll be a planter, not a luna. I'll have my own plantation and I'll hire my own men. We'll have money enough so you won't have to sleep with anyone but me. *(possessively)* I hate the thought of other men touching you. Especially Kam. You're not seeing that scoundrel anymore, are you? *(she shakes her head; he speaks desiringly)* You're spoiled. French perfume, cigarettes, silk stockings . . . in the middle of nowhere. You fancy yourself a lady, don't you, Li-Tai?

LI-TAI: I have my ways. *(to herself)* Sometimes I wonder which is more oppressive—the heat of the sun or the lust of a man.

FOOK: You know you couldn't survive here without me, Li-Tai. Don't forget where you were when I rescued you. You didn't have one decent outfit to your name and you were frail as a bean thread. It was easy as picking fruit off the ground. If I hadn't taken you, you would have rotted. *(pauses)* We'll be loading the mules tomorrow . . . I'll be back Sunday. *(pinches her cheek)* Be nice.

LI-TAI: Bring my cicada!

FOOK *(annoyed):* I'm jealous. *(with amusement)* Imagine that! Jealous of a cicada! A damned cicada. *(He exits.)*

(The porch door opens slightly.)

KAM: Look, someone's coming!

WING: Can you see who?

KAM: Shh.

(The CHINESE LUNA *stumbles out drunk and leaves in the darkness.)*

KAM: It's that sonuvabitch Fook Ming! *(under his breath)* That no-good bitch! She goes for that stuffed cock. *(pushes* WING *toward the door)* Go on, now's your chance!

WING *(resisting):* Don't push me!

KAM: You got cold feet?

WING: I just don't like to be pushed.

KAM: Alright, all right. *(starts to leave)*

WING: Hey, where you going?

KAM: To see somebody.

WING: Yeah? Who?

KAM *(giving him the nod):* What are you waiting for? Someone to take you by the hand? *(reassuringly)* Okay, I'll wait till you go in.

WING *(pats* KAM *on shoulder):* Thanks Kam.

KAM: Remember, take your time, kid. Take a deep breath. Remember what I told you! *(he watches* WING *approach her door)* And don't forget to tell her who sent you!

(Light fades on KAM. WING *takes a deep breath and knocks.)*

LI-TAI *(calling from inside):* Who is it?

WING *(clearing his throat):* My name is Wing Chun . . . Kuo.

(The light inside the cabin comes up as LI-TAI *slowly opens the door. She motions him to enter. He stands there awkwardly.)*

LI-TAI *(stares at him with immediate recognition):* You?

WING *(captivated):* I hope it's not too late.

LI-TAI *(glancing around nervously):* I thought I heard voices. *(returning curiously to* WING*)* You new?

WING: Yes. Three weeks.

LI-TAI: Hoi-ping?

WING *(surprised):* Yes. How did you know?

LI-TAI *(matter-of-factly):* By the way you talk.

WING *(impressed):* You're clever.

LI-TAI *(examining him):* You're good-looking. You look mixed.

WING: I'm Chinese, same as you. I was the best farmer back home.

LI-TAI: I believe it. *(looks at his hands)* Are you good with your hands?

WING *(surprised):* Yes. I can carve things.

LI-TAI *(impressed):* Ah, an artist! *(sounding his name)* Wing Chun. My name is Li-Tai.

WING: Li-Tai. That's pretty. *(pauses)* Where you from?

LI-TAI *(abruptly):* Look. I know you're not here to gossip. You have two dollars?

(He fumbles in his pocket and without looking hands her several bills. She smirks at his naivete and quickly tucks it in her kimono pocket.)

LI-TAI: Sit down.

(He sits.)

LI-TAI: Want something to drink?

WING: Some tea would be nice, thank you.

LI-TAI *(amused laugh):* Tea? How old are you?

WING: Twenty.

LI-TAI *(frowning):* You're lying.

WING *(embarrassed):* Sixteen.

LI-TAI: This your first time?

> *(He nods with embarrassment. She takes a whiskey bottle, uncorks it, pours a glass, and hands it to him.)*

LI-TAI: Drink it. It'll give you confidence.

> *(He takes a big swallow and chokes. She laughs at him.)*

LI-TAI: Slow down. What's your hurry? *(smiling)* Talk to me.

WING *(still embarrassed):* About what?

LI-TAI: About you.

WING *(blushing):* There's not much to tell.

LI-TAI: Why not?

WING *(takes a gulp, then blurts):* My name is Wing and I like to eat duck gizzards.

> *(She bursts out laughing, then he laughs, too.)*

WING: On the first day of school, I remember the teacher asked us to introduce ourselves.

LI-TAI: And that was what you said.

WING: I couldn't think of anything else!

LI-TAI *(mockingly):* You still can't.

WING *(frustrated):* I don't know why I'm so tongue-tied. *(finishes his glass)*

LI-TAI: Talking is not important. *(refills his glass)* There are other ways to communicate. *(pours herself one, clicks his glass, then slumps on the bed with her glass in a provocative manner)* Your parents have a bride picked out for you yet?

WING: No. *(pauses)* My parents are dead.

LI-TAI: I'm sorry.

WING: My father died here. At Kahuku.

LI-TAI: Oh? *(surprised)* What was his name?

WING: Lau Hing. Kuo Lau Hing.

> *(She freezes at the recognition of his name.)*

WING: He was one of those Sandalwood boys who never made it back.

LI-TAI *(trembling):* How old were you when he left?

WING: I was just a baby.

(Struck by the resemblance, she cups his face with her hands.)

LI-TAI: Let me look at you!

WING *(embarrassed):* What's the matter? Why are you looking at me like that?

LI-TAI *(marveling):* You remind me of someone.

WING: I'm as good as any man on Kahuku.

LI-TAI *(disdainfully):* The average man here is a pig. You don't want to be like them, do you?

WING: One flop in the family is enough. It's no secret. Lau Hing was a bum.

LI-TAI: How can a son talk about his own father in that way?

WING: And how can a father treat his family that way? Why should I pretend he was somebody he wasn't? *(somberly)* He was no-body to me. Nothing.

LI-TAI *(stung with guilt):* Your mother? She loved him?

WING *(disgustedly):* She died. He lied to her. He lied to her every month for two years! When he got tired of lying, he stopped writing altogether. She didn't hear from him again. Then one day, she gets this letter saying he's dead. *(bitterly)* You want to know what killed him? *(pauses)* Opium. The money he should have sent home, he squandered on himself! *(pauses)* They shipped his trunk back. She thought it was his bones. When she opened it, she fainted. The box was empty except for his hat and a few personal belongings. His body was never re-covered they said, because he had drowned in the ocean. *(with cruel irony)* That's why I'm here. To redeem a dead man.

LI-TAI: You think you'll succeed?

WING: I'm not sending my ghost in an empty box home. Life is too short! *(listening to the sound of rain)* It's raining again.

LI-TAI: It's always raining. There's no escape. *(with a sense of fore-boding)* You do what you can do to forget. And survive. *(picks up a fan and begins moodily fanning herself)* I can't decide what's more boring. Living out here in the middle of nowhere or raising chickens in a puny plot back home.

WING: Why did you come here?

LI-TAI: A lady in the village told me that Hawai'i was paradise. She said there was hardly anything to do there but suck on big, fat, juicy sugarcane—sweeter than honey. I was crazy for cane and waited for the day to come here. When my mother died, my father remarried. My new mother didn't like a girl with bound feet who talked back. So I told her to send me to Hawai'i. She sold me to a rich old merchant on the Big Island. I cried and begged to go back home. But I was his number four concubine. His favorite. Four is a bad luck number. So when the old man suffered a stroke in my bedroom, they, of course, blamed it on me. Number one wife, who was always jealous of me, picked up my red slippers and threw them at my face. Then she beat me with a bamboo rod and called me a good-for-nothing slave girl! *(laughs bitterly)* They lit firecrackers when Fook Ming took me. To rid my evil spirit. Some paradise. *(moved by* WING'S *look of compassion)* Tell me, what do they say about me?

WING *(blushing):* Who?

LI-TAI: The men. What do the men say about Li-Tai?

*(*LAU HING *crosses from the wing toward* LI-TAI.*)*

WING: Nothing. *(admiringly)* Just that you're beautiful.

LAU *(passionately):* You're beautiful!

*(*LI-TAI *turns and sees* LAU.*)*

LI-TAI: Who sent you here?

WING: No one, I swear!

LI-TAI *(frightened by* Lau's *apparition):* Why do you come? *(cautiously)* What do you want from me?

WING *(apologetic and earnest):* I came to you because I need a woman.

LAU *(echoing simultaneously):* I came to you because I need a woman.

LI-TAI *(scornfully):* How much is your pleasure worth? Two dollars? All the money you have?

WING *(ardently):* Everything!

LAU: Everything!

LI-TAI *(with a nervous laugh):* So you need a woman. But not just any woman? *(crosses to a table and lights a candle in a glass holder)* You want one with experience? One who can guide you into manhood? *(puts out the kerosene lamp, picks up the candle, and turns to him)* Someone who can open your eyes and wipe the clouds from them. *(crosses to him)* Because you're not a little boy anymore. *(continues her cross to the bed)* And Mama can't help you. *(places candle on bedside table, then lies down)* But I can. *(coyly)* Come here.

(He takes a nervous breath and crosses to her. He halts in front of her. LAU turns and watches them.)

LI-TAI: Are you afraid of me?

(She reaches for him and pulls him down to his knees. She puts his hand to her face and he slowly strokes her cheek as if discovering a woman's skin for the first time. He continues touching and stroking her face, neck, arms, and shoulders, gently and innocently.)

LI-TAI: You're pure as the lily's hidden leaf. *(gazing intently at him)* I see little torches flickering in your eyes!

WING *(with nervous passion):* They burn for you.

LI-TAI: You should stay away from fire.

WING: Why? We sacrifice to the gods with fire.

LI-TAI: Forget the gods. There's only you and I here. And the huge ocean, which surrounds us.

(She pulls him to her. She takes his hands and examines them as if remembering something from the past. She gently presses them to her cheeks. Then she pulls him alongside her on the

bed. He removes her embroidered slippers, gently, then caresses her feet. LAU approaches the pair, mesmerized.)

WING: Does that feel good? *(she moans softly)* They're so tiny.

LI-TAI *(sighs):* Oh your hands . . . they feel like water!

LAU *(echoing):* . . . they feel like water!

LI-TAI *(matter-of-factly):* I'm made for pleasure. Not marriage. Family, cooking, raising babies. I wouldn't be good for that. *(a sad laugh)* I'm only good for one thing. *(provocatively)* And you, what are you good for?

(He kisses her feet. By now, LAU is standing a short distance from the couple, watching and experiencing every nuance of gesture as if reliving it. She leans over and unfastens his shirt. She takes in his young torso and gently runs her fingers over him. He takes her fingertips and gently bites them. She withdraws her hands, unloosens the kimono around her shoulders till it reveals her nakedness. LAU HING moves in closer to watch. WING reaches to touch her, but she coyly pulls away and recovers herself with the kimono. He pulls her to him and pulls open her kimono as if unveiling a miracle. Struck by this first experience of womanly beauty, he stares in awe of her.)

LAU *(passionately):* You're beautiful!

(WING takes her into his arms. We hear the pounding rain amid her soft moans as they kiss. Fade out.)

Scene Five

(Downstage left.)

LAU: "When a dog comes, then riches . . . When a pig comes, then woes . . . When a cat comes, run quickly . . . And buy mourning clothes." *(whittles with a carving knife the final touches to a puppet as he speaks)* Chance. Everything, chance! Every gambler knows it. Every farmer knows it. If nature's not with you, you're just out of luck. One flood can wipe your field clean; one disease can finish you off. You see the cane? They grow straight and tall against the wind. Just give them plenty of sunshine and water. But if blight comes *(indicating, with stylized gestures, the puppet's futile struggle with supernatural forces)*, there's nothing can save it. *(to the puppet)* It's the hand of Yuk Wong Dai Dei. Heaven and earth. No man on earth can stop him. If a man does you wrong you can kill him. But once cane rot sets in, who do you blame?

(Fade out.)

Scene Six

(The next morning. LI-TAI *awakens beside* WING. *She contemplates his slumbering face. She raises her hand lovingly to stroke his features but refrains to keep from disturbing him. She throws on a light robe and climbs out of bed.* WING *stirs.)*

WING *(looks around, disoriented, then horrified):* Oh my god, it's morning! How could I fall asleep! *(gets up and starts frantically putting on his clothes)* I gotta get back.

LI-TAI *(calmly):* Wait. I'll fix breakfast. You can't work on an empty stomach.

WING: Next time.

LI-TAI *(resolutely):* Maybe there won't be a next time.

WING *(confused):* I don't understand.

LI-TAI *(a bit forcefully):* Stay here.

WING: I can't. *(reassuringly)* Look, I'll be back.

LI-TAI *(skeptically):* When?

WING: Next Saturday?

LI-TAI *(demanding):* Tomorrow!

WING *(embarrassed):* I-I . . . can't afford . . .

LI-TAI *(offended):* I won't take your money. I don't want it. Just don't treat me like some whore.

WING *(taking her by the shoulder):* What's gotten into you?

LI-TAI *(pulling away):* You tell me. *(sarcastically)* You're a man. Oh what's the use! The sun flattens down on you like an iron and all you can do is lie there and whimper. *(a sigh of disgust)* Some paradise.

WING: You give in to bitterness.

LI-TAI: They said, "'You will never want to leave!" *(with bitter irony)* I never asked to come. *(reminiscing)* I was only twenty when I came to Kahuku . . . *(turning away from him)* . . .and the easy life. I've been here too long! *(gesturing at the landscape)* Like those mountains that never move. *(thinking aloud)* What do you think happens to us when we die?

WING *(decisively):* We go on living in the afterlife.

LI-TAI: No we don't. We wither and die.

WING: Don't you believe in immortality?

LI-TAI *(firmly):* No.

WING: Everything lives in the soul.

LI-TAI: Everything dies in the heart.

WING: That's not Chinese!

LI-TAI: Maybe I'm not Chinese.

WING: Don't you believe in fate?

LI-TAI: No.

WING: Why not?

LI-TAI: Because fate is destiny. I don't believe in destiny. It's our own hand that pulls us down, not some god's. We answer to ourselves.

WING: I don't know about that . . . *(romantically)* I was lying in the dark, unable to sleep, so I listened to sounds. The soft feet of rain, the rustling of boughs and leaves, ten thousand voices of crickets . . . I heard the grass talk to the wind. I heard the cicada's song.

LI-TAI *(amused):* What did it sing?

WING: It sang good evening to the stars.

LI-TAI: And what did the stars answer?

WING: The stars answered that they were lonely.

LI-TAI: Why were they lonely?

WING: Because they shined alone in the sky.

LI-TAI *(laughing):* Did they sing in Chinese?

WING: In a language beyond words. Did you ever try, when you were a kid, to pick out one star in the sky, then try to find that same star the next night? You can't. But you keep looking anyhow. When I first looked at you, I had this feeling fate brought us together. *(looks at her meaningfully)* Things happen for a reason.

LI-TAI: I don't believe that. Things just happen. We make them happen. We stumble into traps. We live, we die.

WING *(intrigued):* You're not like the women back home.

LI-TAI: They all think like one person. The young girls talk like old women and the old women are ignorant and superstitious. In China you're born old before you can walk. As a woman you're allowed to do only one thing. Please men. I've spent my whole life doing that! *(matter-of-factly)* You see this body? It's not mine. It belongs to Kahuku Plantation. My skin even smells like burnt cane!

WING: And what about your heart?

LI-TAI: I cut it out. Long ago.

WING: Then what was it I felt last night? *(with certainty)* I've known you before.

LI-TAI: Last night I was drunk! So were you. *(begins primping before the mirror)* What happened to all the years? I look in the mirror and count each new gray hair. *(sadly)* Time has no respect for a woman.

WING *(looking at her reflection from behind):* You have a beautiful face, a true face. With features that sing. *(tenderly)* Your brows describe the mists of Kweilin.

LI-TAI *(laughs):* What do my wrinkles reveal?

WING: The soft rays of the moon.

LI-TAI: A waning moon?

WING: No. A full one. *(dramatically)* I was reborn last night.

LI-TAI *(laughing):* Don't make me laugh.

WING: I mean it. *(puts his arms shyly around her)*

LI-TAI: Don't be foolish. *(scoffing)* I'm old enough to be your mother!

WING: The soul has no age.

LI-TAI *(sighs)*: You remind me of a man I loved fifteen years ago.

WING: Who was that?

LI-TAI *(elusively)*: A man who was a cicada. *(thoughtfully)* Did you know the cicada dies after he mates?

WING *(optimistically)*: Yes, but he is resurrected from the grave he leaves behind.

> *(WING kisses her, then exits. A spot on LAU, kneeling in the cabin. He is folding a red Chinese robe in a ceremonial manner. She gives a start. Fade out).*

Scene Seven

> *(Break time. Several weeks have passed. KAM enters mopping the sweat off his face as he puts down his machete. WING follows exhausted and lays his machete down. KAM ladles some water from a barrel for himself, then for WING.)*

WING: Thanks for covering me.

KAM: Sonuvabitch! Is it her again? How can you afford to go so much?

WING *(worried)*: What did you tell the boss?

KAM *(facetiously)*: I said you were in the outhouse with diarrhea.

WING *(gloomily)*: Very funny.

KAM: I'm not covering for you anymore. I'm warning you!

WING: Okay, okay! *(nervously)* What do you know about Li-Tai?

KAM *(suspiciously)*: Why?

WING *(with a deep breath)*: I want to marry her.

KAM *(shocked)*: You're joking! *(contemptuously)* She's a prostitute.

WING: Different flowers have a way with different eyes. *(defensively)* Besides, you said yourself some of the men marry prostitutes.

KAM *(angrily)*: Listen, kid, you don't know what you're talking about. You don't go marry the first prostitute you jump in bed with. That's crazy! Soak your head in cold water and get back to the fields. *(nastily)* Did she tell you who she is?

WING: I don't care about the past.

KAM: Oh you don't, do you? Did she tell you she's Fook Ming's concubine? Huh? Did she tell you how he keeps her in that cabin all to himself? How he visits her on Sundays and Mondays? How the rest of the week he sets her up with the men?

WING *(stubbornly):* I don't care about him.

KAM *(shaking his head):* You're not the first you know. Don't think you're the only one who's tried. *(nastily)* More men have crawled into Li-Tai's bed than lice. They don't call her "The Cocoon" for nothing. She's used up. You stay away. I'm telling you, she's no good. She's poison. *(shaming him)* What would your parents think? You chasing after a slut?

WING *(grabs KAM angrily by the collar):* Don't call her names, you hear me? You're jealous because you want her too!

KAM *(confessing guiltily):* That's right. I want her too. I'd be lying if I said I didn't.

WING: Are you in love with her?

KAM *(angrily):* What man around here isn't in love with Li-Tai? What man here doesn't want her? The question is what man is crazy enough to give everything up for her?

WING: I am.

KAM *(sighs):* I know. That's what worries me. *(pauses)* You don't know the danger you're in. I seen one fella waste himself over her. He was a top cutter too. The best on Kahuku. Worked like the devil to buy her off Fook Ming, but when she refused him, he went mad. He deserted one night, went to her cabin, but she just laughed at him. He couldn't take it. Went completely insane. Poor Lau Hing.

WING *(paling):* Lau Hing Kuo?

KAM *(surprised):* Yeah, that was his name. Did you know him?

WING *(softly):* He was my father.

KAM *(hits himself in the head):* I talk too much.

WING: Then my father never went back to China because of her?

KAM *(shaking his head):* Li-Tai bewitched him. He was so heart-broken, he killed himself.

WING *(with shame):* If it's true, then I should hate her.

KAM *(gravely):* It's true. Everybody knows about Li-Tai and your father.

(LAU crosses behind WING. WING stands there frozen in utter disbelief and shock. KAM shakes his head desparingly.)

KAM: You ask me, you've jumped from the net into the frying pan! When you think of what you left to come here, it makes no damn difference. Back home you'd plow the field and pray for rain. Even though you might not eat, at least it's your land. Here, you don't starve, but you work like an ox for some other sonuvabitch's land. Not only that, you don't live like a normal man. *(with indignation)* Look at me, I should be married by now. I should have a wife to screw. I should have a roomful of kids to take care of me in my old age. Instead I waste my time gambling, smoking opium, and falling in love with prostitutes. Like Li Tai.

(Fade out.)

Scene Eight

(The magical song of a flute fills the air. On stage right, LAU is on his hands and knees stalking a cicada. At his side are LI-TAI's cricket cage and his wrapped bundle. He mimes catching the insect and carefully putting it in the cage, eyeing it with fascination. As the light comes up on the men stage left, LAU sits back in reverie, listening to the cicada's song. It is three months later on the plantation. The men are bedraggled from a long day of cane loading. WING ladles water into tin cups for each of them.)

KAM *(massaging his aching shouder as he grumbles):* God sits on his holy ass, while we labor like ants! If we die, who cares? *(with disgust)* Look at this hand! Can't even grip the machete. Can't even hold a pair of chopsticks, it's so swollen. *(trying to make a fist to curse the sky)* I may be an insignificant speck, but I got some feelings! *(mopping his forehead with his sleeve)* There must be all of ten suns out there! Each one burns hotter then the rest. We're ants pushing crumbs. No matter how many rows we level, we're always behind. The cane's as endless as sky. *(observing the sullen, hard-working WING)* Except you, you're inhuman. You blast through that jungle like you got a bee up your ass. You got endurance, Wing, but you also got no consideration. *(a warning tone)* Making it hard on the rest of us, you know? No one can pair up with you! They say you cut ahead and cause their cane to fall. *(with begrudging admiration)* You hit the stalk, it falls. Other fellas hit five, six times, it just shakes. You got one swift machete—like you been born to it. You gonna make me lose face, little brother! *(scolding)* All work and no play's unnatural, Wing. Go to town. Relax. *(raising an eyebrow)* Meet some new friends, yeah? *(pauses)* Come with me tonight! There's some tall, yellow-haired wahine with mango breasts and asses like breadfruit. Lots of huluhulu. Hairy legs are beastly.

WING *(disinterested):* You go ahead, Kam.

KAM *(exasperated):* Goddam, Wing, Li-Tai's not the only woman in the world! You'd think she was Kwan Yin on earth! There's lots more where she comes from. She's common as opihi!

WING *(spins around with fists clenched):* Shut your mouth or I'll kill you!

KAM *(holding his arms up to protect himself):* Hold it, boy! I'm only trying to help. I was the one who introduced you to her! *(guiltily)* That's why I feel responsible. That's why when the fellas talk, I'm the one who defends you.

WING *(annoyed):* Why should you defend me?

KAM: They say things about you and her.

WING: What do I care what those bastards say?

KAM: They say, "Like father, like son."

WING *(with angry suspicion):* How do they know Lau's my father? I never told anyone. *(grabbing him angrily by the collar)* Except you.

KAM *(uneasily):* Maybe she told them!

WING *(threatening):* You're lying!

KAM *(a matter-of-fact confession):* Anyhow they were bound to find out, even if I didn't tell. *(struggling free)* Since you came along, she's stopped seeing anybody else. *(pauses)* They say you cursed her.

WING *(confused):* What the hell are you talking about?

KAM: Li-Tai is fading. She's an opium eater. You haven't been over there, have you? *(no reply)* She's consumed. She's wasted to nothing. The same way your father did. They say you caused it, to avenge him. I told them they were crazy. Fook's the one who's no good. He's the haoles' bootlicker. He's turned her into a ghost.

(FOOK MING *enters, crossing to* WING.)

FOOK: You fellas did decent work. I'm gonna let you off early this afternoon to make up for last night.

BOTH MEN *(mechanically):* Thank you. *(Both men turn to go.)*

FOOK: Oh, Wing. (WING *remains*) I been watching you. You're strong worker. In fact, one of the best cutters Kahuku's ever had. I like the way you go about your business. No funny stuff. Not like the others. I have to ride whip on 'em to keep 'em awake. You don't give me problems. You're solid, steady. No tricks. The big boss likes you. I like you too. *(studying* WING*)* I want you to be my back-up boy. You get a raise from three to four dollars a month. You keep the men in line, you see to it the harvest is in on time. Can you handle it?

WING *(with mechanical politeness):* Yes sir.

FOOK: Good. I think I can trust you. *(confidentially)* Let me warn you. Once you leave China, it's every Chinaman for himself. The minute you turn your back, there's always someone in the shadow, waiting to stick a knife in you. I would be careful of my friends if I were you. That Kam is a troublemaker. Friendship runs thin with him. Take it from me, the only real thing here . . . *(drops a silver dollar at* WING's *foot)* . . .is this.

(Fade out.)

Scene Nine

(Nighttime. The song of a cicada fills the silence. LI-TAI *is lying on the bed in an opium stupor. There is a loud knocking on the door. It is* WING *returning after an absence.* LI-TAI *appears oblivious to the noise, but the banging continues.)*

LI-TAI *(shouting):* Go away! Go away!

(The door opens. WING *stands in the doorway staring, shocked at the spectacle of* LI-TAI *in her degenerated, euphoric state. She does not appear aware of his presence.)*

WING: Li-Tai!

(She recognizes his voice but doesn't stir.)

WING: It's me, Wing. *(approaching tentatively)* I hear you're sick.

LI-TAI *(to herself):* Three months.

WING *(confessing):* I tried to put you out of my mind.

LI-TAI: Who are you?

WING *(bewildered at her unkempt state):* What's happened to you? Why are you doing this?

LI-TAI: What are you doing here?

WING *(with resolve):* I want to know something. *(demanding)* I need to know.

(She absently picks up the pipe.)

WING: You knew he was my father.

LI-TAI *(distractedly):* What are you talking about?

WING *(impatient):* Quit pretending. Lau Hing Quo. I told you he was my father! *(seizes the pipe violently)*

LI-TAI *(grabbing for the pipe):* Give me that!

(He jerks it away from her.)

LI-TAI: Damn you, give it to me!

WING *(accusatory):* You were my father's lover, weren't you?

LI-TAI *(evasively):* I had many lovers!

WING *(resentfully):* Then he never meant anything to you, did he? You used him. *(hurt)* The same way you used me. *(rage mounting)* You knew he was my father, but you didn't care. I told you who my father was and yet you made love to me. How could you? What kind of a woman are you?

LI-TAI *(coldly):* You're not man enough to know.

WING: You bitch! *(slaps her on the cheek and then is stunned by his own violence)* I-I never hit a woman before!

LI-TAI *(evenly):* Lau Hing never hit me.

WING *(jealously):* How else was my father better than me?

LI-TAI *(acidly):* He knew how to treat a woman.

WING *(grabs the pipe and plays a sadistic keep-away with her):* How badly do you want this? Enough to inch over here on your belly? Show your true self, Li-Tai! Show me your white belly! Show me how you can crawl. *(sadistically)* CRAWL! I want you to crawl to me! *(tormenting)* Tell me, lizard woman, I want to know! *(with increasing cruelty)* Tell me how he treated you! *(grabbing her by the hair)* Was he better than me, huh?

(She fights her tears.)

WING: Or have you already forgotten? *(lets go of her in disgust, snaps the pipe in two)* Here, bitch! *(throws it on the floor)*

(She crawls to the broken pipe.)

WING: Why don't you kill yourself. Get it over with!

LI-TAI *(demanding):* No, you kill me! Kill me! That's what you want, isn't it? *(picks up the broken pipe and stares absently at it)* I waited. I left the porch light on. I listened for your footsteps, your knock. I didn't sleep or eat. All I heard was the cicada. And the wind. Then it struck me that all my life I have done nothing but wait for a man. I waited for your father. And I waited for you.

WING *(accusatory):* You killed him!

LI-TAI *(with a sad laugh):* He wanted to marry me. *(cynically)* What kind of a future would we have had? A plantation runaway and a pei-pa girl?

WING: He was obsessed with you.

LI-TAI: He was obsessed with escaping.

WING: You were his dream. He betrayed everything for you.

LI-TAI: Go ahead and believe what you want. What does it matter now? *(listening)* Did you know if there was no sound, there would be nothing to measure time? Sometimes everything becomes so still, even the heart stops beating. Your mind just crawls inside itself like a hole.

WING *(bitterly):* For you he destroyed mother.

LI-TAI: He never loved her.

WING: You're spiteful. Hateful.

LI-TAI: I thought you were different. But you're not. If I'm spiteful and hateful, it's because you men made me this way. Lau was kind. I thought you were too. But you're cruel. Lau understood me, because he was different too. He had mixed blood. It runs in you too. They called him Heungsan Jai, "Sandalwood Boy," from Sandalwood Mountains. *(pauses)* I knew you were your father's son before you even told me. His face was etched on yours. You came in from his shadow.

WING: My father would have gone back, if it wasn't for you.

LI-TAI *(sadly):* You hate me, don't you? Don't you think I've suffered? How can you be so righteous? So sure of me. It wasn't because of me. It was your family. Lau swore he'd never go back. They treated him like dirt!

WING: Stop lying!

LI-TAI: Your grandfather brought a Hawaiian mistress back with him to China and she died shortly after giving birth to your father. When your grandfather died, the property was divided, and your father was cheated out of his share of land. Because he was a half-breed. Lau's marriage was arranged by a relative he barely knew. He never loved your mother. Lau loved me!

WING *(yelling):* Shut up!

LI-TAI: Look at yourself in the mirror, "Sandalwood Boy"! Find what's missing!

WING *(snatches the broken pipe and violently hurls the pieces against the wall):* SHUT UP! SHUT UP! *(jealously)* He still haunts you.

LI-TAI: He's dead.

WING: Tell me one thing. I've got to know. Do you love me, Li-Tai? Or is it my father you love?

LI-TAI: When you didn't come, I wanted to die. Is that love?

WING: Answer me!

LI-TAI: I love you.

WING: When I came here, I wanted to kill you. I wanted to hurt you. Then I took one look at you and I knew I couldn't pretend. I can't hate you, Li-Tai. *(pauses)* Give this up!

LI-TAI: I can't.

WING: Give up Fook Ming!

LI-TAI *(with a bitter laugh):* Fook Ming is impotent. I give him the illusion of virility. For that he pays me.

WING *(indicating her state):* This is how he pays you!

LI-TAI: It's my choice.

WING: Leave him.

LI-TAI: Don't be foolish.

WING: I'll leave Kahuku and take you with me. We'll go to Honolulu.

LI-TAI: Look at me! I'm not a young woman.

WING: You're scared. Everyone on this plantation is scared!

LI-TAI: Yes I am. I look in the mirror, but the lines and shadows don't go away. I think I'm looking at a stranger, then I realize the stranger is me. The young woman I thought I was is gone. Just a memory.

WING *(fervently):* If we can't change our past lives, then let us, at least, have our future! *(pauses)* Remember what I said about fate bringing us together? I believe it now more than ever.

LI-TAI *(trembling):* No.

WING: There's nothing to be afraid of. Trust me.

LI-TAI: It's too late.

WING: Don't you want to be happy?

LI-TAI: Happy? I thought only babies and idiots were happy!

WING: I'm good with my hands. I have skills. I can find a job in

Honolulu. Back home, I carved the temple statues. I made Kwan Yin so beautiful, she brought tears to the villagers' eyes. My Kwan Kung was so fierce he frightened away temple thieves. If I can't do wood carving I can always farm. I heard about some rice farmers who are doing real well in marshland near Waikiki. And some taro planters in a valley called Manoa too. *(bitterly)* I can do more than cut cane!

LI-TAI *(worried):* What about Fook Ming?

WING: He won't be able to find us. We'll change our names and our family histories. We'll start all over.

LI-TAI *(thoughtfully):* I like that. I like the idea of starting over.

WING: I'll build you a house with twenty rooms and a courtyard with fruit trees and night-blooming jasmine. We'll plant seeds wherever we go and I'll carve the eight immortals over our front door so fate will smile upon us.

LI-TAI *(wistful):* You dream!

WING: I'll come for you on the ninth day of the ninth moon.

(Lights fade on couple and light comes up on LAU *with his bundle at his feet.)*

LAU: Everything can be understood in a moment, even if nothing is seen. *(holds up the red robe)* This robe belongs to someone on this side. I will take it to her. *(fondles the garment as if it were alive and makes the sleeves dance sensuously before his eyes)* Every night her empty robe dances in the wind and her sleeves get tangled in the boughs. The moon has just come to light her small house. *(he listens)* Listen to the wind. It's the only voice among the leaves. See how quiet the air has become! Darkness awaits her. *(he turns towards cabin)*

(Fade out.)

Scene Ten

(Three weeks later in the heavy rain of the afternoon. Distant thunder. LI-TAI *is packing. There is a knock on the door.)*

LI-TAI *(with nervous anticipation and indecision about what to do with the suitcase):* Wing?

(The knocking continues. She quickly hides the suitcase under the bed, then opens the door. She is surprised to see a rain-soaked KAM.)

LI-TAI: What are you doing here?

KAM *(awkwardly):* May I come in, Li-Tai?

LI-TAI: I thought I told you never to come back.

KAM *(with urgency):* It's important Li-Tai. It concerns you and Wing Chun.

LI-TAI *(suspiciously):* Come in.

*(*KAM *enters.)*

KAM *(brushing wet hair from his forehead):* Something has been bothering me. *(pauses)* I know the last time we left on bad terms. I have no hard feelings. I hope you don't either. *(groping)* After all, we're all Chinese, aren't we? We all came here for the same reason—why shouldn't we all get along and help each other?

LI-TAI: Get to the point, Kam.

KAM *(nervously):* Do you have some water?

LI-TAI *(pours him a glass):* Sit down.

KAM *(gulping gratefully):* Thank you. *(sits)* I want to apologize.

LI-TAI *(skeptical):* That's decent of you.

KAM: For those things I said to you. I've come to talk about you and Wing.

LI-TAI *(icily):* What concern is that of yours?

KAM: I only want to help, Li-Tai. *(rubbing his knees)* You don't know how hard it is for a man. Thousands of miles from home. Nothing to look at but field after rotten field of cane and empty sky. *(painfully)* You're a beautiful woman. Men fall in love with you. *(pauses)* It's no wonder Wing follows his father's footsteps . . .

LI-TAI *(upset):* I won't listen to this.

KAM: First Lau Hing, now Wing. Who next, Li-Tai?

LI-TAI: Get out!

KAM: Do you know that Wing is Lau Hing's son?

LI-TAI *(shaken):* Is this what you've come to tell me?

KAM: You must stop seeing Wing.

LI-TAI: You can't stop me!

KAM *(scrutinizing her):* It doesn't make a difference to you then? Why did you do it?

LI-TAI *(angrily):* You were the one who sent him here! Have you forgotten?

KAM *(defensively):* Do you think I'd be so vile as to do something like that if I'd known? I sent him as a gesture. A kind of peace offering. I know I'm pretty low-down, but I'm not the devil. I don't play with the gods' rules, no more than I can change what's happened. *(pauses)* It's not for me to judge. That is up to heaven. *(pauses)* But think of what you're doing. Think! Wing wants to make good. Not like his father. In ten years he had gone from top cutter at Kahuku to a skeleton. *(pauses)* They blamed you for his suicide, Li-Tai.

(Light on LAU HING standing in the plantation.)

LI-TAI *(bitterly):* Of course. If a man is weak, it's the fault of the woman. Do you think I have the power to change men's lives? Am I the one who profits from the cane? Am I the one who put you here? Why don't you blame yourself? I'll tell you why. Because you're all scared! *(pauses)* At least Lau Hing had the guts to escape. *(painfully)* He deserted and came to me. He wanted me to run away with him. I refused. I was scared. Not him. He was ready to give up everything for his freedom. But I couldn't. *(ashamed)* I was a coward. What kind of a life would we have? Taking in laundry, shoveling horse dung, scrubbing white folks' dirt? I told him I wanted more than he could give. I told him I didn't want to see him anymore. *(pauses)* He stared at me as if I was mad. Then he left. I didn't see him again. *(pauses)* Then one day I was walking by the water ditch. I heard a moan. When I got close, I saw Lau Hing lying there on the ground . . .

(A spot on LAU *twisting the puppet's limbs as if trying to tear them apart. Then he drops the puppet in a fit of despair and gives a wrenching, soundless cry of pain.)*

LI-TAI *(distraught):* He was rolling in mud, kicking his feet up in the air and drooling like a baby. It was revolting! I turned and ran. I ran all the way home without stopping. I still can see him, lying there, vivid as ever. He disappeared soon after. They said he'd drowned himself. His body was never found.

(Fade on LAU *staring absently at the inert puppet.)*

KAM *(sadly):* One cannot trifle with the world. Lau failed his family. He failed you.

LI-TAI *(solemnly):* No. That's a lie. Lau didn't fail me. *(pauses)* I was the one who failed him. I promised to go with him, but in the end I didn't have the courage.

KAM: You were right not to go with him. What a fool!

LI-TAI: Even though I loved him, even though I wanted to, I couldn't face what was on the other side.

KAM: You've survived. That's enough.

LI-TAI: No, it isn't enough.

KAM: For godsakes, if I can stumble through the day half-awake, I'm ahead! The moment I'm awake, I'm pulled by the smell of cane and the lash of the whip. What choice do I have? I cut that cane and I don't ask questions. I get my four dollars and I spend it. That's life.

LI-TAI: No. Life is going after what you want, no matter what. *(pauses)* I was only six when my mother died. They led me to a small fire. I had to jump over for purification. But I was terrified. I screamed hysterically. I can still see their angry faces. *(pauses)* That day Lau insisted I run away with him to the mainland, I became terrified. The idea of freedom was as frightening as death.

KAM: The problem with you, Li-Tai, is you think too much. You should have been born a man.

LI-TAI: Men want to believe there's a difference between the way men and women think when there isn't.

KAM *(admonishing):* For a girl, to be without talent is itself a virtue.

LI-TAI *(curtly):* Virtue without talent is worthless. One may as well be an insect.

KAM *(amused):* I admire a headstrong woman. *(swallowing)* You've been through a lot. You don't need no more troubles. Neither do I. In nine months my contract will be up. Then I'll be a free man. *(building up courage)* I'm not a rich man. I'm not a young man, but I can take care of you. I can satisfy you . . . *(puts a nervous hand on her leg; she pulls away)* You won't even let me touch you! Do I repulse you? *(cruelly)* I bet you open up for the young ones . . . like Wing!

LI-TAI *(pulling away):* Get out!

KAM *(guiltily):* I'm sorry. I didn't mean it.

LI-TAI *(contemptuously):* You're wasting my time. Get out.

KAM *(rising):* I can give you a decent life. I can take you away from this. *(angrily)* What can that kid give you, huh? A grave in Kahuku? Is that what you want? Don't be stupid. You're no rosebud. Look at yourself.

(LAU *enters carrying the cricket cage in one hand and the red robe folded over his arm. He watches* LI-TAI *from across the room.)*

KAM: You're a stubborn woman, Li-Tai. *(pauses)* Good afternoon. *(bows stiffly)* Thanks for the water. This rain never lets up, does it? *(wipes his sweaty palms on his pants, then exits)*

(LI-TAI *crosses to the bed and pulls a suitcase out from underneath.* LAU *crosses with the bundle and folded kimono on top. She looks up, startled, at* LAU.)

LI-TAI: Lau Hing! Why are you here?

LAU: I've left Kahuku.

LI-TAI: You deserted.

LAU: You're coming with me, Li-Tai.

LI-TAI: I'm not going with you, Lau.

LAU: You promised.

LI-TAI: I've changed my mind.

LAU: Why?

LI-TAI: I'm a woman, Lau. There's nothing out there but desolation.

LAU: This life is good enough for you?

LI-TAI: What can you give me?

LAU *(presenting her with the bundle)*: My soul.

LI-TAI *(terrified)*: No!

LAU: You must return my bones. These bones are weary. They have waited so long for the earth. I have carried them all these years. An empty grave awaits me across the ocean. I cannot rest until these bones return to China. I must journey home. Come with me, Li-Tai. It is time. I have come to free you. I was a prisoner of Kahuku, just as you are. Now together we can walk through water and fire. *(extends his arms)* Come!

LI-TAI: I can't go with you Lau. *(with resolve)* I'm going with Wing!

LAU: Wing is my flesh. *(whispering)* He was sent here. You are the only one who can help him. Don't be afraid, Li-Tai! Trust me. Trust yourself. *(approaches her)* Remember the little girl? Go back to her. She needs you. Can't you hear her calling? You must save her. Jump! The flames won't hurt you. From water to fire. Jump! Over ocean into air. Reach! Into your heart. Into the heart of heaven. Redemption lies there. Li-Tai, come!

(LAU *hands her the bundle, which she accepts. He then removes the red robe on top and holds it up for her to wear. She crosses to him in trancelike submission. He helps her slowly and ceremoniously into the open fire robe. Fade out.)*

Scene Eleven

(*Outside* LI-TAI's *cabin. Dusk.* WING *approaches with a hastily wrapped bundle thrown over his shoulder. He is suddenly cut off by* FOOK MING, *approaching from the opposite direction.*)

FOOK *(suspiciously)*: You going someplace?

WING: I'm going to see Li-Tai.

FOOK: What are you doing with that goddam bundle? *(no reply)* Are you planning on going somewhere, Wing?

WING: Fook Ming, I don't want any trouble.

FOOK: Don't tell me you're running away? You've only been here a year!

WING: I can't finish my contract.

FOOK: Why, that's too bad. You have only four years to go. You owe Kahuku thirteen hundred dollars for passage, room, and board.

WING: I will pay it back.

FOOK: You will pay it back. Right here on Kahuku! *(anger increasing)* Why did you stop here? *(yells)* Answer me, you sonuvabitch!

WING: I'm taking Li-Tai with me.

FOOK: Over my dead body. *(seething)* You think you can come here, still wet behind the ears and scheme for my woman behind my back?

WING: She doesn't love you.

FOOK *(exploding):* Li-Tai is mine! I own her. Every hair on her body, every inch of her flesh and bones is paid for in gold.

WING: You don't own her soul.

FOOK *(laughing uproariously):* So you, Wing Chun, have come to claim her soul, huh? What a hero. Too stupid to know you should never meddle with another man's property. It's a shame you have to learn the hard way. Because now, Wing boy . . . *(pulls out a knife)* . . . I will have to kill you!

(They struggle with the knife. FOOK *is about to stab* WING, *when* KAM SU *suddenly appears and grabs* FOOK *from behind. The knife falls to the ground,* WING *seizes it.)*

FOOK *(desperately):* Don't do it, Wing. Don't kill me! Please! You won't get away with it. You'll hang!

(Just as WING *is about to plunge the knife into* FOOK, WING *comes to his senses and drops the knife on the ground.* KAM *suddenly retrieves the knife and plunges it into* FOOK's *belly.* FOOK *stares at him for one moment before he crumples and falls dead.)*

KAM (*staring at the lifeless body*): That's for every man who's died on Kahuku. For every goddam wasted life! (*to a shocked* WING) I know where you're going! You're making a mistake.

WING: I got nothing against you. Leave me alone.

KAM (*angrily*): She was mine until you came along! *She was mine!!*

WING (*steadily*): I don't want to fight you, Kam.

KAM (*with an ironical laugh*): When my contract was up, I was going back to China. I was going to take her with me.

WING: She doesn't love you, Kam.

KAM: She would have come, if you hadn't spoiled everything! (*with growing desperation*) I know Li-Tai. She would have come with me. I know she would have!

WING (*trying to reason*): You could come with us.

KAM (*deeply offended*): I ought to kill you!

WING: You got one murder on your hands, Kam. You want another? Is it worth it?

KAM (*laughing bitterly*): I'm a free man today. Do you know what that means? That means I can walk off this plantation and never look back. That means I can change my name and become a new man. Who knows? I might even get rich! (*reaches inside his pocket*) I got nothing holding me back! (*hysterically, he pulls out a fistful of coins, which spills onto the ground*) You see this money? I got more! I been saving for this day, kid! Look at me, look at me! Do I look like a Gold Mountain Boy? Do I look prosperous to you? (*pauses*) Or do I look like some dried-up sinner? (*throws the money on the ground as if it was dirt*) Take it! Take it! Take this dirty money! Take it!

WING: I can't take your money, Kam.

KAM (*commanding*): Give it to her!

WING: She doesn't want it, either!

KAM (*suspiciously*): You're speaking for her now, huh? (*a surly nod*) So that's the way it is. I might have known. (*confessing frankly*) I wanted to kill you and her. That's why I came. To put a stop to everything. But when I saw Fook, everything came to a head.

I had to put a stop to everything. I had to. *(sincerely)* You understand? It had to be done. (WING *nods*) I don't want to know where you're going or what you're going to do. (KAM *turns to leave*)

WING: Where you going?

KAM *(stops to think):* Honolulu. I like the sound of that name. Hono-lu-lu. Sounds like a woman's name. Maybe I can start a gambling house there. *(grins)* Who knows?

WING *(shaking his head):* I don't understand you, Kam.

KAM *(with an ironic laugh):* I don't understand myself! *(an afterthought)* Oh, a word of advice. Watch out for the haoles if you go to Honolulu. They are a two-faced, cunning lot. I heard tell about a fella who bought a plot of land for a taro patch from some haoles. As it turned out, they didn't even own the land. It was owned by the Church. But by the time he found out, he had already planted and seeded the whole damn plot! So watch out. They'll crucify you.

WING: I will.

(They bow farewell to each other. KAM *runs off. Fade out.)*

Scene Twelve

(LI-TAI'S *cabin. Night. Cicadas.* LI-TAI *is dying. She is lying in bed in the red robe and* LAU'S *bundle is at her feet.)*

WING *(rushing over to her in alarm, taking her hands):* Li-Tai! Li-Tai!

LI-TAI *(very weakly):* Wing, I'm sorry. I can't go with you. There's little time.

WING *(determinedly):* I won't leave without you!

LI-TAI: You must. Or everything will have been a loss. I have a message for you. *(points to the bundle at her feet)* You must take this to Kwantung and bury it. They are the bones of your father. He gave them to me for safe burial. Lau died before he could fulfill his duty as a husband and father. Now you must complete his task. Now you are the keeper of his bones. Return home with them. Your father has waited a long time. *(squeezes his hand)* So have I. *(pauses)* Go home, Wing. Go home before it's too late.

WING *(desperately):* Don't leave me, Li-Tai, don't leave me!

LI-TAI: You were right from the first. We are old souls, you and I. Our destinies were locked. But now you have a chance to be free. Don't wander as your father and I did. Return these bones where they belong. They are part of you, Wing. Part of me. Home. I am ready to go home. Now. Home . . .

(She loses consciousness. Her fingers fall limp from his hands and she dies. WING struggles against breaking down. Calmly, he places one final kiss on her lips and covers her slowly with the blanket. He turns his attention then to the bundle, lifts it ceremoniously with the growing revelation of its intrinsic meaning. He carries the bundle in his arms, as if it was alive, outside. He stares sadly into the horizon. We hear the mournful melody of KAM'S voice from afar:)

> Hawaii, Hawaii
> so far, far from home,
> Hawaii, Hawaii
> My bones ache and my heart breaks,
> thinking about the one I left behind.
>
> Hawaii, Hawaii
> so far, far from home,
> Hawaii, Hawaii
> Don't let me die of misery.
> Don't bury me under the cane fields
> of Hawaii, Hawaii . . .

(Fade out.)

End of Play

Velina
Hasu
Houston

I grew up in Junction City, Kansas, a small town that survives on agriculture and the military, next door to Fort Riley, a U.S. Army base. I lived in a community of Japanese American families and Amerasian offspring. The mothers are natives of Japan, and the fathers are American men of various racial extractions who served in World War II and met their international brides during the U.S. occupation of Japan. Junction City also has a large number of European, Korean, Vietnamese, and Thai international brides.

My mother, Setsuko Takechi, was born in Matsuyama, Japan, and grew up in Imabari. Her provincial Kansai upbringing and unique steel chrysanthemum strength and grace afforded me a childhood rich in culture that shaped my behavior, customs, politics, philosophy, ethics, cultural identity, culinary skills and tastes, and spiritual outlook. My father, Lemo, was born in Linden, Alabama. His parents were dead before he was twelve, thus forcing him into manhood at an early age. He moved to New York and eventually volunteered to serve in World War II. I am a child of war, as are most Amerasians. Without war, my existence may have been an impossibility. My father's gentle spirit was eroded by combat and the racism to which soldiers of color were exposed. My mother suffered the loss of economic stability, dignity, national pride, and family in combat, as well as the suicide of her father, and the premature death of her mother. And she watched as America tested the atomic bomb on the Japanese. These events, in part catalyzed by World War II, helped to conceive me.

My father died when I was eleven. I helped my mother arrange for the funeral because she felt uncomfortable dealing with the many Americans with whom we had to interact in order to put him to rest. We chose a lilac-colored casket. I still remember staring vividly at my father's corpse buffeted against ivory satin in that shiny lilac box. I remember how the ground sank under my feet at the cemetery and how the flowers seemed so dull and pointless drifting over his casket as it lowered into the ground. My childhood was over. As my political battles as an Amerasian wage on, I often think of a line from my play *Tea:* "I was born in a storm . . . and it's never stopped raining." But I have learned to manage the rain to bear the fruit of survival, the fruit of a beautiful child, and the fruit of art.

Encouraged by my mother, I began writing haiku at the age of six. When I was twelve, a teacher said my poetry was very visual and urged me to write a play. It was then that I fell in love for the first time in my life. I fell in love with dramatic literature. I wrote my first play at the age of thirteen. I turned to dramatic literature full force and wrote many plays in order to learn by doing. I was exercising muscles that I had never exercised before. I was learning how to tone and refine them and then maintain the balance. It is a lifelong process for the serious playwright. I went to Kansas State University, where I was an honors student in journalism, mass communications, theater, and philosophy. I stayed in Kansas to be with my widowed mother because the rules of my culture expect nothing less. When she remarried, I left the Midwest. I went to the University of California at Los Angeles, where I studied with Richard Walter and Theodore Apstein and earned a master of fine arts in theater and playwriting.

I am an assistant professor at the University of Southern California School of Theater. I teach playwriting and modern dramatic literature, including the study and analysis of Asian American plays. I am cofounder and president of The Amerasian League, a nonprofit organization dedicated to educational awareness of Amerasian culture. I present poetry readings and lectures in the United States and Japan on various aspects of theater; Amerasian, Japanese, or Japanese American culture; and African American–Asian American relations. All of my work is dedicated to my mother, Setsuko, and my son, Kiyoshi, whom I rear on my own in my favorite American city—Santa Monica. Kiyoshi is a gifted child who attends a private school, Wildwood Elementary, and a Japanese school, Kumon Institute. His upbringing is rich with Japanese and American cultural influences; he enjoys Japanese food and practices Japanese customs diligently. He often asks me, "Mommy, why do Americans wear shoes in the house?" or "Mommy, I get tired of the American kids asking me what I'm eating for lunch when I eat o-manju and musubi." These are questions I also asked my mother at his age. Kiyoshi has written five plays and three short stories. When he grows up, he says he wants to be a playwright and a professor and take care of me "when you get littler than me." I have one older sister, Rika, a doctoral candidate in international marketing relations with an emphasis on the Japanese market, who is married to Brian Ten, a Santa Monica architect. Our older adoptive brother,

Joji Kawada Houston, one of the first Amerasians born after World War II, disappeared in 1984.

I write because I must. It is as natural and necessary as breathing. Fusae Takechi, my maternal grandmother, was known throughout the Ehime prefecture for being very "handy and gifted," able, people would say, to knit a dress in a day. My mother can devour classical Japanese literature in a day and sew a hanten for my son as quickly. I have inherited this dedication and speed. I never suffer writer's block; in fact, to me it is a myth. I am prolific and write quickly. I never run out of ideas. If anything, too many ideas seduce my imagination and I have to hold them at bay. These are blessings that I *never* take for granted. As I noted in this book's introduction, the plays I write must give something to the world in which we live; they must recycle our emotions, spirit, and intellect to refuel and improve the world—not destroy it. They must reflect a social consciousness without losing a sense of the personal. Their vision must remain inextricably tied to the never-ending exploration and excavation of the human condition in the hope of enlightening as well as entertaining an audience. My plays explore the politics of living, broadly defined, taking into account how we guide, influence, empower, and manage every aspect of our lives.

In *Tea* I examine the politics of war, love, culture, class, racism, and nationalism. The play focuses on the lives of five Japanese women who married American servicemen during the U.S. occupation of their homeland. It takes place in Junction City and is based on my family history and the histories of several women whom I knew while growing up. After the first death occurs in the Japanese community—a violent suicide—four women come together to clean up the house of the deceased woman and are forced, in the wake of her death, to explore their own realities and excavate the secrets that have been buried in their souls for so long. The spirit of the dead woman, stuck in limbo because she left her earthly existence without settling accounts—accounts that relate to her mental health, cultural environment, and domestic abuse, among other things—returns to be their guide, to try to force them to come to terms with their own cultural and emotional dislocation. This journey is realized through the use of lyric imagery, poetry, and a structure that blends naturalism with Japanese theater techniques, time travel, and characterization devices that allow me to tell several complex stories in a short amount of time. In his review of the Odyssey Theatre Ensemble production in 1991, Don Shirley of the *Los Angeles Times* said about the women in the play, "Attracted to America by young love and by the self-confidence of the victorious young nation, they had no idea of how stranded and unhappy they would feel in the Great Plains. . . . That national self-confidence now feels like a choking insularity." Shirley noted that the play "is an impassioned and impressionistic look at these [Japanese] women and, by extension, at some of the implications of one of today's trendiest buzzwords: 'multiculturalism.' Although her play is set in Kansas nearly 30 years ago, Houston's concerns are equally those of Los Angeles in 1991."[1] Reviewing the same production, Sandra Kreiswirth of the Santa Monica *Outlook* called the play "funny, warm and ultimately heartbreaking" and said that the women "came to America clutching their own culture while dreaming of things unknown and new. For some, those dreams turned out to be nightmares; for others, disappointments."[2] The women in the play, like my mother and my sister and myself, are caught between two worlds and there simply is no resolution.

Asa Ga Kimashita is the first play in a trilogy of plays that includes *American Dreams* and *Tea*. *American Dreams* focuses on Creed, the African–Native American soldier we meet in *Asa Ga Kimashita*, bringing Setsuko, the heroine of *Asa Ga Kimashita*, home to New York. He returns to face his family's rejection of his interracial marriage and his bitter discovery that the American melting pot is merely a myth. *Asa Ga Kimashita* is a story that I formulated during my late teenage years, based on extensive discussions I had with my mother about our family history in Japan related to the World War II experience. This peculiarly Japanese play is also part of the African American experience, by virtue of its exploration of a Japanese woman's interracial romance with an African–Native American. In addition, the play speaks of a new era, not only for Japan and for America, but also for the world. That era is taking hold now as Japan and America enter a new century as culturally diverse nations that are part of a shrinking global village.

[1]Don Shirley, "*Tea* and Empathy: Velina Hasu Houston's Heartfelt Stories of Japanese War Brides," *Los Angeles Times' Calendar*, 29 January 1991.
[2]Sandra Kreiswirth, Santa Monica *Outlook*, 1 Febeuary 1991.

Indeed, they are the two powerful forces controlling the Pacific Rim, and politically they are at odds with one another again. It makes me realize my biculturalism more than ever. In an unpublished academic critique of my plays, Shirley Geok-lin Lim said about *Asa Ga Kimashita*, "[It] is a fascinating coming-out play. . . . [but] the play's sympathies are nowhere certain. Even as it attacks the feudal [Japanese] constructions that impose narrow limits on women's lives, it critiques the social reforms that the American military government in Japan forced upon a resisting population."[3] My sympathies belong to two countries; it can be no other way because I am a Japanese Amerasian. I cannot take sides. Japan rose out of the ashes of the atomic bomb with assistance from America. The Japanese were neither arrogant nor racist in their time of need. Today Americans use the term *nationalist sentiment* to defend their Japan-bashing, but often it is merely a euphemism for racism. We have seen this euphemism offered before in our history, such as the nationalist sentiment (read: hysteria) that led to American *citizens* who were one-eighth Japanese or more being detained in concentration camps during World War II.

Because of racism, American citizens of Japanese descent cannot celebrate their Japanese heritage without comment or even punishment. Irish Americans celebrate their Irish heritage and wear shamrocks on their day of national Irish pride. German Americans celebrate Oktoberfest. Can one imagine the backlash if Americans of Japanese descent had a day of national Japanese pride and wore a symbol of that pride? Even when we are withdrawn and silent about our pride in our heritage, we are detained in camps, beaten to death with a bat (Vincent Chin, a Chinese American, was mistaken for Japanese and beaten to death by two out-of-work European American auto workers), called pro-Japan, or assaulted (a Japanese woman was assaulted by European American women in a Southern California night club for speaking Japanese). German, Dutch, or Italian companies buy American firms and real estate with no mention of it in the press. If a Japanese company attempts the same, the media makes it a political event that is not without racism itself and that

---

[3] Shirley Geok-lin Lim, unpublished critique offered at Asian American Cultural Transformations Conference, University of California at Santa Barbara, California, April 1991.

fans the flames of racism in the American public. The "Buy America" campaign currently sweeping the nation is problematic in that it is difficult to ascertain just exactly what is American and probably will prove to be another way to practice racism while hiding behind a euphemism. American cars are made with parts from Latin or Asian countries, and Japanese cars are often made in America by American workers. It reminds me of myself: made in Japan and America with Japanese and American parts. But I cannot be bought. While I vociferously challenge America-bashing whenever I am in Japan, I also always will be one of the first to challenge Japan-bashing in America. Japan is my motherland; America is my fatherland. God bless them both. In my writing and politics, I will continue to look at the world through eyes that love both countries, from a vantage point that sees the beauty and the shortcomings of each nation.

Above and beyond these sociopolitical aspects of *Asa Ga Kimashita,* the play is first and foremost a story about love and the ethics of responsibility—both familial and romantic. My Japanese grandfather was a landowner who married a poor, but beautiful, provincial girl whose outlook on life pushed beyond the limited borders of her native Japan. That worldly vision was passed on to her youngest daughter, my mother. It perhaps imbued her with the courage necessary to trust in loving someone from a different culture and, ultimately, to leave the familiarity of her homeland to join her love in his country. Each character in this play must examine the meaning of duty—to country, to maintaining the old order in the face of Japan's defeat, to family, to sibling, to spouse, to love. These examinations are made amid the cacophony of the U.S. occupation of Japan as it struggles to transform Japan from a colonialist empire to a peaceful democracy. The patriarch in the play can barely come to grips with his country's defeat, much less face the indignity of losing his estate to Yankee democracy. The dilemma is one that human beings face again and again—how to accept change, how to accept the stripping away of dignity with some semblance of grace, how to let go of the familiar and move on into completely uncertain territory. In this play, the characters face these questions in different, compelling ways; a bittersweet conclusion leaves us on the doorstep of a new world. As the character of Fusae Shimada (based on my grandmother) says in the play, "There is nothing but the present moment—the one we can grasp in our fists and feel."

That is the singular collective realization that provides the family in the play the spiritual sustenance necessary to move forward with hope for survival.

This play truly began its birth around a small, low, circular table warped while onboard a ship that brought my family from Yokohama to Seattle. The table sat in my family's living room in our house in Junction City. It was the center of our tea time, a time when my mother reflected upon her past and the numerous seeming impossibilities that brought her and my father together and that paved the way for her Amerasian children. It was there that she told me about her beloved persimmon orchard, a place to where she escaped as a child and adolescent to dream. This remnant of her childhood is the source of the orchard in *Asa Ga Kimashita*.

I will continue to write about what I know, think, and dream and what moves my soul and heart. I will never cease to be political because I will never cease being female or being a multiracial, multicultural person of color. I am most grateful to theater audiences in America for their support of my plays.

Plays	Production History
Necessities	Old Globe Theatre (1991, world premiere), Purple Rose Theater (1993)
Tea	Manhattan Theatre Club (1987, world premiere), Old Globe Theatre (1988), Interstate Firehouse Cultural Center (1988), Whole Theatre (1989), Theatre-Works (1990), Kumu Kahua (1990, 1991 Hawai'i Tour Production), Odyssey Theatre Ensemble (1991), The Bishop State Museum of Hawai'i and Kumu Kahua (1991), Mount Holyoke College (1991), Syracuse Stage (1991), Theatre of Yugen (1992), Horizons Theatre (1992), Georgetown University (1993)

Asa Ga Kimashita	University of California at Los Angeles (1981), East West Players (1984); Nova Theater/ Pacific Rim Productions, San Francisco (1985), Kumu Kahua (1991), Massman Theatre, University of Southern California (1991), State University of New York at Geneseo (1991)
American Dreams	Negro Ensemble Company (1984, world premiere), L.A. Theatre Works and National Public Radio/KCRW (1991)
Thirst	Asian American Theatre Company (1986, world premiere)
The Legend of Bobbi Chicago (a musical)	Commissioned by The Mark Taper Forum (as a play, *Tips on How to Store Breast Milk*, 1985)
Tokyo Rose	Commissioned project in development, producers Barbara Trembley and Joan Tewkesbury
Father I Must Have Rice (one-act play)	Ensemble Studio Theatre, L.A. (1987, world premiere)
Petals and Thorns (one-act play)	University of California at Los Angeles (1982), Ensemble Studio Theatre, L.A. (1987)
Albatross	Old Globe Theatre, Manhattan Theatre Club, Arizona Theatre Company (staged readings and workshops)
Christmas Cake	Kumu Kahua (1992, workshop production), East West Players (1991, staged reading)
Kokoro Kara (From the Heart)	

Broken English	Odyssey Theatre Ensemble (1991, staged reading)
Kapi'olani's Faith	Kumu Kahua (1991, staged reading)
My Life A Loaded Gun	Old Globe Theatre (1989, staged reading and workshop)
Plantation (new play)	
Tokyo Valentine (new play)	East West Players (1992, staged reading)
The Voice That Cries in the Wind (new play)	
O-manju (new play)	
Alabama Rain (new play)	
Amerasia Lives: The Amerasian Diaspora Chronicles (new play)	
Mister Los Angeles (new play)	
The Confusion of Tongues (one-act play)	St. Augustine's By-the-Sea (1991)
The Canaanite Woman (one-act play)	
The Matsuyama Mirror (one-act play)	
A Place for Kalamatea (one-act play)	
Zyanya (a one-act Noh play)	

Film and Television

Summer Knowledge (Columbia Pictures; producers: Sidney Poitier, Cedric Scott)

Hishoku (Alternate Current International, Inc.; producer: Margaret Smilow)

Kalito (American Film Institute)

War Brides (Taft Entertainment)

Journey Home (PBS/KCET)

Poetry, Prose, Articles

Green Tea Girl in Orange Pekoe Country (poetry collection, excerpts published nationally)

"On Being Mixed Japanese," *Pacific Citizen* (December 1986)

"The Past Meets the Future: A Cultural Essay," *Amerasia Journal* (1991)

"The Challenge of Diversity for African Americans and Asian Americans," *The Multiracial Asian Times* (November 1991)

Awards and Honors

Remy Martin New Vision Award from Sidney Poitier, the American Film Institute, and Remy Martin (1992); Top 100 Asian Americans of 1991 by *Transpacific* magazine; California Arts Council Performing Arts Fellow (1991); James Zumberge Research and Innovation Fund Grantee (1991); VESTA Award for positive images of women in the arts from The Women's Building, Los Angeles (1991); Japanese American Woman of Merit 1890–1990 by the National Japanese American Historical Society (1991); *Los Angeles Times* and *DramaLogue* Critics' Choice (for *Tea*, 1991); *Kalito* honored in "Celebrating Women's Work" by Northern California Women in Film and Television (1991); honorary co-chairperson for New York Asian Women's Center Tenth Anniversary Celebration (1991); Los Angeles Endowment for the Arts Fellow (1991); McKnight Foundation Fellow (1989); best ten plays of 1988 for Old Globe Theatre production of *Tea* by Sylvie Drake, *Los Angeles Times*; *DramaLogue* Outstanding Achievement in Theatre Award for Old Globe production of *Tea* (1988); Sidney F. Brody literature fellow (1988); San Diego Drama Critics Circle Award for Old Globe production of *Tea* (1988); chosen as member of U.S.-Soviet Cultural Exchange Theater Roundtable, The Mark Taper Forum (1987); twice-named

Rockefeller Foundation playwriting fellow (1984, 1987); best ten plays written by women worldwide for *Tea* by Susan Smith Blackburn Prize of London (1986); national first prize, American Multicultural Playwrights' Festival for *Tea* (1986); Who's Who in American Women (1985); *L.A. Weekly* Drama Critics' Award for *Asa Ga Kimashita* (1984); *DramaLogue* Outstanding Achievement in Theater Award for *Asa Ga Kimashita* (5 Awards, 1984); Author of the Year, Friends of Little Tokyo, Los Angeles (1984); national first prize, Lorraine Hansberry Playwriting Award (1982); national first prize, The David Library Playwriting Award for American Freedom (1982); Best New Plays of 1982 for *Petals and Thorns,* by Los Angeles's Company of Angels; *Kansas City Star* Scholar (1979); *Mademoiselle* magazine Honorary College Board (1976–79); and new play achievement award, American College Theatre Festival Regional, St. Louis, for *Switchboard* (1976).

Asa Ga Kimashita

(Morning Has Broken)

Velina Hasu Houston

CAST OF CHARACTERS

Kiheida Shimada, 60
Fusae Shimada, 53, his wife
Setsuko Shimada, 20, their daughter
Haruko Shimada, 25, their daughter
Hajime Takemoto, 30
Fumiko Kitagawa, 30, Kiheida's niece
Creed Banks, 33, an African American
Mitchell Daniels, 38, an African American
Dr. Watanabe, 44, a physician
Yoko Sagami, 18, the Shimada maid

Time and Place

1945–1946. Ehime Prefecture, the cities of Matsuyama
and Imabari; island of Shikoku, Japan.

Setting

A remote, provincial estate consisting of a home, yard
with flower garden, and the beginnings of a
persimmon orchard, which leads offstage. Of the
house, an anteroom, a "living room,"
bedchambers, and a hallway are visible.

Playwright's note: This play is meant to be performed without an
intermission.

Prologue

(Matsuyama, 1945. Twilight fades in downstage, center, simultaneously with a cacophonous blend of classic Japanese music and World War II–era American music. This is accompanied by the sound of B-29 bombs exploding and the offstage cries of people fleeing for their lives. Enter SETSUKO SHIMADA, *a demure, petite girl of twenty with a gentle, pretty face. But, at this moment, that face is smudged with dirt. Her kimono is torn; she is generally disheveled. She has lost one shoe. She stares straight ahead at the audience and the cries and explosions fade to a bare murmur. She removes a handkerchief from her kimono sleeve, takes locusts from it, and eats them contemplatively.)*

SETSUKO: A beast wrestles with my soul. It comes at night, hiding in the crash of the midnight tide, arrogant and white, powerful and persistent. Who owns this creature? Who unleashes him here, as he comes to abort our lives and devour our dreams? Yesterday, I climbed in my persimmon orchard to stare at the stars of Obon, the sea in July, and happy children. . . . I was one of them. Today, I eat locusts. *(extends a locust toward the audience and smiles gently as she withdraws the offering)* The stars move over to make room for the terror. Its eyes flicker fire and bodies go up in smoke. My schoolmate jumps into the river, curling in death, breasts melting into belly into thighs. And I am whole and unmelted. The beast spares me and yet my heart is on fire. *(a beat)* Mother? Can you hear me? They can take my country, but they cannot take you.

(The bombs and cries fade up as SETSUKO *gathers her locusts hurriedly and looks around in fear. Enter* KIHEIDA SHIMADA, *her portly, dignified father. They stare at one another with great sadness and urgency. He carries a futon [thick Japanese coverlet], which he "soaks" in the river. He takes rope out of his sleeve and hoists* SETSUKO *on his back.* SETSUKO *climbs onto his back and clings to him in her fear. He pats her hand to calm her. The bombs grow nearer and louder. He pulls the futon over her back, and ties her and the futon around his torso. He begins crawling as the sound of the atomic bomb detonating*

fills the theater, and the offstage cries of death and pain echo. The lights cast an eerie glow as he crawls offstage. They exit. Blackout with the voiceover bridging into Scene One.)

Scene One

(Imabari, 1946. In the darkness, the sound of a voiceover is heard, that of General Douglas MacArthur's announcement of the Japanese surrender to the United States, signifying the end of World War II. It is brief, simply the announcement of the surrender of the Imperial Forces. As it ends, the twilight darkness of the predawn fades in simultaneously with the sound of offstage bombing. It is a faint and dreamlike reverberation mixed with traditional shakuhachi music. The bombing crescendoes as a light fades in on the face of KIHEIDA SHIMADA, *who sleeps in the living room of his home. The remnants of his sake drinking are evident on the table.* KIHEIDA *awakens in fright. Anguished, he tries to stop the sound of the bombs, which are being imagined in his head. As he shakes his head furiously, the sound of the bombs and shakuhachi fade and are replaced with the somber instrumental music of "Kimi Ga Yo," the Japanese national anthem. He touches objects in the room as if to affirm his reality. He steps onto the porch and stretches as the light of morning fades in. He shakes the nightmare out again and wipes sweat from his brow. He straightens his traditional Japanese garments and deeply breathes in the air, glad to be alive. He espies a broken piece of fencing. He frowns and adjusts it. It falls again. He shrugs, determined to remain cheerful. Music fades out. Presently,* HAJIME TAKE-MOTO, *thirty, enters carrying a wooden box of produce. He wears work clothes. Well built with a rigid, handsome face, he carries a mutilated glass bottle, which he thrusts into his pocket upon seeing* KIHEIDA.)

HAJIME: Good morning, Shimada-san.

KIHEIDA: Ah, ohayo, Takemoto-san.

*(*HAJIME *presses on.)*

KIHEIDA: Chotto. You drove all night. Sit. Rest.

(KIHEIDA *gives him a cigarette. With deferential hesitation,* HAJIME *sets down the box and sits on it.*)

KIHEIDA: What a nightmare I had: fire bombs everywhere again . . . my wife falling like she did last year, during the air raids . . . Setsuko cringing by the river, waiting for death. Sometimes I never want to sleep. Sometimes I never want to wake up. You look like you have not slept at all.

HAJIME: I had to drive back from the mountains late. So much wood. I did not want to make the police suspicious. Shimada-san, I am almost done with a fence around the farm, then I must get to work on your inn. I want to rebuild your house in the city as soon as possible, too.

KIHEIDA: Government is tightening up on lumber sales since this occupation started. How can we rebuild without wood?

HAJIME *(with shame):* With my black market work, I have too much lumber. *(a bow)* It is yours, Shimada-san. Your gift of the land tract my father worked for you is appreciated.

KIHEIDA: You are industrious. You deserve a start in life. Land, a wife with a sturdy soul, and several sons.

HAJIME *(with shame):* This black market makes my hands feel dirty. *(spits at the ground)* American pigs.

KIHEIDA: I suppose it is necessary to rebuild the old Nippon.

HAJIME: A new Nippon.

KIHEIDA *(adamantly):* Ia. The old.

HAJIME: How can it ever be the same again? *(shows him the bottle)* Look. Here is the old, melted by Yankee fire bombs. I found it in Matsuyama in the ruins of your house.

KIHEIDA: Hajime-kun, I am sorry you lost your parents in the war, but you still have your brother. And since you have made your intentions clear about my Haruko . . .

HAJIME: . . . she is so much like my mother . . . *(as* KIHEIDA *studies him, he looks away evasively)* I know she will make a proper wife.

KIHEIDA: The best. And, when I am gone, you will have all the Shimada farmland for your own.

HAJIME: All of it? A mere peasant like me?

KIHEIDA: All of my tenant farmers will serve you dutifully.

HAJIME *(warily):* But what of MacArthur's land resettlement? Large tenant farms like this one are now against the law.

KIHEIDA: Whose law? There is only Japanese law.

HAJIME *(with respect):* Your land tracts will be given to the peasants. Something called "democracy."

KIHEIDA: Democracy? It sounds like a disease. This land has been in my family for centuries. It saved us during the war and it will be my final home.

HAJIME: But the Yankees will come and—

KIHEIDA: *My home,* Takemoto-kun.

(FUSAE SHIMADA *enters with a tray of tea and a plate with sliced persimmons and a whole persimmon. She is a striking woman, small but sturdy, tired but with elegance in her carriage. Her long, graying hair is bound in a braid. She wears a kimono. She bows.* HAJIME *bows;* KIHEIDA *nods his head.)*

HAJIME: Ohayo gozaimasu.

FUSAE: Ohayo gozaimasu, Takemoto-san.

KIHEIDA *(calling to her like a servant):* Oi.

(KIHEIDA *reaches for fruit. She feeds him a slice. He smiles, enjoying the attention.)*

FUSAE: Fresh from the orchard. I picked them on my morning walk.

KIHEIDA: You do not walk. You float through the orchard dreaming like a poet.

FUSAE: Do not flatter an old woman so. I savor my morning walks in the orchard.

KIHEIDA: And you shall have them always.

FUSAE: When I came here as a young bride, the orchard was a ship in which my mind could travel anywhere.

KIHEIDA *(to* HAJIME, *with amusement):* Women and their dreams are so troublesome.

FUSAE: You also should cultivate dreams.

KIHEIDA: I cultivate land.

FUSAE: Dreams can outlive the land.

KIHEIDA: Dreams produce nothing but heartache. *(a beat, to* HAJIME) Do you dream?

HAJIME: Why, no, sir.

KIHEIDA: Smart man.

(FUSAE *offers* HAJIME *some fruit. He accepts it with a bow of his head. As she hands the plate to* HAJIME, KIHEIDA *immediately takes it for himself and devours another slice of fruit. He is oblivious to his rudeness, though* FUSAE *and* HAJIME *exchange a glance.* HAJIME *finds it amusing.* FUSAE *removes a letter from her kimono. Upon seeing it,* KIHEIDA'S *countenance darkens.)*

FUSAE: Otoosan. I ask again. Please read this letter.

KIHEIDA: Nan ka?

FUSAE: You know what it is. *(to* HAJIME) It came two weeks ago.

HAJIME *(nods knowingly):* The Yankee pigs are coming for your land, Shimada-san.

(HARUKO SHIMADA, *twenty-five, enters. In kimono, she is a handsome woman with an air of seriousness and devotion. The essence of deference, she is reluctant to interrupt.)*

HARUKO: Ohayo gozaimasu.

HAJIME: Ah, ohayo, Haruko-san.

HARUKO *(flustered by* HAJIME'S *attention):* How are you this morning?

HAJIME: Now I am very well. *(offers her something wrapped in rice paper)* Doozo.

HARUKO: Doomo arigato. *(opens it to reveal a beautiful red leaf)* How exquisite.

HAJIME: I found it in the mountains.

HARUKO: May I keep it, Otoosan?

KIHEIDA *(beaming):* I suppose.

HARUKO *(sees the produce):* Mah, so many fruits and vegetables! *(inspects the box)*

HAJIME *(stops her):* Be careful! *(takes out a small package)* Poison.

HARUKO: Poison?

KIHEIDA: Nan ka? It isn't that bad yet, is it, Takemoto-kun? *(laughs)*

HAJIME: Many rodents in the country now. They feasted for so long on the bodies left behind by the bombs that they wait to be fed again.

HARUKO: We must save the best cucumbers for next week. I shall tell Yoko to make o-tsukemono for Setsuko.

HAJIME *(trying to hide his interest):* Setsuko-san is coming home?

HARUKO: She never should have left, not with Mother feeling ill.

FUSAE: I have never felt better. And Setsuko is not coming home for burdens. She is coming home for the joy of family.

HARUKO: Yes, Mother. You are quite right. Setsuko must be working hard at dressmaking school.

FUSAE: So do not belabor or exaggerate my fatigue.

KIHEIDA: Setsuko's telegram says she is tired of staying in Kobe and listening to her cousin's mouth all the time. That is why she is coming home.

FUSAE: Otoosan. Setchan never said that about Fumiko. She has been at dressmaking school for five months. Too long. She wants to return to the quiet of the country.

HAJIME: She is a high-spirited girl. The country will be boring to her now.

KIHEIDA: Well, she belongs here. Too many Yankee vermin in Kobe.

HARUKO: That is why I did not consider dressmaking school.

KIHEIDA: My wise one. The Yankees have tails, you know, like a beast. They rape you if you so much as look at them.

FUSAE: They do not have tails.

KIHEIDA: How do you know?

FUSAE: Because they are human and humans do not have tails. Do not worry about Setchan. I am sure cousin Fumiko is taking care of her.

KIHEIDA: I have my doubts about Fumiko as a suitable companion. Your niece is too . . .

FUSAE: Independent?

KIHEIDA: Yes. Too independent. Like you. *(the couple exchange a smile)* Takemoto-kun, why don't you accompany Haruko for a walk in my beautiful orchard? The trees are full of persimmons, just waiting to be picked, like the heart of a young girl.

HAJIME: But my work.

KIHEIDA: Ah, iki nasai, iki nasai. I will take care of this.

(KIHEIDA *watches with pleasure as* HAJIME *and* HARUKO *prepare to exit.)*

HARUKO: So kind of you to accompany me, Takemoto-san.

HAJIME: Please, Haruko-san . . . call me Hajime.

(They exit as she blushes at his forwardness.)

KIHEIDA: Yoko!

(The tiny, humble YOKO SAGAMI *enters. She is eighteen. She wears work garments.)*

YOKO: Hai.

KIHEIDA *(an order)*: Sake, sake!

(YOKO *and* FUSAE *exchange a disapproving glance with regard to his tone.* YOKO *bows and exits.* KIHEIDA *picks up the whole persimmon, polishes it, and admires its sheen as he holds it up.)*

KIHEIDA: The taste of the future, my wife. Soon our daughters will marry and all will be well. The inn will be rebuilt and the farmland will thrive again. Yes, trust in Takemoto-kun. He's an enterprising young man.

FUSAE: It is not easy to rebuild the past.

KIHEIDA: There is only the past. The future always is uncertain.

FUSAE *(holds out the letter)*: Otoosan, please. We must respect the occupation. This letter from the American general, it says . . .

KIHEIDA *(throws the letter aside)*: Occupation. Yankee word for stealing our land and spreading mindless democracy.

FUSAE *(retrieves the letter):* We may only have a few acres of rice left. The orchard is a certain loss. *(a beat)* Anta, I have been thinking . . . what if we divided up the land ourselves and took a step toward being part of this future that the Americans plan for us?

KIHEIDA: Have you lost your mind? This estate has been managed to perfection, passed from father to son for millennia. You ask me to turn it over to peasants? For free? Did you read those books our guest left at the inn? Americans did not give their land to their slaves. Democracy seems a matter of mere convenience and privilege.

FUSAE: If we act now, strangers will not come into our midst waving documents and guns and telling us who shall have what part of our land. And that will not be the end of it. Next we will have to entertain Americans at our inn.

KIHEIDA *(a sharp, cutting glance at her):* No more hairy white devils at my inn.

FUSAE *(quietly):* Please, if you must speak of him, refer to him with the same respect he gave to you.

KIHEIDA: The Dutchman. *(a momentarily quiet voice)* No more. *(tends to one of his plants to calm himself)*

FUSAE: The Yankees control our country now.

KIHEIDA: Our Imperial Forces will rise again. Nippon has *never* lost a war.

FUSAE: Until a year ago.

KIHEIDA: I should not discuss politics with you.

FUSAE: They may be politics, Otoosan, but they are also truth.

KIHEIDA: Sometimes you talk as if you want our country to change.

FUSAE: No. The war has been everyone's tragedy. *(sits as if resigned to her fate)* It is so quiet here in the country. Matsuyama was a nice city.

KIHEIDA: *Is* a nice city.

FUSAE: Only the ghost of it remains. So here we are in the country. I walk the orchard and pick persimmon blossoms to hide in my books and remember after the orchard is gone.

KIHEIDA: You will pick persimmons here when you are ninety.

FUSAE: Once the tenants take over the land, they will grow rice. It is more profitable than the fruit.

KIHEIDA: The orchard is a part of you. It will remain intact.

FUSAE: Will they let us continue to live here?

KIHEIDA: Living here is good.

FUSAE: Yes.

KIHEIDA: Perhaps it is my presence that tarnishes the luster of the provincial life.

FUSAE *(finding him ridiculous):* Otoosan, please.

(KIHEIDA grunts, ignores her, and prepares a game of go. FUSAE straightens up as YOKO returns with KIHEIDA's sake. She serves it shrouded in her meekness.)

YOKO: May I treat you with anything else, Shimada-san?

KIHEIDA: Do you have dreams, too, Yoko, like my wife and my daughters?

YOKO *(surprised at the question):* Why, yes!

KIHEIDA: Do you dream of dresses and the best tea?

YOKO: No, Shimada-san.

KIHEIDA: What do you dream about then?

YOKO *(proudly):* Of living like an empress.

KIHEIDA *(laughs):* And how does an empress live?

YOKO: I am not certain.

KIHEIDA *(to FUSAE):* See? They dream only of uncertainties. How can they manage land with such limited vision?

FUSAE: Yoko-chan, you may go. Thank you. Bring us more fruit, please.

YOKO: Yes. *(looks at KIHEIDA without speaking)*

KIHEIDA *(impatiently):* Yes? What is it?

YOKO: I dream of lipstick as red as persimmon, too!

(YOKO *runs out. As* FUSAE *prepares to exit:*)

KIHEIDA: Oi.

FUSAE: Hai.

KIHEIDA: It *is* quiet here, na.

FUSAE: Sometimes I sleep so much, I think I will keep on sleeping forever.

KIHEIDA: I am sorry you are in pain. *(placing blame)* Yankee pigs.

FUSAE: The Americans did not do this to me. The doctor said the pains are not related to the fall.

KIHEIDA: I remember you running in the early morning light. Darkness and confusion, bombs falling everywhere. I tried to catch you, but you ran so much faster than me. Like a deer. People trampled over you. *(a beat)* I will bring in a city doctor to see you.

FUSAE: Do not make such a fuss.

KIHEIDA: Fusae. The country would be *too* quiet without you.

(*He feigns deep, vocal involvement in his game to evade emotion. As she watches him with affection, blackout.*)

Scene Two

(*Lights fade in downstage right accompanied by the sounds of a city. Kobe, Japan. Enter* SETSUKO. *She wears a beautiful kimono and walks with a slow, graceful gait. She carries an armful of books, a furoshiki full of dressmaking paraphernalia, and a packet of patterns in her hand. Her cousin* FUMIKO *dressed in American clothes, walks briskly a step ahead of her.* FUMIKO *is willful; she knows she is lovely. She wears an American ensemble including hat and gloves. Offstage, a horn beeps and a U.S. Army helmet rolls onstage in front of the women. They stop abruptly and look in the direction from which it came. Enter* CREED, *a handsome and regal African American with a gentle smile.* FUMIKO'S *eyes grow wide at the sight of* CREED. *But* CREED *sees only Setsuko, who is immediately shy and deferential.* SETSUKO *drops down on her knees and bows, not looking up at him.* FUMIKO *screams in shock and faints.* SETSUKO *is afraid to get up and help her.* CREED *takes out a handkerchief and pats* FUMIKO'S *brow.)*

SETSUKO: Please forgive our clumsiness, honorable American.

CREED: You didn't do anything wrong. Is she going to be okay?

SETSUKO *(still not looking up):* She has never seen . . . one of you. *(a beat)* I have never seen one of you either. *(looks and quickly looks away)*

CREED: A colored man, you mean.

SETSUKO: Yes. We apologize for our rudeness.

CREED: Maybe I was driving too fast—or paying attention to something other than my driving. Miss? Please stand up or look up or something.

SETSUKO *(barely daring to look up):* Forgive me.

CREED: Will you please stop apologizing? There's so much charm in this country that I just might choke on it. Gee, she's really out cold.

SETSUKO *(represses a giggle, as does* CREED*):* It is funny to see her in this state. She is usually so . . . perfect.

(FUMIKO *starts to revive. She sees* CREED *and screams again.* SETSUKO *muffles it with her hand.* FUMIKO *sits up and stares at* CREED.*)*

FUMIKO: What are you?

CREED *(a gentle smile):* A human being.

FUMIKO: I am sorry. I've never seen one quite like you. What do they call you?

CREED: Negro, colored, other things I don't want to repeat in front of ladies. But I call myself a colored man because my mama was red and my papa was brown.

FUMIKO: Are there many of you . . . colored skins?

CREED: Brown, yellow, dark brown. You name it. We got it.

(SETSUKO *retrieves the helmet, bows, and hands it to* CREED.*)*

231

CREED: Thank you. Would you ladies like a ride in my jeep?

FUMIKO *(points toward audience)*: Look, Setchan! That mama-san is already staring at us! Like we just dropped off the moon or something! *(waves at the offstage mama-san, speaks to mama-san)* "God bless America!" "Hail to the emperor!"

SETSUKO: Fumiko-san, enough. A crowd is gathering.

FUMIKO *(to CREED)*: We would love to take that ride. What is your name?

CREED: Creed Banks.

SETSUKO: A pleasure to make your acquaintance, sir.

FUMIKO: Oh stop with the bowing, cousin! *(to CREED)* She is from the provinces. She does not know that you people do not bow.

(CREED helps her stand and SETSUKO dusts dirt from her dress. He bows to SETSUKO.)

CREED: Very pleased to make your acquaintance. *(quickly, to FUMIKO without a bow)* And yours, too. *(smiles and bows formally)*

(FUMIKO stares at CREED again in renewed awe, as CREED picks up SETSUKO's belongings and gestures for them to go ahead of him toward the offstage jeep. She breaks out in a grin, having decided that she likes him.)

FUMIKO: Imagine that! A brown American!

(Lights crossfade to Scene Three.)

Scene Three

(Later that evening at the SHIMADA estate. KIHEIDA tends to the flowers in his garden as YOKO cleans in the house. Enter SETSUKO. She wears a kimono and carries a valise, a furoshiki full of gifts, and a branch of persimmon tree with a fruit on it. She manages to walk up behind her father without his taking notice. A smile on her face, she leans over and whispers in his ear.)

SETSUKO: Otoosan. Tadaima.

KIHEIDA *(jumps in surprise)*: Ah! Setchan! *(they bow formally)* Oi, oi.

FUSAE *(offstage)*: Hai, hai. (FUSAE *emerges from the upstage exit.* YOKO *bows in the doorway.)*

YOKO *(excitedly)*: Setchan. Okaeri nasai.

FUSAE *(exuberant at her daughter's return)*: Okaeri nasai. It is good to have you home.

SETSUKO: I walked through the orchard first. *(a beat)* It looked different. When I picked the fruit, I thought I heard a woman sigh with mournful exhaustion. The sound echoed through the orchard and came back to wrap around me.

FUSAE: Spirits of peasants who knew nothing but toiling our land all their lives. Sometimes in the dawn, I hear them, too.

SETSUKO: What misery.

KIHEIDA: They had work and we took care of them. What do you propose? That we go work our land ourselves? Will you lift up your pretty kimono and wade knee-deep in the muddy earth to grow rice for the entire prefecture? Will you use your delicate shoulders to tote baskets of persimmons to market?

SETSUKO: If I must, then I will. *(holds the fruit in her hand)* We take these for granted. For people like Yoko-san, they are the finest dessert. I will not ever take them for granted anymore. I have eaten insects to stay alive. I have shredded kimono to use as towels.

KIHEIDA: Enough. All right. I will be nicer to Yoko. What else can I do to appease the spirits?

SETSUKO: What I can do is teach their children English.

KIHEIDA: English? *(laughs)* The Yankees will leave in a few years and it will no longer be the fashion.

SETSUKO: It is not fashion. It is the future.

(KIHEIDA *dismisses her talk with a wave of his hand while mother and daughter exchange a knowing look.* HARUKO *enters from the upstage exit and bows at the doorway as* FUSAE *beckons* SETSUKO *to come inside.)*

SETSUKO: Tadaima, Oneesan.

HARUKO: Okaeri nasai.

(As SETSUKO *removes her shoes and enters, her father following suit,* YOKO *straightens their shoes and then exits to the kitchen.)*

FUSAE: Five months away seems like five years, my little one. But you are home now.

KIHEIDA: Yes. Where it is safe.

SETSUKO: Safe?

KIHEIDA: The islands are infested.

HARUKO: So, ne. *(to* SETSUKO *as if naming a dread disease)* Americans.

(The family sits as YOKO *brings a tray of tea. She and* SETSUKO *exchange intimate smiles.)*

YOKO: Setsuko-san. You look very good. *(exits as* KIHEIDA *waves her away)*

KIHEIDA: So how is Fumiko?

SETSUKO: She is very busy with her new job.

FUSAE: And Kobe?

SETSUKO: Full of foreigners. Many new military buildings.

KIHEIDA: No wonder you wanted to come home.

SETSUKO *(slides a gift toward her father):* Hai. Omiyage.

KIHEIDA: Ah, doomo. *(his mind on other things)* Haruko. How old are you now?

HARUKO: Twenty-five.

KIHEIDA: And, Setsuko, you?

SETSUKO: Twenty.

KIHEIDA: Oi. How old were you when we married?

FUSAE *(a whisper):* Ju-hachi sai.

KIHEIDA: Nan ka? Speak up.

FUSAE: *Eighteen.*

KIHEIDA *(grunts with pleasure):* Time for marriage now that this war is behind us.

(SETSUKO *observes* HARUKO'S *delight.*)

SETSUKO: It seems Oneesan has a secret.

KIHEIDA: Do not worry, Setsuko. I will find someone proper for you, too.

FUSAE *(opens the gift; it is a box of American chocolates):* Ah, sweets.

KIHEIDA: Nan ka.

SETSUKO: American chocolates.

(FUSAE *offers him candy. He examines the box and grunts in disapproval.*)

KIHEIDA: Yankee garbage.

SETSUKO: Fumiko bought it for me at the P.X.

KIHEIDA: P.X.? What is the P.X.?

(HAJIME *enters from the farmland in work clothes.*)

SETSUKO: A store built by Americans.

HAJIME: Good evening.

KIHEIDA: You remember Takemoto-kun.

SETSUKO: Yes. Your father worked our land. You taught me how to ride a bicycle.

HAJIME: I live here now, in the inn. Helping out. I have spent the last six months working on the inn and cleaning up the farmland so we can start harvesting rice again.

KIHEIDA: He works hard, asks for nothing.

HAJIME: You have grown quite a bit from the little girl who used to play in the orchard.

SETSUKO: Yes, that was a precious time.

HAJIME: Well, back on the road for me. Night is the only time to get the lumber out of the mountains.

HARUKO: Be careful, ne, Takemoto-san. Driving at night is tiring.

HAJIME: You are too kind.

KIHEIDA: Come, Hajime-kun. Show me how my fence is progressing before you go. You must eat first, too—with the family, na. *(to* FUSAE*)* Oi. Hajime-kun will be joining us for dinner.

FUSAE: Hai, hai.

(The men exit to the farmland. The women share the candy. HARUKO *appears deep in thought.)*

HARUKO: Okaasan? Why were you so old when you married father?

FUSAE: I did not marry him. He married me.

*(*SETSUKO *finds this amusing;* FUSAE *smiles at her, but* HARUKO *silences her with a firm gaze.)*

FUSAE: Our lives are in your father's hands, ne . . . just as my life was in my father's hands and my mother's life was in her father's hands.

*(*FUSAE *grows tense; she shakes off a rush and holds her hand to her chest as if in pain.* SETSUKO *shows concern, but* FUSAE *smiles and dismisses it.)*

FUSAE: I am going to rest before dinner.

HARUKO: Hai, Okaasan.

*(*FUSAE *exits upstage as the girls stand and bow.)*

SETSUKO: Haruko? Is Mother not feeling well?

HARUKO *(evasive)*: She is tired. We are all tired from working to make everything like it was. *(retrieves a basket, removes persimmons from it, and begins to polish them;* SETSUKO *observes)*

SETSUKO: Why didn't anyone write me about Okaasan's exhaustion?

HARUKO: It is the breast injury from her fall.

SETSUKO: When I left for Kobe, it was almost healed.

HARUKO: Ie. Infection.

SETSUKO *(tries to hide her fear)*: Is she . . . is she going to be all right?

HARUKO: Her nerves are bad. *(a beat)* The war affects us all in strange ways, ne. Sometimes she shakes so hard that she cannot knit anymore. Remember how she used to be able to knit a dress in a day? *(a beat)* Setchan, if I ever get married, promise me you will stay here and take care of her.

SETSUKO: You know I will.

HARUKO: It may require you putting off marriage.

SETSUKO *(she nods; a beat)*: Oneesan. How do you think Mother felt when she had to marry a stranger.

HARUKO: Her father knew him. He was not a stranger.

SETSUKO: At least a woman cannot blame her own stupidity for making the wrong choice.

HARUKO *(lost in her own concerns)*: Setchan, I am an old maid. Mother was younger than us when she married Father.

SETSUKO: We are young, Oneesan.

HARUKO: No . . . we are unforgivably old.

SETSUKO *(with gentle amusement)*: Takemoto-san seems willing to forgive you, my "ancient" sister.

(HARUKO *stops polishing the fruit and sits back with a smile. They giggle.* SETSUKO *removes a small gift from her handbag and gives it to* HARUKO.)

SETSUKO: Hai. Omiyage.

HARUKO *(opens it quickly; it's a hair ornament)*: Mah! Kirei desho!

(HARUKO *kneels in front of* SETSUKO, *who arranges* HARUKO'S *hair with the ornament.*)

HARUKO: Setchan, can you not see us both, side by side with our husbands, our children playing in the garden? The inn will be busy. We will be in Matsuyama again. And there will be four, no maybe six, grandchildren for our deserving parents.

(SETSUKO *places the ornament as* HARUKO *beams with joy.*)

SETSUKO: Dreams can be exhausting, ne . . .

HARUKO: Not mine. Are yours? *(as* SETSUKO *hesitates)* You never speak of your dreams, Setchan.

SETSUKO: My dreams are too daring sometimes.

HARUKO: Tell me a dream.

SETSUKO: No . . . I think not. *(a pause)* Oneesan? What does it feel like to be . . . in love?

HARUKO *(dreamily, truly feeling what she's saying):* Well . . . I do not actually know . . . but I imagine it feels like being caressed by the wings of a million fluttering butterflies . . .

SETSUKO *(a gentle smile):* Artful conjecture.

HARUKO *(composing herself):* Well, as I said, I do not actually know.

SETSUKO *(testing the waters):* Fumiko says many Japanese are marrying Americans. (HARUKO *gasps*) Honto, yo. I saw it with my own eyes, many mixed couples in Kobe.

HARUKO: Ignorance. *(firmly)* Japan has given us grace. We owe much. *(a thoughtful warning)* Besides, white men are strange, Setchan. They eat with little shovels. You have to remind them to remove their shoes at the door. They insist on holding your hand when you walk. They kiss you when everyone can see. Honto yo. They have no respect for women. No respect at all.

SETSUKO: Not all Americans are like that.

HARUKO: Ie. Barbarians, all of them. I have heard the stories. Remember the day of the big bombs? Father had to rescue you with the futon? You called them devils that day. You cursed them.

SETSUKO: That was war.

HARUKO: It still is war, Setchan, as long as they try to control our lives.

SETSUKO: Mother says people from different countries have a lot to learn from each other.

HARUKO: She had no business saying that to you.

SETSUKO: But we know why she said it. *(with hesitation)* Because of the yellow-haired man who stayed at the inn many years ago. The professor.

HARUKO *(alarmed):* You remember him?

SETSUKO: Clearly. Okaasan's friend.

HARUKO: But you were so young. *(a beat)* We must not speak of him.

SETSUKO: He was a nice kind of different. Hair as yellow as an egg yolk and eyes sea-blue. How could I forget him? *(a beat)* How could she?

HARUKO: Yellow-haired animal. He is like all the rest. They come here looking for treasures of the Far East. They see us and think we are one of them, a thing to possess, to wear on their fingers like gold rings.

SETSUKO: He wasn't like that, was he?

HARUKO: White pig.

SETSUKO: Oneesan! Such language!

HARUKO: I want everything to be like it was before the war.

SETSUKO: But that can never be, sister. We must go on with our lives.

HARUKO *(her mind on other things):* Setchan. Takemoto-san asked me to call him Hajime! (SETSUKO *smiles*) I think my marriage to Hajime-san is being arranged!

SETSUKO: See? Your life will grow rich with love and happy children. I am glad to be home to share your joy with you.

HARUKO: Truly?

SETSUKO: And to see Father and Mother again. It is difficult to be away from Mother for too long. And it is so comfortable and quiet here in the country. I can think here.

HARUKO: Think about what?

SETSUKO: About living my life.

HARUKO: Our parents plan well for us.

SETSUKO: But they did not plan for war.

HARUKO: The Americans will go back to their country one day and things will get back to normal.

SETSUKO: Will they?

HARUKO: May I tell you a secret? I thought you would meet a foreign devil and leave Nippon.

SETSUKO *(careful disbelief):* No.

HARUKO: Yes. That was my nightmare. They cast spells, you know. Worse than demons.

SETSUKO: Well, I am home now and I am never going away again, Oneesan.

HARUKO: Setchan, even after I am married, I will help you take care of Okaasan. You won't have to do it all yourself. I know you are young, and you like to travel around Nippon and do new things. I want you to have that freedom until you marry.

SETSUKO: Thank you. That means a lot to me.

HARUKO: Come. Let me show you the beautiful red leaf Takemoto-san brought back from the forest.

SETSUKO: A personal gift for you?

HARUKO: I asked Otoosan if I could keep it.

SETSUKO: When a man gives a gift of nature, it is quite serious.

HARUKO: Yes, little sister. *(a smile)* It is the beginning of my life.

(The women exit upstage as lights crossfade to Scene Four.)

Scene Four

(Music—"Tokyo Boogie Woogie," a postwar popular Japanese song—fades in as lights fade up. The next day. KIHEIDA *again adjusts the fence.* SETSUKO *passes by in the background reading a book. He smiles at this sighting and watches her as she disappears offstage. He goes into the house and moves a flower in an ikebana arrangement. Unsatisfied, he returns it to its original position. He feels the soil. Finding it dry, he takes the plant and exits to the kitchen. Immediately,* FUMIKO *enters from the roadway. She wears another American dress, gloves, and a hat. She looks around.)*

FUMIKO: Gomen kudasai! Gomen kudasai! Setchan?

(She shrugs, sits on the porch, and removes a silver cigarette box from her handbag. She takes out a cigarette, lights it, and enjoys the first drag. KIHEIDA *enters unseen by her and looks at his niece in shock.)*

KIHEIDA: Fumiko!

FUMIKO: Ara! Ojisan! *(smiles coyly as she tries to conceal the ciga-*

rette behind her) Kon'nichi wa. It has been a long time. *(bows low and daintily)*

KIHEIDA: What are you wearing?

FUMIKO *(twirls around to give a full effect):* Clothes.

KIHEIDA: Yankee clothes.

FUMIKO: Hai.

KIHEIDA *(points at her cigarette):* Hora!

FUMIKO: Ah, gomen nasai.

KIHEIDA: It is not like you. Bad manners.

FUMIKO *(she puts it out in the plant he carries; he reacts with mock indignation):* There is so much to remember when one is Japanese, ne? I've been working hard, Ojisan. Allow me at least one vice.

(He puts down his plant, removes the cigarette from it, and puts it in an ashtray. Exposing her legs in the process, FUMIKO perches on the porch and removes her high heels. Her uncle watches, shaking his head as she comes into the house. She smiles and embraces him, knowing what his reaction will be.)

KIHEIDA *(jumps in shock):* Have you gone mad?

FUMIKO: A Western custom, Ojisan.

KIHEIDA: In America, young ladies fondle their uncles?

FUMIKO: It is a sign of family affection. *(slips him a package of American cigarettes)* I have not seen you in a while, Uncle.

KIHEIDA *(takes the cigarettes and puts them in his kimono; she offers him a light and he waves her away):* All right. Enough Western indulgence. Go upstairs. Change into proper clothes.

FUMIKO *(a smile):* No.

(KIHEIDA laughs with enjoyment and pours sake. She quickly intercedes and pours it for him.)

FUMIKO: Sake, sake, sake, ne?

KIHEIDA *(laughs again at being caught):* Tell me, did you go out and buy a dress just for me?

FUMIKO: Oh, Ojisan, Setchan has told me how you fret over the Americans. Don't worry. What I wear has no bearing on the future of Nippon.

KIHEIDA: Ha. First our women put on dresses, then cut their hair, and smoke like men. What next? *(grunts)* Better dead than to let the Yankees change our lives.

FUMIKO: The Yankees are not changing my life; *I* am changing my life. All respect, Ojisan, but I have to take care of myself now.

KIHEIDA: Look at you, dressed like American whore.

FUMIKO: Ojisan, women have been wearing dresses in Nippon for several years now. Just because you are so old-fashioned—

KIHEIDA: Bad influence for Setsuko.

FUMIKO *(sharply):* No. *(more softly)* I am a good girl. But I believe in freedom, Ojisan, and I intend to have it and everything that comes with it.

KIHEIDA: You see what your Yankee freedom has done? You live in Kobe, a beautiful city ravaged by Yankee fire bombs, your own parents victims of them. How can you strut about in American clothes as Yankees walk in their ashes?

FUMIKO *(somberly):* I do not look back, Ojisan.

(He grunts in dissent as SETSUKO enters from the orchard with a basket of fruit. Upon seeing FUMIKO, SETSUKO runs to the porch, removes her shoes and enters the house.)

SETSUKO: Kon'nichi wa, Fumi-chan!

FUMIKO: Ah, kon'nichi wa, Setchan!

(They practice an embrace. KIHEIDA claps his hands together to separate them.)

KIHEIDA: Western indulgence.

FUMIKO: Mah, this constant harping about Americans. Ojisan, no Yankees are knocking at your door, and if they were, they'd probably make great sake partners for you, ne.

KIHEIDA: You have been struck by the moonlight once too often, niece.

(FUMIKO *and* SETSUKO *stifle laughter. As* KIHEIDA *reaches for his sake,* FUMIKO *moves it out of his grasp. On second thought, she pours some for herself.* SETSUKO *bows her head in amusement.* KIHEIDA *looks at his niece and simply shakes his head.* HAJIME *enters from the orchard and bows. He eyes* FUMIKO *with guarded suspicion.)*

HAJIME: Shimada-san, the fence is done. I ask that you inspect it.

KIHEIDA: Hai. Just a minute. Takemoto-kun, my niece, Kitagawa Fumiko-san. Fumiko, this is Takemoto Hajime-san.

HAJIME: Yes. You live in Kobe, do you not, Kitagawa-san?

FUMIKO: Why, yes.

HAJIME: My brother lives there.

FUMIKO: Ah. *(a beat as* HAJIME *continues to stare at her)* Yes?

HAJIME: You dress this way all the time. And always wear the hat and the gloves.

FUMIKO: Yes.

HAJIME: And you live just outside of the city, in a small white house?

FUMIKO: Yes.

HAJIME: I have heard of you.

FUMIKO: Is that so?

HAJIME: You are an—

SETSUKO *(sharply cuts him off):* Takemoto-san, you are being impolite.

HAJIME *(to* KIHEIDA): Excuse my insolence. *(to* FUMIKO) My brother knew of you when you lived here and he saw you in Kobe. I hear you have interesting friends.

SETSUKO: Kobe is full of interesting people, Takemoto-san.

KIHEIDA *(laughs):* Knowing my niece, she probably entertains all kinds of people—bohemians, actors . . . *(entreats* HAJIME *to laugh)*

FUMIKO *(stares icily at* HAJIME): Go ahead and laugh, but there will be many more like me.

KIHEIDA: Fumiko, you do not have to work. You know you are welcome to live here. *(to* HAJIME, *with apology)* She is a governess
for my wife's relatives.

HAJIME: Shimada-san, I think you should know—

FUMIKO: Shall I tell him, Takemoto-san? Or do you require the
pleasure?

HAJIME: She is an interpreter, Shimada-san.

KIHEIDA: Ah, for our government. Well, it is war time. We must all
help in whatever ways we can.

HAJIME: She does not work for the Empire.

FUMIKO *(bows to* KIHEIDA): Forgive me, ne, Ojisan. I work for the
consulate . . . the United States consulate.

*(*KIHEIDA *absorbs this, tries to pour sake, and finds none is left.
He looks at his cup and wipes off* FUMIKO's *lipstick. He looks
at her somberly.)*

KIHEIDA: How old are you, Fumiko?

FUMIKO: Thirty.

HAJIME: Thirty?

KIHEIDA: Thirty.

HAJIME: You should have been married by now, war or no war.

KIHEIDA: Takemoto-kun, please.

HAJIME *(to* KIHEIDA): Many Japanese spy for the Yankees and
many of them are women. They make friends with the Yankee
G.I.s and—

FUMIKO *(looks at* HAJIME): You are quite the annoyance, ne.

SETSUKO: Takemoto-san. My cousin likes to talk too much. She
would never make a good spy.

(As the women laugh, KIHEIDA *grunts in dismissal, in a good
humor but having heard enough of this female banter. He prepares to exit to the orchard with* HAJIME, *but stops.)*

KIHEIDA *(he glances at* FUMIKO): Hajime-kun, this brother of yours,
is he single?

FUMIKO: Ojisan!

(FUMIKO *giggles as the men exit,* HAJIME *turning at the last minute to gaze at* SETSUKO. *As soon as the men are gone,* FUMIKO's *mock giggling fades into seriousness. She gives her cousin a gentle smile. In the background,* KIHEIDA *and* HAJIME *can be seen speaking.* HAJIME *speaks in earnest while the words weigh heavily on* KIHEIDA. *He nods and nods, as* HAJIME *leads him away offstage.*)

FUMIKO: Setchan. Come back to Kobe with me. You know Creed-san's tour of duty is almost over.

SETSUKO: Fumiko, I left Kobe because I cannot see him anymore.

FUMIKO: Baka, ne. You love him. You cannot just run away from it like this. Why all of a sudden?

SETSUKO: A few days ago, I saw a woman with her half-Yankee baby. Her mother walked beside her, crying in public and hanging her head in shame.

FUMIKO: So?

SETSUKO: Your parents died in the war. Mine are still alive and I never want to make them feel like that.

FUMIKO: But you have been seeing Creed-san for almost a year.

SETSUKO: Seven months. *(a beat)* Fumi-chan, even if I did decide to see him—while he is still in Nippon—it would be difficult. I have to take care of Mother.

FUMIKO: I thought she was all right now.

SETSUKO: She has pains. The village doctor is baffled.

FUMIKO: Ara. Poor thing. But, Setchan, she cannot live forever, even if we both want her to. After she is gone, you still have to make a life for yourself.

SETSUKO: Living in Kobe with you, I really began to think I could walk onto a ship and go to America to be with Creed. *(a beat)* It was silly dreaming.

FUMIKO: Well, it is no silly dream for me, Setchan. I am going to America with Billy. I am going to be Mrs. Billy Davenport!

SETSUKO: If he comes back for you.

FUMIKO: He will come back. Listen to the American song he sang for me *(tune of "Red River Valley")* "From this Japan they say I am going. I will miss your bright eyes and sweet soul. For I know, love, that you are my sunshine. And without you my heart will grow cold."

(SETSUKO *and* FUMIKO *share a quiet smile that makes both of their eyes moisten. They practice a hug as* HARUKO *enters from upstage. Not expecting to see* FUMIKO *and not understanding the embrace, she is jarred.)*

HARUKO: Fumiko-san?

(FUMIKO, *overcome with emotion, tries to hug* HARUKO, *who flits away nervously.)*

FUMIKO: Ah, Haru-chan. How are you, little bird?

HARUKO: Thank you. I am comfortable. And you?

FUMIKO: I am filled with hope and possibilities.

HARUKO *(finding* FUMIKO *eccentric):* Fumi-chan, Setchan told me about all the Yankee buta in Kobe. Have you seen them, too?

FUMIKO: Yes, I see one every once in a while.

HARUKO *(pitying her):* Honto? Otoosan says they are pink like a pig, tall, and hairy. How can you stand to walk beside them?

FUMIKO: I stand it.

HARUKO: Do they smell?

FUMIKO: A new scent.

HARUKO: Can you imagine being alone with one of them? I am sure they do not take off their shoes. It is a guarantee they do not take a bath every night. They do not like our food. They do not know our language. Their ears and noses are so big!

FUMIKO: Haruko . . . What if I told you I was seeing an American?

HARUKO *(laughs):* Such jokes, Fumi-chan.

FUMIKO: From Boston. He has green eyes and the kindness of a woman. (HARUKO's *laughter ceases)* It is a secret, ne.

HARUKO: You are serious.

FUMIKO: I have never been more serious.

HARUKO: Baka, ne. What is the matter with you?

FUMIKO: I fell in love with him.

HARUKO: I knew it wasn't a good idea for you to live in Kobe by yourself. As soon as we heard your parents had died, Otoosan should have made you come to the country. And then when he allowed Setchan to go live with you. That was too much. *(a beat)* At least Setsuko knows her own head. She would never be wild like you.

SETSUKO: Oneesan, I have met Fumiko-san's friend; he is very nice.

HARUKO: You've *talked* to a barbarian?

SETSUKO: You have never traveled out of the provinces, Haruko-san. You have never even seen an American. I know the war was a bad experience for us all, but it's over now. Americans and Japanese are living together in Kobe and Tokyo and all the other American bases in Nippon. *(a beat)* It is only natural that some of those people are going to fall in love.

HARUKO *(to FUMIKO)*: You go back to Kobe, ne, Fumiko-san. You have no place here. *(she gets up to go, stops, and looks at FUMIKO)* Are you not afraid that I will tell my father?

FUMIKO: I am not afraid of anything. I cannot afford to be.

(HARUKO exits.)

FUMIKO: You must come back with me.

SETSUKO: Can you not see that it would cause my father great pain?

FUMIKO: And when your father is dead? Then what? Who will tell you how to live your life? Who can get back the dreams that you throw away today?

SETSUKO: I cannot be selfish.

FUMIKO: And I cannot be stupid.

(KIHEIDA reenters. His face is grave and withdrawn. He does not look at either SETSUKO or FUMIKO. Both women bow to him.)

SETSUKO: Does the fence look as beautiful as before, Father?

KIHEIDA: Its beauty is not important. Its function is my concern. *(a beat)* Setsuko. You are not to return to Kobe again. In fact, you will not be leaving the estate again.

SETSUKO: Yes, Father.

KIHEIDA (to FUMIKO): First Takemoto-san tells me you work for the Yankees and now Haruko-san tells me you sleep with them, too. You are no longer my niece.

FUMIKO: This is a new era for Nippon, Uncle.

KIHEIDA: It may be a new era, but I am an old man and I live by old ways.

FUMIKO: If she wants to come to Kobe, she can come.

SETSUKO: If I *want* to come . . .

KIHEIDA: She will go nowhere, or she will go with the knowledge that she no longer has a family.

FUMIKO: This provincial close-mindedness and arrogance is what brought our country to its knees.

(KIHEIDA *advances on her as if angry enough to strike her, but he restrains himself.* FUMIKO *is shocked into silence.*)

FUMIKO: We cannot go on living like this.

SETSUKO: It takes a long time for the caterpillar to become the butterfly, ne, Fumiko-san. Yes, Nippon is changing, but she must change in her own way.

FUMIKO: She doesn't get her way anymore. It is the morning after a terrible storm and the Yankee benevolence is something we must respect.

KIHEIDA: Your way of showing respect is a disgrace. Take leave of us, Fumiko-san.

FUMIKO (bows deeply): Uncle. (reaches out to embrace Setsuko, but KIHEIDA bars her path) Setchan, be well.

SETSUKO: Good luck to you, cousin.

(FUMIKO, saddened, departs, exiting offstage.)

KIHEIDA: You agree with her brazenness, do you not, little one?

SETSUKO: I am not so little anymore, Father, but, yes, I agree that a new day is coming and we must be ready for it or expire.

KIHEIDA: Your cousin. She is leaving us.

SETSUKO: You asked her to leave, did you not?

KIHEIDA: I mean she is going to . . . to America, yes?

(SETSUKO *nods. She tries to exit but stops when her father gazes at her directly.*)

KIHEIDA: I require a cup of tea, little dove.

SETSUKO: Would you like anything else, Father?

KIHEIDA: Yes. *(a beat)* I would like a promise from you.

SETSUKO: I cannot promise anyone anything in these times, Father. I can only follow my instincts and they have led me here, to the sanctuary of our home.

(*Lost in thought,* KIHEIDA *begins to exit.*)

KIHEIDA *(speaking to himself):* Yes. You will be safe here. *(exits)*

SETSUKO: If only being safe was all that I wanted out of life.

(*Lights crossfade to two spotlights, one downstage right and one downstage left.* SETSUKO *and* CREED *appear in these. He writes a letter; she does the same. They alternately contemplate words and write.*)

SETSUKO: I pledge my love to you.

CREED: I never expected to fall in love.

SETSUKO: I am not worthy of you, as my country is to blame for this terrible war.

CREED: I'm not worthy of you, as we have killed your people and ravaged your country.

SETSUKO: Nothing in my history or upbringing prepared me for falling in love with a foreigner.

CREED: The thought of living without you is unbearable.

SETSUKO: America is so far away. How could people ever accept me? How could they forget the war?

CREED: Life isn't easy in America, Setsuko. People are nearly hysterical about Japanese Americans, so I'm sure it would be twice as difficult for you. The "land of the free" is a myth they don't even sell to Negroes. But, I swear to God, I'll protect you. I'll give you the best life I can.

SETSUKO: My mother is not well. I must be near her.

CREED: I know it is too much to expect you to marry a colored man and leave your country, but . . .

SETSUKO: Are there persimmons in America?

CREED: I don't care what happens. I'm always going to love you. I wish you could hear me. I wish you could know how you have become all women to me.

(The spotlights begin to merge in the middle, a blue light out of time. The couple draw closer to each other as SETSUKO *speaks:)*

SETSUKO: You draw near and the beast retreats in the shadows. I can see the stars and children smile again. This is magic. You have given me back my dreams.

(Close now, they touch each others' faces and finally kiss deeply. But SETSUKO *looks up suddenly in fear and runs out as* CREED *looks around in bewilderment. Blackout. Lights cross-fade to Scene Five.)*

Scene Five

(A week later. Peace reigns in the Shimada household. It is twilight. FUMIKO *appears. She sneaks into the house, startling* YOKO, *who sleeps in the front room. She cups her hands over* YOKO's *mouth.)*

FUMIKO: Keep quiet. I must see Setsuko.

YOKO: You are not supposed to be here!

FUMIKO: Wake her and bring her here. Be quiet.

YOKO: I will not help you take her away from us.

*(*FUMIKO *thinks quickly and takes a tube of lipstick from her purse.)*

FUMIKO: Here. A gift for you.

YOKO: Kuchibeni!

*(*YOKO, *totally disarmed, takes the gift and* FUMIKO's *compact. She applies the lipstick on much too liberally. She looks like a clown. Both the women stifle giggles.)*

YOKO: Is it American-made? (FUMIKO's *nod thrills her*) Yankee lipstick, mah!

(YOKO *willingly exits to do* FUMIKO's *bidding. Shortly,* SETSUKO *appears, her head still full of sleep.* YOKO *ties up her yukata as* FUMIKO *helps.*)

SETSUKO: What has happened?

(FUMIKO *stares at* YOKO, *who is all ears.*)

FUMIKO: You must come with me to the pier. *(to* YOKO*)* Is the lipstick thick enough to keep your lips sealed?

(YOKO *nods as* FUMIKO *and* SETSUKO *exit. The sound of the tide fades in. Lights crossfade to an area downstage that represents the pier. As* SETSUKO *and* FUMIKO *appear on bicycles, the tide sounds fade out. The women get off their bicycles and walk downstage.* FUMIKO *is looking for someone.*)

SETSUKO: Why have you done this, Fumiko-san?

FUMIKO: Do not ask me. Ask him. Or ask yourself.

(CREED *enters. In his military dress uniform, the handsome African American first sergeant walks with a regal bearing.* FUMIKO *disappears as* CREED *approaches* SETSUKO.*)

SETSUKO: Creed.

CREED: Setsuko.

SETSUKO: Did Fumiko deliver my letter?

CREED: Yes. I read it many times.

SETSUKO: You look well.

CREED: Setsuko . . . in a few weeks, I am leaving Japan forever.

SETSUKO: There is no forever, Creed. I have told you this. Now is all there is, nothing more than the present moment.

CREED: I had hoped that we could have "now."

SETSUKO: You are thirteen years older than me. I was a little girl when you became a man.

CREED: But you're a woman now. This war has given you a wisdom beyond your years.

SETSUKO *(finally looks at him):* I wish I could say yes and go with you to your America, but this is my home.

CREED: But you love me.

SETSUKO: Yes. That is the word I ascribe to this feeling.

CREED: Setsuko, my mother left the reservation to be with my father.

SETSUKO: What is a reservation?

CREED: A place where they keep Indians.

SETSUKO: Who is "they"?

CREED: Americans.

SETSUKO: But aren't Indians Americans?

CREED: Yes.

SETSUKO: So you are already mixed up.

CREED: Mixed.

SETSUKO: Do you ever think about how our children would live in this world? Not Japanese, not Indian, not colored?

CREED: They would live with honesty, just like we have. They would be all three races—something new. *(a beat)* Setsuko, haven't you ever asked your father for anything? Haven't you ever told him you were going to do something and then did it?

SETSUKO: Once I told him I was going to cut my hair . . . and I cut my hair.

CREED: And what did he do?

SETSUKO: He shouted at me and treated me like a girl who would cut off her hair.

CREED: Tell him you will cut your hair again.

(She shakes her head. He stands behind her and touches her hair.)

CREED: Don't you want to? *(she steps away)* You must cut it.

SETSUKO: He will not allow it.

CREED: You'll cut it, if that's what you want. Setsuko, it only happens like this once. There comes a time when a daughter, regardless of where she is from, becomes a woman. Like my mother. She left everything behind for my father.

SETSUKO: And you are asking me to do the same for you. You are asking me to leave behind my family and my country . . . for you.

CREED *(humbly):* Yes.

SETSUKO: You must understand, Creed. When I look into my father's eyes, it is not his anger about the war or his hatred of Americans that weakens me. It is this overwhelming sadness that everything is lost—our livelihood, our pride, and our purity. My father does not know how to go on. I have to be here to help him. *(a beat)* As you see, my hair is long again. *(a beat)* I was wrong to cut it, and I will never cut it again.

CREED: I've always cut my own hair and never considered it anybody's business when I did it.

SETSUKO: And *you* are an American.

(CREED *fumbles with his cap and it falls to the ground.* SETSUKO *sweeps it up, bows to him, smiles, and hands it to him. On second thought, she takes it and carefully places it on his head. She finds just the right angle to complement his face. He tries to smile. Both are sad.)*

SETSUKO: I will try to come to the pier to say good-bye to you, but my mother is ill.

CREED: Yes. I'm sorry to hear that she's ill. Can I do anything? Maybe bring medicines for her?

SETSUKO: A doctor from Osaka will be here next week to see why her pain persists.

CREED: Setsuko, do you think you might change your mind about going?

SETSUKO: No.

CREED: Are you absolutely certain?

SETSUKO: You must go. *(a beat)* Do not forget me.

(FUMIKO *appears. She sees the failure on their faces and it saddens her.)*

FUMIKO: We cannot make you think differently about these matters?

SETSUKO: You are looking at raindrops, Fumiko. I must consider the storm.

(CREED *walks toward* FUMIKO *and they are about to exit.*)

CREED: Setsuko. Promise me one thing. If you do change your mind . . .

(*He stops, as if giving up. But she stares at him and offers a smile that encourages him.*)

SETSUKO: Yes?

CREED: Fumiko will always know where to find me. I will come back for you. Somehow, some way. I mean it.

SETSUKO: I do not doubt you for a moment.

(*He runs back and brazenly kisses her. They stand back and look at one another, and then embrace with great affection.* FUMIKO *bows to her, and* FUMIKO *and* CREED *exit.* SETSUKO *gets on her bicycle. She is about to depart as the glow of a cigarette in the darkness stops her. Fearing her safety, she backs up and trips over her bicycle. She falls. Her kimono opens to reveal her calves. Before she can get up, the man—*HAJIME—*behind the cigarette glow appears. He stands over her and stares at her legs.*)

HAJIME: So now I know your secret dreams, Setsuko.

(SETSUKO *covers her legs, stands, and glares at* HAJIME.)

SETSUKO: You know nothing.

HAJIME: I know everything about you. Because I've loved you since the first time I showed you how to ride a bicycle.

SETSUKO (*looking at him as if he has lost his senses; trying to remain calm*): I was eight then. You were eighteen.

(*She tries to move away. He stops her.*)

HAJIME: But you had the face of an angel.

SETSUKO: Leave me alone, Takemoto-san.

(*He tries to impede her progress. He almost cannot restrain his passion for her.*)

SETSUKO: Stop it!

HAJIME: Please. Hear me out.

SETSUKO *(realizes his intentions, indignant):* You are my sister's intended.

HAJIME *(reaching out to touch her):* You and I are meant for each other—a strong man and a strong woman.

(He touches her and she pulls away. He grabs her and holds onto her tightly. She is not strong enough to break the embrace.)

HAJIME: I can take care of you in the way you are accustomed. You can live on your father's estate your life long, have your children there, and walk in your persimmon orchard reading your endless books.

SETSUKO: My father is not going to give you our land. He has made promises to you only because of Haruko.

HAJIME *(throwing her aside):* The land will be mine. It is *my* father's right. It is the one thing the Yankees are good for.

SETSUKO: You stay out of my way, you behind of a raccoon. *(a beat, with a resolution that frightens him)* I shall never speak to you again.

(She cuts a sharp, brisk path around him; mounts her bicycle. He pulls her off the bicycle and forces her to kiss him. She bites his lip and he jumps back in pain.)

HAJIME: Itai. Is this what the Yankee pigs teach a young lady?

SETSUKO: You are a beast.

(She exits. For a moment, he is forlorn, but, as he grinds his cigarette out in the dirt, his forlornness turns to bitter determination as lights crossfade to Scene Six.)

Scene Six

(Lights downstage, right. It is day. MITCHELL DANIELS, *a handsome African American soldier, posts a sign in Japanese on a tree. He has several other signs tucked under his arm. He exits. Shortly,* YOKO *walks by carrying a basket full of vegetables.*

She stops and struggles to read the sign. What she reads amazes her and excites her. She is full of hope and glee. She stands with a new pride and straightens her yukata. SETSUKO *appears.)*

SETSUKO: What is it, Yoko-chan?

YOKO: It is the land resettlement law! I thought it was only gossip, but it is true!

SETSUKO *(reads from the sign):* "Landlords will be required to make a gift of land to each tenant who has managed landlord's properties for . . . ." *(she shakes off an emotional chill)* So . . . the future begins.

YOKO: What will I do? How will I manage?

SETSUKO: Come. Let me help you with these vegetables.

YOKO: Oh no, no. Too heavy for you.

SETSUKO: Nonsense. *(a beat)* Yoko, what will you do with your land?

YOKO: I will build a house and grow rice so I can live. And I will grow a persimmon orchard for you and your mother.

(The two stare at each other with understanding and affection and carry the basket of vegetables off together. Lights crossfade to Scene Seven.)

Scene Seven

(As lights come up on the house, YOKO *serves tea and fruit to* FUSAE *and* KIHEIDA. FUSAE *begins to pare the fruit, but it is too tiring.* YOKO *takes over for her and enjoys being able to hear their conversation.)*

FUSAE: I tell you, I do not wish to see a doctor.

KIHEIDA: It is not a choice.

FUSAE: A lack of choices has never stopped me before.

*(*KIHEIDA *coughs and the smell of his breath makes* FUSAE *draw back.* YOKO *draws back, too, but is afraid to insult* KIHEIDA, *so she smiles at him instead.)*

FUSAE: You smell like sake and it is only nine o'clock.

(He playfully pulls at her kimono; she is not amused. He laughs and tries to embrace her again. She shrinks back in pain. YOKO *runs out in embarrassment.)*

KIHEIDA: What is it?

FUSAE: The pain in my breast comes back again and again. There. It's gone away now.

(And so he tries to touch her again. She pulls away gently and reties her obi.)

KIHEIDA: In this way, you have not been a good wife.

FUSAE: In this way, you have found many other "wives." Your trips to Tokyo grew quite frequent before the war.

KIHEIDA: I will not go to Tokyo again, if that is what you want.

FUSAE: No. You will only go to another city instead or back to the girl in Kumamachi.

KIHEIDA: I have always had to go somewhere. You were so busy at the inn, managing it like a man.

FUSAE: Someone had to do it.

KIHEIDA: You liked the work, especially because of our Dutch "guest."

FUSAE: He was that and only that. A guest.

KIHEIDA: You spent a lot of time . . . walking in the orchard with him.

FUSAE: He was teaching me English.

KIHEIDA: Yes. I am certain he was a very good teacher.

FUSAE: He was . . . different. *(a beat)* Otoosan, ne, that was a long time ago. We are husband and wife. *(a beat)* That is not going to change.

KIHEIDA: Unfortunately for you.

FUSAE: Do not degrade yourself so. It is unbecoming for a gentleman.

KIHEIDA: I am not a gentleman. Not anymore. Not without land. Not without an empire to be proud of.

(He grunts, removes a flask from his kimono sleeve, and is about to pour more sake. She tries to take it away but cannot.)

FUSAE: Very well. Drink yourself to death.

KIHEIDA: Helps me to forget the war. Helps me to forget . . . this marriage.

FUSAE: You pointed your finger at a poor farmer's daughter, and I became yet another possession for a rich man's son. So do not blame me for this life, ne. I have given you everything.

KIHEIDA: And, so, I must drink.

(He lifts his flask again and she firmly snatches it from him. Anger briefly clouds his face, but it melts in the face of FUSAE's irritation. He sighs in defeat and busies himself with polishing a plant. HAJIME rushes in and stops short at the sight of FUSAE. YOKO enters with more fruit and a letter. When she sees HAJIME, she is flustered and embarrassed. He nods his head to her in appreciation. FUSAE observes this exchange with concern. YOKO hands the letter to FUSAE, who reads it.)

FUSAE: It is from the government of the occupational forces. It is about the land.

(KIHEIDA grabs the letter and tears it up. FUSAE has had enough. She motions for YOKO to help her and the women exit. KIHEIDA quickly retrieves his sake and offers it to HAJIME, who declines with a shake of his head. KIHEIDA looks at the pieces of torn letter.)

HAJIME: You must obey the law, Shimada-san. That letter ordered the division of your land into fifty tracts.

KIHEIDA Fifty tracts! What am I to live on? A single acre? I will have nothing to pass on to you.

HAJIME: My family has been awarded two tracts.

KIHEIDA: Well. You will be richer than I.

HAJIME: Even Sagami-san has been awarded a full tract.

KIHEIDA: Who is Sagami-san?

HAJIME *(quietly):* He was the father of Yoko, your maid.

KIHEIDA: But he is dead.

HAJIME: The land will go to Yoko-san.

KIHEIDA: A maid? A woman being given land! What will she build on it? Trees that grow dresses and lipstick?

HAJIME *(soberly):* She will grow rice.

KIHEIDA *(as the reality sets in):* This is imminent? (HAJIME *nods;* KIHEIDA *whispers)* Tell me the truth. What can I do when the Yankees come?

HAJIME *(summoning courage):* They have already come.

KIHEIDA: For the land?

HAJIME: For other more . . . important things.

KIHEIDA *(nodding):* You mean this Yankee boyfriend of my niece's.

HAJIME: A dark Yankee came to the pier and met with Setsuko last night.

KIHEIDA: You lie.

HAJIME: Ask her. He was brown like a Polynesian.

KIHEIDA: Surely, Setsuko would never—

*(*KIHEIDA *begins to leave, but* HAJIME *stops him.)*

HAJIME: Sir . . . I want to ask for the hand of your daughter.

KIHEIDA *(brightening):* How generous of you. I thought without the land you might feel less inclined to marry Haruko.

HAJIME: . . . I wish to ask for . . . Setsuko-san's hand . . .

KIHEIDA: You speak foolishness. The oldest must marry first.

HAJIME *(in earnest):* But it is certain that Haruko will marry one of our own. Setsuko? Her attitude demands a quick marriage. If I am intruding, I am sorry. I will return to my work now.

*(*HAJIME *bows abruptly.* KIHEIDA *firmly halts him. The two men exchange a look.)*

KIHEIDA: You have always looked at Setsuko like you were a thirsty man and she was the last cup of tea in the land.

*(*HAJIME, *ashamed, looks downward.)*

HAJIME: For me, she is.

259

KIHEIDA: Were this any other time, I would slap you and order you off of my land.

HAJIME: But now it is my land, too.

KIHEIDA: You wish to take everything I have?

HAJIME: Setsuko is to be my wife then?

KIHEIDA: I cannot fight the tide.

(As HAJIME *restrains his elation and rushes to leave,* SETSUKO *enters. They collide. She moves away from him quickly.* HAJIME *stops and looks at* KIHEIDA *for guidance.*)

KIHEIDA: Setsuko. You are to be married.

(*Startled,* SETSUKO *tries to regain her composure.*)

KIHEIDA: The man I have . . . chosen for you is Takemoto-san.

SETSUKO: What?

KIHEIDA: Because of your unforgivable indiscretion, it will be your responsibility to tell your sister. I expect you to do this by sunset.

(KIHEIDA *marches from the room, pained by what he has had to do.* SETSUKO *looks at* HAJIME *with loathing and disgust.* HARUKO *appears outside. She has picked a bouquet of flowers and a basket of persimmons. She enters the house and smiles. The smile quickly dissipates as she measures the tension in the house. She extends the flowers to* HAJIME.)

HARUKO: I picked these for you.

(*He takes them and bows humbly and repeatedly.* SETSUKO *takes the flowers back and forces them into* HARUKO'S *confused hands.*)

HARUKO: What are you doing?

SETSUKO: You must take them back, keep them for yourself.

HARUKO (*a whisper to* SETSUKO): He is my intended, ne, Setchan.

SETSUKO (*eyes trained on* HAJIME): Oneesan . . . sometimes things do not turn out the way we expect.

HARUKO (*still confused, another whisper*): Do not worry, Setchan. Father will find a nice boy for you, too, and—

SETSUKO *(with urgency):* Oneesan.

(The urgency startles HARUKO.*)*

HARUKO: What is the matter with you?

SETSUKO: Father intends to make me marry Takemoto-san.

(Shock rolls through HARUKO's *body, leaving her speechless. Her basket of persimmons falls.)*

SETSUKO: It is not my wish. It is—

HAJIME: That is enough, Setsuko. Leave us.

SETSUKO: By all means. After all, this is of your doing.

*(*SETSUKO *exits.* HARUKO *tries to leave, too, but* HAJIME *gently restrains her. She avoids his apologetic gaze. He begins to help her pick up the fruit. They reach for the same persimmon at the same time and his hand comes to rest upon hers. She tries to pull away, but he holds on. Finally, she yanks away and falls back on the ground from the effort.)*

HAJIME: Haruko!

(He tries to help her. She resists, composes herself, sits, and ignores him. Nervously, she cuts a slice of fruit.)

HAJIME: You are always tending to your father's persimmons. Don't you ever want to do something else?

(He picks up a persimmon and studies it.)

HAJIME: Haven't you ever wanted to crush one of these or throw it?

(He throws the persimmon. She shrieks and retrieves it, eyeing him with disbelief.)

HAJIME: Don't you get tired of them? Don't you ever want to go to the market and buy apples or grapes?

(He bites into a fruit and frowns.)

HAJIME: Bitter taste.

(She snatches the fruit from him.)

HARUKO: They are always sweet. I have always liked persimmons. Always.

HAJIME: Haruko-san, please understand, I had to ask him—

HARUKO: *You* asked *him?*

HAJIME: The war has changed us all in different ways. I had always hoped that one day I would marry into your family. I knew it was understood that I would marry you. I *did* want to build a life with you, Haruko-san, but your sister is . . . different. I need that difference now. I want it.

(She tries to leave. He stops her.)

HAJIME: Haruko-san.

(She jerks away, tempering her loathing. She bows politely, with extreme formality.)

HARUKO: I . . . welcome you to our family . . . Takemoto-san.

(She abruptly exits. He picks up a forgotten persimmon, polishes it, and shakes his head in self-loathing.)

Scene Eight

(MITCHELL DANIELS enters the Shimada property. He looks around in confusion. YOKO appears in the house with a bucket. She leaves the house and comes face to face with DANIELS. She stares at him for a moment and then screams in shock.)

DANIELS: Miss. Don't be alarmed. I'm here representing the United States government.

(Another scream from the hysterical YOKO.)

DANIELS: Miss! I'm here on official business.

(Her screams bring FUSAE and KIHEIDA to the anteroom. Both are shocked and alarmed at the sight of DANIELS. DANIELS uncomfortably bows as YOKO runs screaming offstage.)

DANIELS: Hello. I'm Captain Mitchell Daniels, United States Army.

FUSAE: Forgive our maid. She has never been out of the provinces.

KIHEIDA: You are trespassing on private property.

DANIELS *(an eternal, diplomatic smile):* Actually, your property is just what I've come to discuss with you. Are you Mr. Kiheida Shimada? (KIHEIDA *looks away;* DANIELS *presses on)* We've sent you numerous letters indicating our need to facilitate the new land resettlement policies as ordered by General Douglas MacArthur.

KIHEIDA *(surprised):* You mean you are not my daughter's friend?

DANIELS: Sir, I don't have the slightest idea what you are talking about.

*(*FUSAE *is relieved.* KIHEIDA'S *relief lasts only a moment.)*

DANIELS: Sir, if you will give me a few minutes of your time, I need to go over a map of your land and indicate the new boundaries for you. Your tenants are eager to stake their claims and—

KIHEIDA: Takemoto-san! Takemoto-san!

*(*HAJIME, *obviously hard at work, enters with work gloves and work apron on. He stops short at the sight of* DANIELS. *Obviously, he also is confused.)*

KIHEIDA: Takemoto-san, this man has come to take my land . . . in the name of war.

DANIELS: No, sir. In the name of democracy. And peace.

KIHEIDA: Accompany him back to the pier.

DANIELS: But sir, I have a letter from—

*(*KIHEIDA *snatches the letter and tears it up.)*

DANIELS: Sir, if you don't cooperate, I will have to arrest you.

KIHEIDA: This was my father's land and his father's land before him.

DANIELS: I understand, sir, and I respect that. It's just that things are going to have to be a little different around here from now on.

HAJIME: Shimada-san, shall I meet with him in your stead?

*(*FUSAE *finally steps forward and bows to* DANIELS.*)*

FUSAE: I will meet with him.

KIHEIDA: You will do no such thing.

FUSAE *(smiling at* DANIELS *with gentleness):* Do come in, Captain. I have managed this household for years and today I *must* manage it.

*(*KIHEIDA, *though shocked, is powerless to stop his wife or the bold American as* DANIELS *steps into the house and automatically removes his shoes.)*

FUSAE: Please leave your weapons here.

(Surprised, DANIELS deposits a holstered gun at the door.)

DANIELS: Oh, I also need to speak with a Miss Yoko Sagami.

FUSAE: Yoko? Our maid?

(YOKO appears humbly.)

YOKO: I am Yoko Sagami.

DANIELS: I would like to talk to you about a land inheritance, Miss Sagami.

FUSAE: Will she get part of the orchard? I would like her to have part of the orchard.

(YOKO's demeanor takes on a sense of pride and artificial bearing as KIHEIDA watches in alarm. She bows to FUSAE, who takes her hand and leads her out. HAJIME enjoys the change in YOKO. DANIELS, YOKO, and FUSAE exit into the house and offstage. KIHEIDA stares at the gun and starts to move toward it, but HAJIME yanks his arm away and restrains him. Lights crossfade to downstage. Dusk. The gun and captain's shoes are gone. The land map is laid out on a table. KIHEIDA pores over it meticulously and grunts with dismay. HAJIME enters from the field.)

HAJIME: What was the Yankee's verdict?

KIHEIDA: I am left with one-tenth of my land. One-tenth.

HAJIME: And the doctor?

KIHEIDA: He is with my wife now.

(DR. WATANABE, forty-four, a pleasant-looking Japanese, enters the anteroom. KIHEIDA jumps up anxiously. FUSAE follows him. She forces a cheerfulness.)

KIHEIDA: Is everything all right?

FUSAE: You worry too much, ne, Otoosan.

KIHEIDA *(to the doctor):* But is she all right?

DR. WATANABE *(a tone of resolve):* Everything will be all right. I have given her some new medicine. What she has is a tumor in the uppermost section of her left breast—

KIHEIDA *(fearing the worst):* And?

DR. WATANABE: She has—

FUSAE: All the time in the world.

> (DR. WATANABE *casts a stern glance at* FUSAE, *but it softens as the gracious woman takes him by the arm and leads him to the door.)*

FUSAE: Dr. Watanabe, please give my blessings to your cousin in Osaka.

KIHEIDA: Osaka. I am told the city is a virtual wasteland.

DR. WATANABE *(his mind whisks to the weightier issue of the country):* It was. But the Americans are helping us rebuild.

KIHEIDA: Doctor, they took away my land. Is there nothing I can do about this disgrace?

DR. WATANABE: Now is not a time to think about disgrace. It is a time to think about survival.

FUSAE *(softly):* Yes.

KIHEIDA: Then I have lost all sense of time.

> (FUSAE *and the doctor exchange a look of understanding, and the doctor takes leave. She turns and stares at* HAJIME, *wanting to make him uncomfortable so he will leave. He finally does.)*

FUSAE: It is thievery, you know.

KIHEIDA *(stares at the map):* Yes. We finally agree.

FUSAE: I mean what that young man has done to our daughters' hearts.

> (FUSAE *suffers a pain. It passes and she smiles reassuringly at* KIHEIDA. *But he knows.)*

KIHEIDA: You must rest.

FUSAE: When there is little time left, I refuse to spend it in bed.

KIHEIDA *(accepting fate):* I see. *(a beat)* How can I make you more comfortable?

FUSAE: You have never asked me that in my entire life with you. *(a beat)* I have only one wish.

KIHEIDA: Wish it.

FUSAE: I wish for the freedom of my youngest child.

KIHEIDA: Do you know what that freedom may bring?

(SETSUKO *enters with tea. She serves her parents.*)

SETSUKO: What did the doctor say, Mother?

(HARUKO *arrives behind her with a light snack.* KIHEIDA *cannot take seeing his daughters together, though neither of them will look at him. He stands and exits.*)

HARUKO: Will you have an operation?

FUSAE *(shakes her head):* Before I am gone, I hope your father will see the error of his ways.

(*The truth slowly sinks in and* SETSUKO *lays her head on her mother's lap in sadness.*)

HARUKO: Poor father! He must be feeling awful.

(HARUKO *runs from the room and exits.* FUSAE *rocks* SETSUKO *back and forth.* SETSUKO *sits up, looks around, and slips a small package from her kimono sleeve.*)

SETSUKO: A present for you.

(FUSAE *opens it. It is a silk American dress. She is delighted.*)

FUSAE: How lovely.

SETSUKO: I thought of all the times you sewed us American-style dresses and father burned them. I wanted you to have one for your birthday, but—

FUSAE: I know. My birthday is another six months away . . . Let us be optimistic. I will wear it for you when May comes.

SETSUKO *(takes a book from her kimono sleeve):* And a new book. An ancient tale of romance.

FUSAE: My favorite kind of tale. Does it end happily?

SETSUKO *(quietly):* No.

FUSAE *(a sigh tempered with a gentle smile):* I suppose they never do. My mother used to say that is how we grow—through loss. The day I burned my mother's ashes, I became old.

SETSUKO: And so I will be old.

FUSAE: I fight to live and be strong so you will remain young.

SETSUKO *(daring to ask):* Mother?

FUSAE: Yes, my child.

SETSUKO: Mother . . . have you . . . have you never been in love?

FUSAE *(a smile):* Like in the novel perhaps?

SETSUKO *(bows her head):* I am sorry. I should not ask this.

FUSAE *(another smile):* But you ask because you are your mother's daughter.

(KIHEIDA *appears in the hallway and is unable to stop himself from eavesdropping.)*

FUSAE: I came to love your father, despite the fact he plucked me from my father's arms as if I were a fruit for consumption. Maybe these are our ways, but something inside of me has always rankled at the idea of men taking women. It is uncivilized, don't you think? *(a beat, a faraway look in her eyes)* But your father was my choice in a way, too. In the provinces, the old ones say that a reliable mule is always better than a wild horse.

SETSUKO: And you chose the . . . mule. (FUSAE *nods)* Over the horse, the man who came to the inn.

FUSAE: You were only five when he was here. Such memory. The gentle man from Amsterdam.

SETSUKO: And you . . . loved him?

FUSAE: And I bid him farewell knowing that I would never see him again. Who is to say that my life in Holland would have been any different than this one? Do dreams diffuse when one crosses over the heady seas? I do not know.

SETSUKO: Mother, when you are gone—

FUSAE: I know, Setchan.

SETSUKO: When you are gone, I may take my freedom.

FUSAE: I would be disappointed in you if you did not.

SETSUKO: Truly?

FUSAE: The war has made us all old, Setchan. And you love a man with brown skin and American eyes.

SETSUKO: But I look in his eyes and I see history. I see dreams, Mother.

FUSAE: And so you grow at a rate I could never even have imagined when I was your age. And if you go to America and make children who are Japanese and American, they will grow in ways that you cannot imagine now. They will have to.

SETSUKO: I am sorry, Mother.

FUSAE: On the contrary. I celebrate in your dreams. *(a beat)* And now, I shall get some rest.

(FUSAE *stands to exit.* KIHEIDA *buries his face in his hands. He fights to compose himself and reenters the room.* FUSAE *exits to the bedchambers.* SETSUKO *immediately rises and begins to exit to the outside of the house.)*

KIHEIDA: Where are you going?

SETSUKO: Outside.

KIHEIDA: For what?

SETSUKO: To walk. In the orchard. I need to think.

KIHEIDA: To think? To think about what? America?

SETSUKO: I am truly sorry, Father. I never meant to bring such pain into your life.

(He *refuses to look at her as she briskly exits. Lights crossfade to the bedchambers as* KIHEIDA *enters and sits on the floor beside* FUSAE, *who lies on her bedding. She offers him a smile, but his eyes are glazed. She leans against him.* YOKO *brings her another blanket and she nods in thanks. With* YOKO'S *help, she places it around their legs for warmth.* KIHEIDA'S *stare makes* YOKO *uncomfortable and nervous.* YOKO *exits.)*

KIHEIDA: Fusae . . . I have not been a good father.

FUSAE: You have done your best.

KIHEIDA: Forty years with you, Fusae. I still remember when my father asked your father to let me marry you.

(He takes her hand and presses it to his face, and then tucks her in tightly under the cover.)

KIHEIDA: Forty years.

FUSAE *(a deep sigh):* Maybe in the next life, our love will be a great one, ne, Otoosan.

(She tries to sleep; he awakens her with a mysterious urgency. She takes note.)

KIHEIDA: Fusae. I am going for a walk.

FUSAE: Yes?

KIHEIDA: The twilight. It will help me forget.

(Again, she tries to sleep; again, he nudges her.)

KIHEIDA: Fusae, I am sorry for all these years. I never meant to take away from your life. The first time I saw you, I told myself that I would give you the best of everything. I said—

FUSAE: Go to sleep, Otoosan. The morning will be here soon.

KIHEIDA: Fusae, my dear one . . .

FUSAE: Sleep, Otoosan. That is the only place where all can be forgotten.

(She quickly dozes off. He caresses her hair and kisses her forehead. He returns to the living room and studies his surroundings as if, again, affirming his reality. He exits to the kitchen as lights crossfade to the anteroom. Immediately, FUSAE sits up in bed and looks around in fear. Seeing nothing, she returns to a fitful sleep. KIHEIDA emerges from the kitchen with a fresh pot of sake and a package of powder. He sits at the table in the anteroom and mixes the powder in his drink. Quickly, he drinks it, finding it extremely distasteful. He wipes his mouth and washes down the taste with more sake. He mixes more, but leaves it on the table. His mobility is distorted and he grows nervous as he sits at the table and removes his spectacles. His energy dissipates. He experiences a sharp pain in his abdominal region, but forces composure. His head begins to nod. He tries to finish the rest of his sake, but drops his cup. Still, he forces a prideful composure. Troubled and sad, he drops his

head again. From the roadway, SETSUKO *reenters. She attempts to be as quiet as possible and enter the house without waking anyone. As she tiptoes, he slowly lifts his head and sees her.)*

KIHEIDA: Setsuko.

SETSUKO: Hai, Otoosan.

KIHEIDA: It is four in the morning.

SETSUKO: So desu ne.

KIHEIDA: Setsuko, I did not raise you to chase after a Yankee soldier.

SETSUKO: I did not grow up dreaming of a Yankee soldier either. *(a beat)* When I was little, I used to climb on the rocks by the sea and stare at ships. I dreamt of being on one of them, sailing to a faraway place where I could be free to sing and laugh and let my hair down.

(He drops his head again.)

SETSUKO: You have been at the sake again, ne, Otoosan.

KIHEIDA: So, na. Sorry for the trouble. *(a pause)* Setsuko. Nippon is not important to you anymore, na.

SETSUKO: Aren't you asking me if *you* aren't important?

KIHEIDA: Nippon. I said Nippon.

SETSUKO: You are very important. You have been a good father.

KIHEIDA: Your mother. She gave you too much spirit.

SETSUKO: And what did you give me, Otoosan?

KIHEIDA *(his last smile):* Stubbornness. Go to sleep, little dove. Dream.

(She smiles and exits. FUSAE'S *sleep grows more fitful.* KIHEIDA *moans and suddenly slumps forward as if sleeping. His body convulses a few times and then is still.* FUSAE *immediately sits up.)*

FUSAE: Yoko!

(A sleepy YOKO *runs into the bedchambers and helps* FUSAE *rise.)*

YOKO: What is the matter? Shall I call for Dr. Watanabe at the inn?

(As fast as FUSAE *can move, they go to the front room.* FUSAE *looks at her husband, picks up the sake, and shakes him.)*

FUSAE: No more of this, Otoosan.

*(*FUSAE *tries to help him sit up; he falls.)*

FUSAE: Otoosan?

(She lifts his arm; it falls, a dead weight.)

FUSAE: Otoosan.

*(*YOKO *begins to scream wildly in panic.* HARUKO *appears at the upstage exit.)*

HARUKO: What has happened? It has been hard to sleep in this house lately, ne.

YOKO: The master! The master is very sick!

*(*HARUKO *looks at* FUSAE'S *face and immediately realizes; she cradles her father in her arms.)*

HARUKO: Otoosan. Yoko, send for the doctor quickly. Hayaku!

*(*YOKO *hyperventilates as* HARUKO *checks* KIHEIDA'S *nonexistent pulse.* HARUKO *begins to weep. She examines the powder remnants on the table with curiosity.* SETSUKO *comes in, having been wakened by the noise.)*

SETSUKO: What has happened?

HARUKO: Otoosan . . .

*(*FUSAE *falls to her knees beside the body.)*

FUSAE *(a whisper):* Haruko.

SETSUKO: Oh no. Oh no.

YOKO: Takemoto-san! Takemoto-san!

(A sleepy, bewildered HAJIME *enters.)*

HAJIME: Did he have too much to drink?

HARUKO: Takemoto-san, what is this?

*(*HARUKO *points to the powder on the table; he rubs it between his fingers as his eyes gaze knowingly at* KIHEIDA.*)*

HAJIME: It is poison. For the rodents. They've been rampant since the war. I bought it earlier this week. To save the persimmons. They eat them ravenously.

SETSUKO: To save the persimmons . . .

(He tries to remove the body; HARUKO *will not let go.* FUSAE *sits at the table, feeling the sake bottle and holding* KIHEIDA'S *glasses in her hands as if trying to touch what is now forever gone.)*

FUSAE: Setsuko.

*(*SETSUKO *goes to her mother's side and holds her arm tightly to steady her.)*

HARUKO *(not looking at* SETSUKO; *anger and despair):* You brought the war right into our own house. This family has never been the same since you became a Yankee lover.

FUSAE: Haruko. *(a pause; firmly)* There is never anything but the present moment, the one we can grasp in our fists and feel.

HARUKO: I cannot forget! *(to* SETSUKO*)* You destroyed him. You have stolen from me the only two people who mattered in my life.

SETSUKO: Oneesan . . . we cannot control the kind of souls the gods choose to give us. I just hope someday you can forgive me for my dreams that seemed to get in everybody's way. And, maybe then, we can look into each other's eyes and find the comfort of sisters and friends.

FUSAE: Haruko. Takemoto-san. Please.

*(*FUSAE *indicates the body; they both carry him out, upstage;* YOKO *follows, trying to be helpful. As lights slowly, slowly fade to the light of dawn,* FUSAE *raises her head. She looks very tired. The spectacles are still in her hand. She studies them as* SETSUKO *watches her religiously.)*

FUSAE: Another morning in this silent countryside.

SETSUKO: So ne.

FUSAE: It used to be, every morning was the same. Until the war.

SETSUKO: Yes.

FUSAE: Otoosan never makes it easy for us, ne.

SETSUKO: I have not made it easy either.

FUSAE: Because you had a dream? No. That really is not so bad. I have had them, too. A long time ago, but I have not forgotten. Sometimes it is easier to fight for your dreams. Maybe this was meant to be such a time.

SETSUKO: You mean if I had dismissed my duty, you would have let me leave you?

FUSAE: You would not have left?

(SETSUKO *shakes her head.*)

SETSUKO: It was not just duty, Mother. It is you . . . you and I . . . you are more than my mother, more than . . .

(FUSAE *holds up a hand gently to silence her daughter.*)

FUSAE: Then I have not taught you well. Setchan, what you might have done is no more shameful than what your father has done to us today. Who is to be the judge? Not I. Certainly not him. These are things no one has any control over.

SETSUKO: But this is my fault.

FUSAE: No one is to blame for the casualties of war. It is not just you, ne. It is the shame of defeat. It is the loss of his land. It is the passing away of all that he ruled. When the kingdom is gone, what job is there for the king? Where does he go? *(a pause)* Setchan . . . if you could still go to America, would you want to?

SETSUKO: I have always wanted to; I simply made the necessary choice.

FUSAE: I will not be here very long, Setchan.

SETSUKO: But I want to be here with you. I want to do the right thing.

FUSAE: Look at me, Setsuko. I did the "right thing" so many years ago. I let go of my dreams and remained with your father. So I am here. If you had gone to America, no matter how hard it might have been for you sometimes, you would never have been here. I have nothing but Haruko and you, and I want you

273

to have your dreams, Setchan. I think you should hold on to them. Hold on tightly.

SETSUKO: Okaasan . . . if I were to go to America, would you, could you come with me?

FUSAE: Setchan . . . I am old.

SETSUKO: But, to think, when I returned to visit, you could be . . .

FUSAE *(silences her, her voice cracking though she seeks composure):* Even when I am gone, we will find each other again. *(a pause)* Come, let us walk in the orchard, like we have walked a hundred times in our lives. (FUSAE *pauses as she stares once again at* KIHEIDA's *spectacles, kisses them gingerly, and slips them into her kimono sleeve.* SETSUKO *helps her to stand.* FUSAE *looks around the room. Her eyes come to rest on a bowl of persimmons. She kneels beside it.)*

FUSAE: . . . Setchan . . . it is good to be alive.

(FUSAE *picks up a persimmon and holds it between the palms of her hands. She lets it roll across her palms, staring at it as lights fade to black.)*

End of Play